# THE NATURE OF ECONOMIC THOUGHT

# THE NATURE OF ECONOMIC THOUGHT

## SELECTED PAPERS 1955–1964


BY

G.L.S.SHACKLE

*Brunner Professor of Economic Science in the University of Liverpool*

CAMBRIDGE

AT THE UNIVERSITY PRESS

1966

CAMBRIDGE UNIVERSITY PRESS
Cambridge, New York, Melbourne, Madrid, Cape Town, Singapore,
São Paulo, Delhi, Dubai, Tokyo, Mexico City

Cambridge University Press
The Edinburgh Building, Cambridge CB2 8RU, UK

Published in the United States of America by Cambridge University Press, New York

www.cambridge.org
Information on this title: www.cambridge.org/9780521147590



First published 1966
First paperback printing 2010

*A catalogue record for this publication is available from the British Library*

*Library of Congress Catalogue Card Number: 66–13989*

ISBN 978-0-521-06278-7 Hardback
ISBN 978-0-521-14759-0 Paperback

*To*

HENRI GUITTON

GUY DEVILLEBICHOT

PAULIN BOISSEAU

# CONTENTS

PART V INTEREST AND INVESTMENT



PART VI CRITICAL REFLECTIONS

# PREFACE

Economics has been defined as the logic of choice. Amongst what, then, are men free to choose? Not amongst situations or events which exist or occur in some objective reality, for when something is actual the time is too late for choosing something else. Not amongst perfectly specified situations or events whose occurrence in some future is somehow guaranteed, for there is no such perfect knowledge and no such guarantee. Men choose amongst their own imaginations of what rival available policies will bring them. Each conceived policy or course of action will in general provide a basis, more or less firm, for many different imagined outcomes. Who knows whether, in seeking to list such outcomes, a man is wholly constrained by his experience and his present circumstances, so that these thoughts are determinate and, if we knew enough, wholly explicable by reference to the past? If they are not capable of being thus wholly explained away, there is room, in this process of listing rival imagined outcomes of a policy, for both *freedom* and *reason*: freedom in creating the objects amongst which there is choice, viz. the bundles of rival outcomes, one bundle for each available policy; and *reason* in choosing amongst these bundles and thus amongst these policies.

Economists have said that their subject is about reason, and some of them have developed it by reason alone from a brief and simple list of axioms taken for granted or even declared to be self-evidently true. But almost none of them have said that their subject is concerned with imagination. Business life may be 'aleatory', but only in the strict sense. The *alea* has six sides and one or other of this known list of contingencies must come up at any throw, for the list is known to be complete. There is no room for new, additional contingencies to be invented; the business man is a gambler but he must not aspire to be a poet. Business may be a game, but the economist treats it as having a book of rules which enable all contingencies to be listed and each to be assigned a probability, a value of a distributional variable. The probabilities may be 'subjective', they may be mere personal judgements and not objective, observed frequencies, but by binding these judgements into a distribution we ensure their coherence. The assumption of complete knowledge (though tacitly assumed as the basis of traditional value-theory) may be absurd in the form of 'perfect foresight', but the assumption of completely listable contingencies, however complex and however astronomically numerous they might be, is regarded as natural and necessary. It is in repudiation of this view that the essays of Part II of this book have been written.

Such radical heresy necessarily colours a man's whole work, not only that part of it where his case comes up to be explicitly argued. Thus in the essays of Part I there will be found my more general view of the nature and value of economics in its past and present forms. In the essays under *Business and Psychology* in Part III I have sought insight, from that same personal viewpoint, into the world of enterprise where the psychic act of *decision*, the chief focus of my own interest, is the fount of success or failure. Part IV is more conventional, but illustrates my many endeavours to appeal direct to business men themselves.

The market system in all its complexity of detail and simplicity of principle is nothing but a vast information-dispenser. It gathers from all persons, businesses and nations information concerning the buying and selling propensities of all these sources of action, computes their resultant in the form of a price and re-transmits this guiding datum to them so that, substituting it for the unknown in their action equations, they can decide what to do. Amongst these prices, or ratios of exchange, there are those between goods here and now and promises of goods later. These *interest rates* play an elusive and tantalizing role in the life of society. They are the chief formal and precise link between today's facts about itself and today's conjectures, hopes and fears about tomorrow. Time is the reason and condition of their being; must they not then be the central lever for controlling the economy? It has long been argued that they are, and Keynes himself wrote largely as though they were. Yet belief in their efficacy and importance fluctuates continually. The circumstances which govern them, their power to influence action, are still the subject of debate. This debate, as it proceeded during the first fifteen years from the end of the second world war, is surveyed in Part V, which consists of the article commissioned by the *Economic Journal* and financed by the Rockefeller Foundation.

Lastly I have included my reviews of three books. Each of these books, in its own way, gave me stimulus and scope for relating my idiosyncrasies to the views of others, and allowed me to illustrate that truth which more and more impresses me, the oneness, the undividedness of the study of man. History and philosophy, political theory, psychology of some sorts and economics all belong in a single Great Theme. Economics is not pure logic but, quite in contrast with such a character, it is part of the endeavour to describe the integral nature of man.

G. L. S. S.

*November 1964*

# ACKNOWLEDGEMENTS

I am most grateful to all those editors of journals and books who have allowed me to include in this collection the pieces which they respectively first published. The names of those places of first publication are listed below. The essays whose titles are given without publication details have not previously been printed.

G.L.S.S.

*12 November 1964*

'The Unity of European Economic Thought', in *Le collettività locali e la costruzione dell'unità europea*. I.S.A.P. (Milan, 1963). (Essay written in March 1961.)

'The Hedgehog and the Fox', *The Indian Journal of Economics*, vol. 34 (1964).

'Keynes and the Nature of Human Affairs', *Weltwirtschaftliches Archiv*, vol. 87 (1961).

'The Ruin of Economy', *Kyklos*, vol. 14 (1961).

'The "Great Theory" in Eclipse', Italian version published in *Mercurio*, vol. 5 (1962).

'Time, Nature, and Decision', in *Money, Growth and Methodology*, ed. Hugo Hegeland (University of Lund, Sweden, 1961).

'The Description of Uncertainty', *La Scuola in Azione*. E.N.I. Scuola di Studi Superiori sugli Idrocarburi, no. 21 (Milan, 1961–62).

'Decision and Uncertainty', French version published in *Futuribles*, no. 26. (Société d'Etudes et de Documentation Economiques, Industrielles et Sociales, 1 March 1962.)

'The Dilemma of History', essay not previously printed, written May 1962.

'Models of Conjecture', essay not previously printed, written June 1963.

'Brief Testament', *Weltwirtschaftliches Archiv*, vol. 82 (1959).

'The Economist's Model of Man', *Occupational Psychology*, vol. 32 (1958).

'Theory and the Business Man', *Scientific Business*, vol. 1, no. 1 (1963).

'Business Men on Business Decisions', *Scottish Journal of Political Economy*, vol. 2 (1955).

'Business and Uncertainty', *Bankers' Magazine*, vol. CLXXXIX (March 1960).

'Scale, Risk and Profit', essay not previously printed, written June 1961.

'Resources and Demands', essay not previously printed, written May 1963.

'The Nature of Inflation', *Company Accountant*, Conference number (1955). (An address given at the Scarborough National Conference.)

'Recent Theories Concerning the Nature and Role of Interest', *Economic Journal*, vol. 71 (1961).

'Battles Long Ago', *Weltwirtschaftliches Archiv*, vol. 89 (1962).

'The Stages of Economic Growth', *Political Studies*, vol. 10 (1962).

'Values and Intentions', *Kyklos*, vol. 15 (1962).

# I

# THE MEANING AND METHOD OF ECONOMICS

# I

# THE UNITY OF EUROPEAN ECONOMIC THOUGHT

To cope with life, a person needs a system of explanation of it. When I am watching a game of cricket, I do not know what will happen next, but I know the sorts of things that can arise as a sequel to this or that event or situation which has just come into being, for I know the rules and purpose of the game. Looking back on the course of a morning's play, I can see a pattern in it. I can trace the successive re-appraisals made by each captain, see the point of his shifts of policy and of his detailed tactics, perceive how the course of play was affected by his decisions, how the effect of these decisions depended on the other side's reactions and responses, and how, in general, the sequence of events 'makes sense'. The rules and purpose of the game constitute my system of explanation of what goes on in the field of play. Were I watching a game of billiards, or an Eastern ritual dance, or an abstract painter at work, I should by no means have the same sense of *familiarity with the strictly unprecedented.* No two events on a cricket field are ever exactly alike, yet to a follower of cricket every event on any cricket field, at any time anywhere, is understandable, and can be seen as in some degree the upshot of recognizable endeavours and constraints.

It is this purpose, of rendering familiar, when they have happened, the unprecedented events of life, which theory serves. Now harmony and concert among any set of nations depends partly on their all interpreting any given event in one and the same basic fashion. If they can see any act as the natural response to a set of circumstances which all of them view in the same light, there will be a basis for ordered discussion and adjustment among them, for 'give and take', for exchange of concessions, for collaboration and even for eventual unity and complete singleness of entity. Theory, therefore, whether political, cultural or economic, is not abstract, remote, unreal, negligible, but practical, immediate, insistent and the very essence of action. Theory is the root of peace.

Science in general can still show enormous differences of opinion. The most striking example is perhaps that of cosmology, where we have the contrast between the steady-state hypothesis which pictures a cosmos with no temporal beginning or end, limitlessly expanding everywhere by a universal mutual retreat of the galaxies and their continual replacement by the creation of fresh matter; and the hypothesis of a primeval atom of unimaginable density, embracing all of what has now been spread, by a vast explosion, through thousands of millions of light-years of space. Some scientists have supposed that by choosing the former hypothesis they could rid themselves of the idea of a creation and of all that goes with it, and some have found that this release admirably suits their political leanings. Theology, indeed, carries us from cosmology to politics. Politics, too, is the background of the question, in biology, whether there can be inheritance of acquired characteristics. The detached, impartial attitude of the natural scientist seems to be something of a myth; he is human like the rest of us.

If even astronomy is political, and the radio-telescope is called in to decide the right form for human institutions, how much more so is economics! How can nations hope to live in friendship, to unite their markets in order to exploit yet more fully the division of labour, to grope, however cautiously, towards a sinking of national identities in a re-created Europeanism such as existed in what we call the Dark Age, if their basic economic preconceptions are radically different?

Those polar opposites, towards one or other of which the world's economic systems approximate more or less, are often compared on the basis of their supposed *efficiency*. Surely this is a misconception or an abuse of language. Efficiency is the ratio of end achieved to means employed, so that if we are concerned with getting mechanical work out of coal, we might measure the efficiency of an engine in foot-pounds lifted per ton of coal burnt. Two different engines might then be legitimately compared. But would it make any sense to say that, for example, a university student was more efficient than a marksman shooting at a target, because the student got 80 per cent of possible marks while the marksman only got 50 per cent of possible bull's-eyes? Is a preacher who converts 10 per cent of those who listen to him less efficient than an advertiser who sells his product to

15 per cent of those who see his advertisement? Because my moving pencil absorbs far fewer calories than a spade, am I more efficient when writing than when gardening? The answers in these examples are too obvious for words. Yet we are constantly told that free enterprise is more, or less, efficient than the exact and detailed planning of the economy. If one country or another is the first to put men upon the moon, that will be a superb, an incomparable achievement. But will it be *more efficient* than enabling 50 million people to choose freely from a great diversity of individual and personal satisfactions? One purpose may be nobler than the other; but if the *ends* are different, and chosen by different people, then comparison of the quantity of *means* will be meaningless. When a nation's economic choices are made by its Government and not, even indirectly, by its citizens, the purposes to which effort is directed will be different from those of a nation of individual decision-makers. We may, on non-economic grounds, hold one scheme of things superior to the other, but we cannot, on economic grounds, claim that one is more efficient than the other: authoritarianism is neither more, nor less, efficient than democracy; it is different in nature and aim. To compare the respective aims themselves is, needless to say, no task for an economist.

Let us, then, put aside the vast and intractable question of how non-elected and elected governments can come to tolerate and live with each other, and concern ourselves only with countries where power and responsibility reside ultimately in the great body of citizens. When the professional economists of these 'western' nations assemble, or meet in private, how far is their mutual understanding and sympathy ready to come to life at a touch because they possess a *general economic theory* in common? Let us consider the shape and method of such a theory, as it would emerge from the works of the most celebrated national representatives of our profession. And to systematize the affair, let us list the questions we would put to each of our witnesses:

1. How do you conceive the source of human action? Is it a mechanical response to objective circumstances, or to circumstances as they are known to the acting subject? What if his knowledge of them is incomplete or false, and indeed how can it be other? What precisely is the role of knowledge, with its inevitable

deficiencies differing from person to person, in allowing the circumstances to elicit action from the individual? Or is action in part spontaneous, creative, uncaused; perhaps constrained but not determined by the subject's knowledge? How in this case can we construct a predictive science of the genesis of events? If action is guided by a *policy*, how can this policy best be condensed into an axiom or axioms? How are human motives to be summarized?

2. The 'total event' in each moment of the whole economy, that is to say, the matrix of proportions in which the numerical values specifying the situation at one instant are changed into those describing the situation at a second instant, will be the combined effect of the efforts of individuals and firms each to realize its own aims. The combining of these efforts will not be a mere addition but an interplay. How does this interplay work? Is the economy to be seen as a machine, an organism, a battlefield or a drill ground, or is its history like an oral saga maintained and embellished by a hundred generations of individual poets?

3. Is economics an explanation of how the economy works and an indicator of what sort of things *can* happen in it, or is it a means of knowing in advance what will in fact happen? Can it support a detailed, exact and far-reaching plan or only guide the continual improvisation of the moment?

In the first of these questions, it will be seen, we are reaching down to the bedrock problem concerning the human condition, the choice of assumption between determinism and non-determinism, a problem which I suspect economists of answering, by implication, in various ways according to the convenience of the argument in hand. Some would say these waters are too deep. I can only ask whether, if we wish to make *decision* an originative act giving its own unpremeditated twist to the spinning yarn of history, we can then consistently claim a *predictive* purpose for economics. But if economics is adrift on these deep waters, we cannot usefully discuss the navigational prospects.

Question 2 is more manageable. To think of the economy as a machine still leaves us free to suppose that its forces take effect instantaneously to produce an equilibrium, or after various time-lags to produce a path of change; or that a pace of change, as in dynamic schemes like those of Harrod, is itself one of those forces. If by contrast we opt for the battlefield model, we need the Theory of Games, and if we elect the drill-ground model we are of course outside the Western world altogether.

The answer to question 3, given by the leaders of a nation's ruling party, will broadly determine the method of economic government adopted. If foresight is possible, then the weight of policy can be allowed to rest on detailed forecasts. The capacity of street and road systems, of railways and airports, of electricity generating stations, of universities and hospitals, that will be required in ten and in twenty years' time, can be discovered and planned for. In short, a *plan* can be made to whose realization the whole current national economic effort can, by fiscal and monetary means, be geared. But if foresight is not of this order of clarity and sureness, if what is *unexpected in detail* (in technical character and in *timing*) must be *expected in general*, then *plans* must give way to *policies*, grand strategy to inspired improvisation, calculation to virtuosity.

To question 1 I doubt whether economists have ever set out to give a deliberate and explicit answer. They seem to me, with a few notable exceptions, to have been, unconsciously, split-minded on this subject, regarding it as interesting and important to trace the psychological mechanism by which there comes about an inevitable and determinate reaction to circumstances. In other words, they have treated the human being as a machine, they have found in self-interest a sort of economic 'force of gravity' whose dictates communicate themselves unmistakably and infallibly to the acting subject; and yet they have used such words as 'cause', which seem out of place in a purely determinist model of the economic universe. If I look at a nearly finished painting, where some human figures are poised, as yet unsupported, above a lake, it may be clear to me that the painter intends to paint a boat in the vacant space. Does it make sense, however, for me to say that the presence of the human figures, and of the water below them, 'causes' the boat to be painted there? It is surely something in the artist's mind, in his total plan or situation, which must in the end be linked with his act of putting a boat in the space upon his canvas? Can we properly say that human needs, and human possession of resources, 'cause' people to work and consume, unless we free them somehow from imprisonment in an inevitable and predestined pattern of events? I would say that if there are to be 'causes' there must be *unpredictable* choice, creative choice, that a 'cause' is a lever which an acting subject is free to move *or not to move*.

It may be that this question, which seeks a *basic statement of the human condition*, though on a general view the most important of all, is for our purpose not very important, since the same two mutually contradictory answers are given by all Western economists: for their own technical purposes, these economists treat men's actions as *wholly analysable*, as capable of being exhibited as the necessary consequence of given circumstances or antecedents; but in their private, intuitive, practical coping with life, in their sense of personal responsibility, in their moment-by-moment decision-making, they treat men's, that is, their own, actions as creative, as spontaneous, as undetermined. Thus, all of us in the Western community of nations are, in this matter, of one mind, or rather, we are all of *two* minds, but the same two. It does not seem to matter.

So to question 2, about the nature of the interplay of rival efforts or opposing forces in the economy. Here, for sixty years, we had near-unanimity. From Walras to the nineteen-thirties the answer about mechanism was general interdependence and a universal tendency towards a comprehensive state of equilibrium which no one would have both the power and the desire to alter in any one particular way. The general equilibrium model was the most intellectually satisfying, the most generally inclusive, efficient, incisive and beautiful construction which economics has ever produced. It answered all questions, it accommodated all forces, factors and facts, it showed the Grand Design of the economy, it left us without doubts or qualms of conscience, with almost nothing to solve, say or do. To this great model many of the greatest figures in the history of our subject contributed, and they came from every quarter of the Western world. Gossen was a German, Jevons an Englishman, Menger an Austrian, Walras a Frenchman, Wicksell a Swede, Pareto an Italian, John Bates Clark an American. These have differed from each other in detail, sometimes have made much of their differences. This very willingness to criticize and this ability to see sharp and clear the lines dividing one version of the

Western theoretical tradition from another were an unconscious tribute and acknowledgement of a fundamental unity. Family quarrels are unintelligible and meaningless, except to members of the family.

The general equilibrium model is no longer looked on as sufficient, for the economic scene of today and yesterday is full of features that it cannot explain. The most omnipresent and inescapable of these features is the use of money. General equilibrium uses a *numéraire* to reduce all goods to a common measure, but it does not include a money in the full modern sense, a money which people can hold as an asset, which is valued only for its general acceptability in exchange and not for any technical qualities which are wanted for their own sake, a money which can be manufactured by mere decree at almost no cost in productive resources; for such a money is incompatible with guaranteed, stable, sustained equilibrium. Such a money enables people to sell goods without buying them, and thus to cause general massive unemployment in defiance of Say's Law. Such a money is valued partly because it makes possible the postponement of effective decision. When we do not know what kind of real equipment, what type of enterprise, will make a profit and avoid a loss, we can retreat into money: thus we can earn without spending, we can save without investing, produce goods without demanding them.

Why does general equilibrium theory exclude, or how does it evade, all this? Because it excludes *uncertainty*, it assumes that economic man knows all he needs to know, can feed his *tastes alone* into a mental computer and obtain unambiguous directions about what to do to secure their maximum satisfaction. Some economists have in recent years made a concession to this aspect of human affairs, which is almost worse than no concession at all, since it betrays a still arrogant assumption of ultimate, unlimited human power. This concession consists in talking about 'incomplete information'. Why do I object to this formula? Because the essence of the human situation is that we can never know how much we do not know. To speak of 'incomplete information' suggests that there is such a thing as 'complete information', *known to be such*. How, in science's name, does one find out how much there is yet to be discovered?

General equilibrium excludes a true money, neglects uncertainty and assumes, not complete knowledge in any full sense, but an extremely limited problem which is artificially reduced to exact and certain solvability. General equilibrium also, as a quite separate matter, excludes *change*. It allows us, of course, to compare different equilibria, and this method, which consists in changing one at a time either the supposed structural parameters, that is, the 'reaction coefficients' of the system, or else its non-economic governing circumstances, such as the distribution of resources amongst different ownerships, is called comparative statics. But this is not the study of change, which surely ought to mean the examination of how one state of affairs arises naturally, or inevitably, from another, by an unbroken evolution described without gaps of time or logic. The rival camps into which today's world is split are engaged in a desperate race to prove to the 'uncommitted' nations that one or other of the two polar opposites, in the economic and political management of affairs, is the best, by helping those uncommitted nations to emerge from poverty and primitive economy into a self-sustaining advance. Thus, instead of equilibrium, the 'take-off' and 'growth' are the engrossing themes.

Lastly, equilibrium depends, for its full theoretical beauty and formal brilliance, on the assumption of *perfect competition*, which knits together firms, industries, individuals with a simplicity equal to that with which gravity seems to bind the physical universe. This, too, has had to go. How can we assume pervasive perfect competition in a world of giant concerns each having assets of a thousand million pounds and employing hundreds of thousands of people? Theory here has responded with a mighty effort. It was not without some excuse that the authors of the *Theory of Games and Economic Behaviour* blew their trumpet and demanded that the walls of Jericho should fall down. The walls of the older economic theory, which in all its various versions depended essentially upon the notions of the differential calculus, upon continuity and derivatives, were perhaps a little shaken but they remain very serviceable. Beside them the new city has been erected, based upon that famous building block, the 'payoff matrix'.

It is, I think, question 3 which is the most dangerous to the cohesiveness of Western economists. It can divide them for several reasons, and all of these reasons seem likely to distribute individuals in one and the same way between two camps. The elaborate plan, to which all private interests are to be subordinated, which solves in an arbitrary but not necessarily indefensible way the problem of balancing the advantage of some citizens, professions, classes and temporal generations of men against the disadvantage of others, and which requires a highly developed statistical basis for its foundation and administration, is the typical and central instrument of socialism. It may often be looked on as the surgeon's knife, the only means of remedying, albeit at the cost of much distress, a plainly unsatisfactory state of affairs; a state of affairs which *all* thinking people recognize as bad, regardless of the incidence of any proposed remedy upon themselves. But the cost, moral as well as economic, of such a plan is deemed too high by many economists. The cost is the loss of power to manoeuvre, the discarding of personal initiative, the repudiation of self-interest as a motive power; above all, perhaps, it is the feeling that to plan men's lives for them, even in the most general and impersonal way, is a usurpation of their right to govern themselves *continuously*.

However, it is not only the *desirability* of a long-term plan, but its *feasibility*, which divides economists. The belief that unprecedented feats of prognosis are now possible has been immensely strengthened by the electronic computer. Basically, belief in the possibility of assured prognosis rests on the belief that the future is a mere *interpretation* or *algebraic manipulation* of the past. *The way things go* must be expressible in a single, stable algebraic formula, if we are to be able to calculate the future. Prognostic power consists in regarding the economic cosmos as a machine; in *describing* this machine, as to its general principles of working, in algebraic terms, the parameters of which have been discovered, statistically, by a careful examination of the historical record and a systematic gathering of current information; and in filling in the blanks of the statement, namely, the recent numerical values of variables, to give the algebra 'something to bite on'. Now the validity of such a procedure depends on two assumptions: first, that the economic cosmos is in fact a machine; secondly, that we can discover enough about this machine, can reach not merely a *superficial* algebraic description which, for some particular historical period, broadly reconciles the behaviour of the set of variables we happen arbitrarily to have picked out, but a true, final grasp of its essential nature, giving due weight to the inconspicuous events which, by a self-regenerative or cumulative process, exert their arcane strength to enormous and unheralded effect.

But what, even in this account of things, can we mean by an *event*? If history is a series of states of affairs, transformed one into another by gradual or abrupt changes, and if this succession of states or, what would be its exact logical equivalent, the succession of changes by which some single initial state is transformed, can be universally *described* by a formula, then no one transformation of one state into another, no 'event', would have any special significance. Such an arbitrarily selected short segment of the pattern of history might be a clue or indicator of what was to follow, but could not be a *source* of what followed. Thus it follows, paradoxically, that what is commonly spoken of as a *dynamic* analysis is, in a deep sense, a timeless and static picture, embodying the conception of 'formulizable history'.

The advent of the electronic computer has made it possible to do an amount of arithmetic formerly inconceivable; to combine and re-combine our numerical data in a process of trial and error which is gigantic in its thoroughness and scope compared with what was formerly within our reach. If the economic cosmos is a machine; if the data we can collect about it are the ultimately meaningful data; then the description of it that we can evolve is going to be rendered more and more perfect by the new electronic tool. We are still left with a peculiar doubt: if a powerful computing laboratory situated, say, at Chicago, and another situated, say, at Moscow, give different descriptions of the economic cosmos, perhaps because the operators of these computers have been unable to treat the cosmos purely as a machine, but have, knowingly or not, fed into it some aspirations, some intended moves of their own, by which the working of the machine will be *modified*, which description are we to believe? When two infallible computing systems are *in contest* with each other, where are we to look for the infallible truth?

May I turn briefly in conclusion to the working methods of some of the great economists? With a brilliant insight, Mr Lawrence E. Fouraker of the Pennsylvania State University has penetrated and exposed the method of Marshall and Keynes:

Their intellects were too proud, resourceful and thorough to go on with the thesis without firmly establishing the connections. Having satisfied themselves, however, they employed a curious device when it came to recording the results of their pursuits. Instead of leading the reader through the intricate analytical processes that their own minds had recently traversed, they would provide a short cut, in the form of an assumption whose purpose was to eliminate consideration of the difficult problem they had faced and solved.*

No student of Keynes can fail to respond with admiring appreciation to this diagnosis. Keynes was an Alexander who loved to cut the Gordian knot, but first he tied up the knot himself, packing into it all the tiresome, irrelevant, non-essential, distracting and preliminary complexities and releasing himself from them at one blow. An example is his formulation of the marginal propensity to consume, which when properly stated is so irresistibly simple, so self-effacing as to pass unnoticed into the reader's mind until it is specially pointed out to him as a Trojan horse stuffed with tacit requirements about the distribution of income and the psychology of personal response to recent changes in income. More striking still is the example of the marginal efficiency of capital, so brilliantly incisive, effective, tidy, arithmetically satisfying and economical of thought, yet so astoundingly silent on the treatment of uncertainty. If the pace of growth of equipment is determined at that point where the demand price and the supply price of equipment are equal, or, equivalently, at that point where the marginal efficiency of capital is no greater than the market rate of interest on loans of money, how is the fact allowed for, that future profits, on which both demand price of equipment and marginal efficiency of capital depend, are a matter essentially of conjecture, of precarious and subjective hopes? Keynes put this essential uncertainty into the *shiftability* of the marginal efficiency schedule, which he thought of as being carried bodily up and down like a boat on the tides of business sentiment.

Do these tremendous short-cuts mean that English economic theory is no more than a sketchy formalizing of intuitions and instinctive judgements? Do they serve pragmatical expediency at the expense of principle, of the real search for radical, all-

* 'The Cambridge Didactic Style', *Journal of Political Economy*, vol. LXVI (February, 1958).

embracing coherence? Again there is the contrast of Marshall's 'partial' analyses of separate, isolated markets, vaguely linked by that curious equivocal concept of perfect competition, where changes of output do not, for the firm, yet do, for the industry, affect the market price, on the one hand; and on the other the general equilibrium of a comprehensively interdependent system, elaborated by Walras and by Pareto in such an immense span of sustained logic. And yet again there is the application of the jewelled adage discovered by Sir Isaiah Berlin: 'The fox knows many things, but the hedgehog knows one big thing.' The one big thing, for us, must, if it exists, be a universal principle of explanation able to cope with all economic phenomena. The nearest we have come to this is the Paretian general equilibrium, far as that is, as I tried to show, from explaining all things. The Marshallian scheme, by contrast, seems like a mountain seen first from one side, then from another, until at last we have seen all of it, but have still to make an effort of imagination to see it in the round.

There is a time, perhaps more than one, in the history of every science when it has its *mystique*: an idea, surprising, vaguely hinting at enormous powers of explanation, and far from being fully understood, takes command of some men's thought and imagination, and is followed to the stars. It is for these men a time of great happiness, a time filled with a sense of purpose, of conquest, of being members of a small *élite*, a time of achievement past and promised, of great prestige and a feeling of being borne upon irresistible waters of success. Such a time, in England, was the 1930's for those who had any share, however humble, in the Keynesian liberation. Whether a man was himself a liberator or a young convert whose feet were scarcely yet entangled in the classical net and was unknowingly eager for release, the time was magical.

The waters have long since receded, leaving, what? It is difficult to believe that if the Western world were again engulfed in a general deep business depression and massive unemployment, the governments would not unhesitatingly start to spend their way out of it. There would in every country be too many alternative leaders and governments vocally making plain the possibility of curing depression by creating and spending public money for any government, except a despotic one, to survive on a policy of leaving business to cure itself. 'We are all Keynesians now,' it has been said, and in a deep pragmatic and political sense this is surely true. Yet Keynes's name and the explicit statement of his ideas are in many places distasteful. The Middle West will have none of him. Little is heard of him in France, except among those in the very van of our science. Germany can dispense with him: why should the country whose 'economic miracle' has been founded on *laisser faire* trouble itself with Keynes's cure for a disease unknown to the modern generation? Countries there are, of course, which had their own lines of advance towards a macro-economic theory. Sweden had a vital contribution to make, a torch lit by Wicksell in the 'nineties and carried forward by Myrdal, Lindahl and their colleagues, pupils and successors. Poland had Kalecki who might have produced a Keynes-like theory on his own, for he had in his head already the germ of the idea. Yet it cannot be said that the Keynesian sunrise lit the whole academic world as that of the 1870's, the subjective revolution, did. The differences between the marginalists were unimportant, and there was in economics in the last quarter of the nineteenth century a true Concert of Europe including, as it were, America. Despite the immensely greater facilities for international movement, despite even the rise of international journals printed in several languages, there is perhaps less theoretical unity today than there was three-quarters of a century ago. This is partly due to the loss of simplicity in our subject. There are so many refinements and fine shades, such pursuit of absolute rigour and high precision, that we have lost the sense of a shapely, orderly and essentially simple body of knowledge. We know many things, but 'the one big thing' is still to seek.

# 2

# THE HEDGEHOG AND THE FOX*

## A SCHEME OF ECONOMIC THEORY

The economists of the nineteenth century wrote books with such titles as *The Principles of Political Economy* or *The Principles of Economics*, thus suggesting that they believed it possible to account for all sides and sorts of economic conduct and organization by a unified, coherent and self-consistent body of propositions. Notwithstanding his disclaimer, Sir John Hicks's *Value and Capital* was virtually a *Principles*. But it is the last that we have had. The year 1939, it seems, was the end of an era in economic theory as in other respects. It is said to be impossible nowadays to write a *Principles* because of the vast complexity and proliferant detail which economic theory now exhibits. But does not such a plea conflict with the very essence and purpose of theory? What is a theory if not a demonstration that a wide diversity of appearances are all illustrations of a single stereotype of associated or sequential circumstances? Theory is simplification, reduction of the manifold variety of the scene to the interplay of a few 'laws'. To say that economic theory has now become too diverse and intricate to be encompassed in one book is an abdication from the theoretician's task. Can we find some more respectable reason for the non-appearance of any new statement of a unified basis of economic theory?

The great explosion in economic theory occurred, I think, in the years immediately following Marshall's death in 1924. In the eleven years from 1926 to 1936 inclusive, six great new branches sprang from the tree. In Sweden, Myrdal and Lindahl inaugurated sequence analysis and brought in the vital concept of the comparison of the *ex-ante* and the *ex-post* image of one and the same segment of the calendar. In England, Mr Sraffa, Sir Roy Harrod and Mrs Joan Robinson, and in the United States Professor Chamberlin, created the theory of monopolistic competition. In England, also, Sir John Hicks and Professor

* With acknowledgements to Sir Isaiah Berlin, whose quotation from Archilochus suggested this title.

R. G. D. Allen (as they now are) worked out in indifference-map form the utility-free theory of consumer's behaviour. Wassily Leontief invented the most beautiful and powerful statistical tool of practical economic policy, perhaps, that we possess, in the input-output analysis of industrial interdependence. The 'new welfare economics', so-called, rose upon the ruins of interpersonal comparisons of utility. And last and most of all, John Maynard Keynes took over the unworkable under-consumptionist theories of J. A. Hobson and others, combined them with Professor Kahn's formulation of the Multiplier, added a theory of the multiplicand in which expectation and uncertainty were given a totally new emphasis and a new essential role, and thus rescued the economics of scarcity from its inherent inability to explain a state of massive unemployment of available productive resources. Keynes's system was immediately seen to be capable of vast developments. The theory of international payments has been revolutionized by it. Theories of the trade cycle have sprung from it, which make the old ones seem almost self-contradictory. And the Harrod–Domar theory of growth has become the basis of an obsession. Do all these ingenious and beautiful constructions rest upon a single set of basic axioms concerning human nature and conduct, human social organization and institutions, and the ultimate defining conditions of conscious life itself? If we cannot unify these constructions, I think it is because of the fundamental differences in the presuppositions they respectively make about time and the implications of time concerning what men can know.

Pareto and his followers, if I have rightly understood them, have taken the view that the notion of equilibrium is central to all economic understanding, and is in effect the same thing as intelligibility. What is not in equilibrium, or seeking it, cannot be analysed, since it is disorderly, irrational and meaningless. I would say myself that equilibrium is a construction by which we enable ourselves to answer Yes to the question whether action can be rational, when we mean by a rational action one which is chosen in full and certain knowledge of all its relevant consequences. The consequences of any action of mine depend upon what actions are being simultaneously chosen by others. This will be true even if, by 'action', we mean a completely specified course of action extending to the furthest time-horizon with which the individual concerns himself. But how can I possibly know, when I choose my own action, what other people are at that same moment deciding to do? Only if there is a pooling of knowledge, a general interchange, amongst all those concerned, of information about the intended action of each. But this knowledge has got to be available to each person before he makes his own choice. Here indeed is a paradox and an apparent impossibility. What we have to suppose is that each person contributes to the common fund of knowledge a range of conditional intentions, the selection amongst them, the choice of that one to which he will eventually commit himself, being dependent on what action is chosen by each other person. This system of conditional intentions, expressed formally as a system of simultaneous equations, may then prove to be in principle solvable, the solution being a prescription of one action for each person, that action, namely, which he would elect out of his whole range of conditional proposals, given that each other person chooses that action which the solution prescribes for him. This is what I mean by a system of equilibrium actions. Equilibrium is rationality and is the sole means of perfect rationality. Now what are the implications of this construction for the nature of existence for those involved? It implies a momentary society, a cosmos of action which effectively exists only for one moment, a timeless system. For even if the actions which are chosen in it occupy a span of time in their performance, yet the acts of choosing these actions must be simultaneous and therefore in effect momentary.

Now, plainly, this is not a realistic picture or model of the world. We are conscious of a sequence of moments, leaving us with an impression or memory of a 'stretch of past time' and an historical story of successive choices and actions, and from this experience we deduce the promise of future sequential moments and a future evolution of states or events in a continuation of history. There can, indeed, be some approximation to the equilibrium model. For, in the economic aspect of life, we do not really need to know the technical details of other people's actions, but only the effect of these actions on our own situation and circumstances, and that effect is exerted, and becomes apparent, through the scarcity it gives rise to in those commodities that we, in rivalry with other people, need and desire, which scarcity makes itself felt in price on the market. The market and the pricing system are a vast computer which is programmed with every person's list of conditional intentions and which then proceeds to solve the total system and prescribe for each person his optimal action, an action optimal for him in view of other people's actions.

The pricing system, if given free play, allows our actions to be quasi-rational. But to emphasize this aspect of things is necessarily to neglect others. We cannot throw the spotlight on one part of life without thereby casting the other parts into relative obscurity. We need theories which will take account of the fact of sequential choices and actions and all that this non-simultaneity of choice implies. For it implies that choices are made by each of us in ignorance of relevant circumstances, namely, the circumstances of that future, yet to be created partly by the choices now being made by other people, which will largely determine the outcome of our own choices. This uncertainty is an absolutely essential and inescapable condition of real life, and equilibrium is that economic model of life which deliberately abstracts from uncertainty and consciously and most ingeniously sets it aside. Thus it is essential to have other models besides equilibrium, ones which rest upon axioms that contradict the presuppositions of equilibrium. And you cannot combine into one general and unified model or theory, models or theories which respectively rest upon mutually incompatible or diametrically opposed assumptions. In these circumstances, a book called a *Principles* could of course still be written. But it would not describe a unified coherent system of ideas, only a collection of models or theories. Must we, then, admit that economics is not a science but a catalogue, at best a loose taxonomy? Is the economist no more than a tinker, willing to turn his hand to the repair of any object, carrying a bag of tools suitably miscellaneous and unrelated?

The tools are not unrelated, for each is a means to discover the actual or the commendable modes of action. But they are diverse, because only 'pure' theories can give us clarity and precision of insight: theories which are pure in the sense that each concentrates on one problem: and because this concentration and purity consists in simplifying their axioms or postulates to those which, at one and the same time, most fully liberate the influences, mechanisms or conditions we wish to study, and most severely inhibit the possible interference with them of anything alien to them or outside them. There is in this matter, as in visual aesthetics, a 'window effect'. How much more interesting, meaningful and suggestive is a scene framed by a window, confined to a small part of the total landscape and heightened in illumination by contrast with a dull or sombre wall! Attention is concentrated, as it were, along a beam, or directed down one particular vista. The viewer feels himself drawn into the scene and involved in it. Something analogous is achieved by rigorous abstraction, which limits a theory to a very few even of those considerations which are recognized to be ultimately inescapable. The one vital and especial respect in which theories must differ from each other for these reasons is that of the meaning and effect which we ascribe in them to time.

We have already looked at a theory which, so far as may be, eliminates or ignores time altogether. Fully rational action can occur only in a momentary or timeless system, because the lapse of time allows choice of actions to be made at dates which follow or precede one another, and which therefore cannot be brought into the scheme of general exchange of commitments. What parts of experience does the momentariness of equilibrium exclude?

Let us be clear about one respect in which the momentary model is entirely true to life: life is experienced 'one moment at a time'. We live in the solitary present. Whatever is actually happening to us or being done by us is happening or being done now. We remember past time and we imagine future time or its content, but we perform or experience these acts of remembering and imagining *now*, in the fleeting, evolving but *sole* moment of present time. But it is these acts of remembering and imagining that most essentially distinguish real life from equilibrium. Our choice of immediate action is made with a view to consequences in the future, and the only existence those consequences can now have, in the moment when choice is being made, is an existence in our imagination. Choice of action is made largely by reference to imagined consequences. Now in the most basic sense the imagination appears to have great freedom. May it not invent and improvise beyond any bounds that anyone can set? In saying that choice of action is choice amongst imaginations, do we destroy all possibility of analysing and making sense of such choice? I would answer this with three suggestions. First, I would say, there are constraints. We can, of course, compose fantasies, we can dream up a world unrelated to that of the experience coming from outside ourselves. But we shall not treat such fictions as having any bearing on our choice of action, because we have consciously released them from any relation to what is possible. Action is chosen with a view to *possible* imagined consequences. Yet this constraint itself is a most peculiar one. For whose is the judgement of what is possible? It is the individual's own. And what he judges to be possible is subject to his own powers of realistic invention, constrained only by his knowledge of what has been discovered of how the natural and human universes work. Thus arises my third suggestion: In judging what is possible, the individual is not working within 'rules of the game' discernible to others. However complete our knowledge might be of the individual's experience and personal history (and in reality this knowledge must of course be fragmentary in the extreme) there is, I would say, no assurance that we could tell in advance what he will invent, what will suddenly present itself to him as possible. But if so, we cannot predict his choice of action, and so we must abandon any hope of predicting history, except, perhaps, for its broadest secular movements. It need scarcely be added that such logical impossibility of prediction is only the final and fundamental obstacle on a road blocked by insuperable practical obstacles. It is inconceivable that enough information could be gathered and processed in time to yield a prediction, even if such information could in principle be sufficient to determine an outcome.

I have now tried to define for you the two extremes of one range of models involving time which, as it seems to me, economics must equip itself with. At one end we have the absence of time: a model which depends essentially on the effective exclusion of time can, I think, be said in a true if paradoxical sense to involve time. This is the model where relevant knowledge possessed by the participants is complete and known by them to be complete. At the other end we have models solely concerned with the structure of decision, that is, with the state of a single mind at a single moment. It is often said that economics deals with the affairs of society, of whole classes or nations of people, and sometimes it is explicitly denied that economics has any concern with the individual. This may have been a justifiable view when the subject-matter of economics was taken to be conduct in face of scarcity and the consequences of that conduct, for scarcity is the same thing as unsatisfied wants, and economists have always repudiated any obligation to explain why wants are what they are. The wants of individuals, taken as given without any examination of the minds of individuals, can be lumped together into the wants of society. But we have long given up the view that economics is no more than the observed or the recommended methods of coping with scarcity. The problem of general unemployment has taught us that economic conduct is a response not only to scarcity but also to a circumstance at least as imperious, namely, uncertainty. And in order to analyse the response to uncertainty we need some insight into the thoughts where uncertainty resides. This is what justifies us when we include, within our range of the economist's instrumental models (his range of insight-tools), one which studies the thoughts of a single person at a single moment.

But we cannot make do with only a single ordering principle, a single range of models, for it is not merely a question of our giving time, in some single role, more or less importance in our models, but of our giving it various roles and various meanings. When we think of time as personal experience or action, it is a solitary moment, even though the very nature and essence of this moment consists in its change into a different moment. But when we think of time as the locus of mechanism, that is, of a sequence of states each later one of which is necessitated by one or more earlier ones, we are taking simultaneous account of several distinct moments, and are giving to each of these distinct moments an equal status in our thought. There is here again some feeling of paradox, but it is easily dissolved. Not time only, but the thinking, feeling and acting human person has more than one role to play. He is a participant in the drama of life and also an observer of that drama. As participant he finds himself bound within the confines of immediacy, of the now. As observer, he can draw together into one structure, one thought-construct, all the moments of history; he can postulate cause and effect or necessary sequence and even, perhaps, conceive of everything that has happened or will happen as the solution of some very complicated differential equation. But however vast the panorama of history that he thus embraces, he contemplates it all in one thought occurring at one moment.

In order to relate to each other models which are thus basically different in character, we need a scheme which can order them on several independent axes. I shall suggest a threefold ordering, in respect of the importance of mechanical, evolutionary and expectational time. We could say that the working of a motor-cycle engine is a long series of controlled experiments, or that it is a human attempt to isolate a small part of the cosmos and set up within it an artificial deterministic subcosmos. The engine is so designed that each phase of a cycle of states or events is naturally and, in a sense, inevitably followed by its proper and desired sequel until the first phase is again itself brought about. If we ask how it is that an engine of a suitable design works in this way, the ultimate answer can only be that the design makes use of the properties of nature. The natural world exhibits certain stereotypes of behaviour. Gas when heated exerts pressure to expand, the heat can be generated by composing this gas of oxygen and a fine mist of petrol vapour and igniting it, and so on. Such an engine suggests itself as an analogy for some of the appearances,the phenomena, of society in its economic life. The so-called business cycle is an idealization of a seeming repetitive pattern of events which resembles in certain formal respects that of the engine. The time occupied by the engine in going through its cycle will, if the throttle is left alone, be constant. The length of the piston-stroke is constant. Above all the sequence of phases is constant. In the record of the quarterly or monthly measurements of the size of the society's general output, the percentage employed of those desiring to be, and so on, we may feel that we discern some rough regularity in the upward and downward swings. The time occupied from peak to peak or from trough to trough, the size of swings and the 'shape-type' of the curve we get if we plot the measurements of output and employment on a diagram may seem to preserve some constancy through a series of successive instances of the cycle. If, now, we believe in the *causal unity* of this pattern of events; if, that is to say, we regard each phase as part of a stereotype which lies across a series of distinct dates, so that the events of one date are part of a structure embracing those of one or more other dates, so that, if the earlier events are different in two instances of the pattern, so will the later events be, and, if the later events of two instances are different, so must the earlier events of these instances have been; and if we direct our attention to this causal unity exclusively; then we are using a model which, for its own quite legitimate purposes, excludes the human act of decision in the sense we have given to this word above, namely, an act which is not purely and merely the inevitable, uniquely possible response to circumstances, the necessary outgrowth of the past, but contains an element of *ex nihilo* invention and origination. The view of society's acts as mechanism is a different view from that of its acts as non-empty decision,* as the creation of emerging history. The binding together of different dates by mechanism, the cutting asunder of different dates by decision: seemingly opposite and conflicting principles. Yet, by high paradox, one is necessary to the other. If there were no stereotypes, no repetitive patterns of small-scale partial determinism, no order in nature and in social nature, decision would be powerless, for there could be no knowing what range of rival hypothetical consequences to assign to any contemplated available act, let alone any feeling certain, on the evidence of the past, what precise, unique result would follow from what present act. Yet though mechanism, or a belief in it, is essential to non-powerless-seeming decision, we still need to keep mechanism and decision as separate principles in our minds and theories; we shall still do well to have separate models of the one and the other.

I sought earlier to contrast action based on complete knowledge, on one hand, and the inventive origination of possible outcomes of available acts, on the other, as the two poles or extremes of one out of many possible systems of ordering theories or models. This particular system orders them according to the importance in them of uncertainty. The equilibrium model has as its whole purpose the total exclusion of uncertainty; the decision model has as its sole concern the study of how men exploit

* The reader who desires to have this and some related terms more fully defined is referred, with apologies for the impracticability of expanding the matter here, to the present writer's *Decision, Order and Time in Human Affairs* (Cambridge University Press, 1961).

that freedom which uncertainty confers upon thought and imagination. In considering mechanism in economic theory we are led to a different system, where the ordering principle is the relative importance of the idea of a structure or stereotype spanning a number of distinct dates so that the events of these respective dates can be looked on as bound together in mathematical functions. Again we have at one extreme the equilibrium model where there is but one effective date. At the other we have those models in which time is no more than a formal space, rendered sterile and fruitless of any essential origination by the reign of a perfect determinism insulated from everything not explicitly included in the model. Such models are self-sufficient and self-contained. They are engines working independently of their surroundings. Such a model is composed of a list of variables (for example, the society's general output or aggregate income, its aggregate net investment, its aggregate consumption) every one of which is shown as depending only on the numerical values assumed by other variables of the list at the same or earlier dates, or on the first, second, etc., derivatives or differences of these other variables with respect to elapsing time. The inclusion of stochastic variables in such a model is an admission rather of the difficulty in practice of making a sufficiently inclusive list of non-stochastic variables, to achieve insulation and determinism, than of the relevance of essential uncertainty.

We have one more axis or ordering system to define. For though the particulars of the business scene may seem chaotic, this fact does not preclude us from seeking some pervasive, permanent and unobtrusive principles, which may conceivably be at work, like the principle of heritable random mutations in biology, gradually modifying the successive generations of those seemingly capricious particular events or entities, and thus effecting an evolution in a steady irreversible current. With this threefold scheme in mind, let us see how some widely studied economic models can be related to each other.

Having proposed in the foregoing a rather personal view of the meaning and purpose of the equilibrium construction, we shall not cite any one example of it. This timeless model serves as the 'origin' of our scheme, representing the 'leftmost'* place in

* According to the ordinary mathematical convention of letting variables, in this case the importance of some meaning of time, increase towards the 'right'.

all three orderings. For a wide coverage, geographically, chronologically and doctrinally, let us take our examples from Cambridge, England, and Cambridge, Massachusetts; from Oxford, Vienna and Stockholm; and from the nineteenth as well as our own century.

Marshall's place in the literature is *sui generis*. Aim and method alike have no parallel or near-parallel, save in the work of some of his disciples, in whose hands, however, the candle-light has been replaced by a harsher and more concentrated ray. Marshall sought to explain the mode of development of firms, industries and societies, recognizing that the source of his observations, later Victorian England, was only one short period in the history of one country, yet hoping to distil and generalize from these observations some principles 'whereby the experience of one time and one age may throw light on the difficulties of another' (*Principles of Economics*, Appendix C, § 4, p. 777). *Marshall's principle* can be summed up thus: The more radical the change, the greater the incentive required to make it worth while, and the longer the period required to effect it economically; and a greater incentive means in practice a larger market or a market of a given size lasting longer; for if the absolute quantity of goods demanded can be supplied over a longer period, a smaller equipment can produce it. Thus all comes down to the length of the period involved: the 'long period' makes payable and possible a more profound development than the 'short period'. Marshall's principle explains the tempo of industrial and commercial development, and the peculiar nature of such development, which is like the successive revelation of fresh horizons by every stage of ascent from sea-level, so that in the very process of growth of firms and industries, economies are achieved which make still greater growth feasible and bring still further possible economies into view. What Marshall sought to describe was the adaptive, exploratory struggle of a species, the line of organisms called firms or industries, towards greater efficiency and mastery of the environment. He sought to describe the modes of economic evolution.

The fashionable literary exercise of tracing the character, content and form of a man's work back to its supposed sources in his heredity, life experience and the history of his times could not, perhaps, be very fruitfully pursued in the case of most economists, who are not usually amongst the major figures on the stage of action and adventure. But with John Maynard Keynes we are, I think, losing much illumination and a sense of the poetic unity which can inform even the supposedly prosaic exertions of those who work in the 'kitchen sink' of sciences, the economists, if we neglect his quite specially interesting career. Keynes, the son of a distinguished economist, early showing a mathematical aptitude which was attentively nurtured even before he went to Eton, and reading the Mathematical Tripos at Cambridge to become a Wrangler (*i.e.* a First Class Honours man), was brought into further contact with the most practical aspect of economics by his appointment to the India Office. While there he launched himself upon a task which, though it might appear unrelated to economics, was, in my own view, a determining influence on what he later achieved. He began to write *A Treatise on Probability*. Now this Treatise on Probability is very different in nature and purpose from those exercises in pure calculation of odds which the phrase 'probability theory' normally conveys. As a branch of mathematics, probability is the business of counting cases and of combining these counts in intricate patterns to conform to stipulated practical forms of random experiment. How different was Keynes's purpose! He asked himself whether rules can be found for interpreting a body of evidence insufficient to yield demonstrable, uniquely certain conclusions, rules such that the inferences or recommendations derived by their aid would be as respectable, as worthy of being accepted and acted on, in the face of an impossibility of getting any more evidence, as if the evidence were in fact sufficient for certainty. What he studied was something very near to the business man's problem of investment decision, when with evidence that cannot be sufficient, since it consists at best of knowledge about the present or past whereas the question depends on circumstances of the future, he has to decide whether or not, now, to order specified specialized expensive equipment.

When, later on, Keynes confronted the paradox of general unemployment in a society still fundamentally constrained by scarcities in all directions, the paradox, that is to say, of a society which needs all the output it can achieve yet leaves large parts of its productive resources idle, it was perhaps natural that he should find the solution in men's awareness of ignorance of the future, an ignorance which is at least as basic a fact of human existence as scarcity itself. An individual or a firm which can command large resources of money can get access to the hope of gain only by exposing itself to the fear of loss. To invest the money, the fund of general purchasing power, in buying specialized equipment exposed to all the uncertainties of obsolescence, fashion and commercial rivalry and hostility, is to invite both hopes and fears. Sometimes the fears will be stronger and liquidity will be preferred. But if there is not enough investment there will be too little production as a whole, and consequently unemployment, for general output is geared to net investment (or more generally, to the 'multiplicand' comprising net investment, the export surplus and part of the government deficit) by the famous Multiplier whose numerical value depends on the society's propensity to consume. Thus it is to the varying depth and oppressiveness of uncertainty of expectation that Keynes ascribes the occurrence of general unemployment.

Keynes's theory was the solution of a paradox. The contrast between his meaning and his method was itself a paradox. And the use made of the component parts or structural members of his theory by some of his younger contemporaries was the greatest paradox of all, for in a sense they ignored his essential vision. Keynes's meaning was the precariousness and fragility of expectations, and the effect on men's decisions of their latent, and sometimes acknowledged, awareness of this instability. His method or formal frame was an equilibrium, a state of affairs where the net investment intended by one sector of society, the enterprisers, was equal to the saving intended by society as a whole. Moreover, although it seems to me perfectly justifiable to speak here of intended investment and intended saving, Keynes himself does not do so, but is even tempted into the fallacy of arguing that because net investment and saving are equal identically and by definition when they are the records of past action, they can be taken as equal to each other always and in all senses. Keynes does not, in fact, use the *ex-ante–ex-post* distinction. His method is therefore one of comparative statics, it consists in a comparison of different equilibria, with a mere hint of some cascade of disorderly events carrying the economy from one equilibrium to another. And in this formal frame the essential meaning of time is expectational time, the imagined history of the future, which each man is free, within bounds of plausibility imposed by his own experience, to invent in his own fashion. But the 'Keynesians', Kalecki and Kaldor, Harrod and Hicks (but not Mrs Joan Robinson) made a quite different sort of construction out of the beams and stanchions which Keynes had given them. They made models which depended on *mechanical* time.

The chief formal difference between Keynes's own construction and those of his principal followers is that Keynes has no equation linking net investment with the other variables of the system, while in the models of regular growth or of the business cycle, in which Harrod, Kalecki, Kaldor, Hicks and others have applied Keynesian ideas to problems beyond that of under-employment equilibrium, net investment is made to depend on general output or its speed of change, on the size of the capital stock, and so on, so as to produce a self-contained system where everything which happens is explained from within the system. This difference is profoundly significant and marks an opposition in basic philosophy. Keynes's concern is to show the occasional or protracted drying-up of enterprise as a consequence of the constitution of human nature and the ordained uncertainty in which human affairs are inescapably conducted. He is thus bound to study the moment, the situation, the interplay of forces which are mutually contemporary in the strictest sense, the uneasy peering over the edge of time. Keynes had been in the thick of the fight, he wrote as a participant. His followers were more detached in experience and outlook. They took the attitude of observers of the scene from without, looking upon a stretch of time and its history without, in effect, assigning to any point of it the status of a meaningful present. They described a structure, not of valuations, expectations and pressures but of objective events occurring at different points of a space or dimension representing extensive time. They treated economics as mechanism. There are, of course, important differences between the particular models. Harrod says:

I regard the fundamental concept in dynamic economics as the rate of increase, just as the state of rest is that of statics. It is the rate of increase that obtains *at a given point of time*, [italics in the original] given the fundamental determinants. In dynamics...we are not, according to my view, concerned with a succession of events through time. The analogy with mechanics is, surely, precise. There we seek to determine the velocity of a particle in consequence of the forces acting upon it at a particular instant.

Despite this interesting passage, where it will be noticed that Harrod positively claims and not merely concedes the analogy between his system and the operation of inanimate forces, we must point out that Harrod's concept of the regularly progressive economy, growing according to a compound interest law, is the solution of a differential equation and thus, since the independent variable is 'time', necessarily involves implicitly the idea of time-lags. Acceleration, though by a limiting process we make it refer to a 'point of time', arises from the comparison of speeds in two intervals, one succeeding the other.

Let me try to sum up the suggestions I have made. In a brilliant passage,* Sir Isaiah Berlin once referred to a line which has been preserved from the poet Archilochus: 'The fox knows many things, but the hedgehog knows one big thing.' Sir Isaiah, and others following him, have compared the hedgehog of this passage to one type of scientist or philosopher and the fox to another. The hedgehog is the system-builder, the seeker after one sole all-encompassing Principle of Nature, a theory which explains everything by a unified conception of what the cosmos is. Such a theory might be itself compact, like the acorn, but able to unfold the whole glory of the heavens and the earth, like the oak which so massively arises in the regularity and beauty of its structure from the minute germ. The fox by contrast is the scientist who is content with a practical and partitioned knowledge, with understanding one thing at a time by reference, in each case, to an ultimately arbitrary pattern or stereotype. Specialists of this sort, working in various departments of knowledge, will doubtless use each other's knowledge as something they can take for granted and which they are not themselves bound to explain or test, and thus out of a variety of particular theories each dealing with a different aspect of affairs, a kind of stepping-stone science may be built up, where transitions in practice are possible but no all-inclusive continuity is achieved.

* Sir Isaiah Berlin, *The Hedgehog and the Fox* (Weidenfeld and Nicholson, 1953).

Even within our own subject, the choice between these two types of endeavour presents itself. General equilibrium, as understood by Pareto, is perhaps an attempt to see the whole economic scene as the manifestation of the free operation of self-interest within a frame of law and order. But this principle tacitly assumes that, while material powers and resources are scarce, knowledge is not scarce, but on the contrary every participant possesses, or can obtain, all knowledge relevant for his own choices. If, with Keynes, we reject this as totally at variance with fact, general equilibrium leaves great questions unexplained. If, with Harrod and others, we believe that continuing growth of the economy's productive power is the condition of its making full use at each date of the productive power it then has, still another kind of model is required. Keynes himself declared that our ultimate ignorance of the future, the awareness of which can inhibit enterprise and cause unemployment, is not something which can be overcome by a more thorough and powerful statistical technique. Yet it is something that we have to cope with. What kind of thoughts can select our actions for us, and give us the sense of εὐδαιμονία in committing ourselves to the course or policy thus chosen, in face of ineluctable uncertainty? This is the question which Keynes ignored and altogether omitted from his discussion, merely assuming that there is some answer to it and that in any case it was necessary to go on and discuss the character and consequences of a situation where men choose their actions irrationally (for that, in effect, is what he said). So yet another type of theory is needed, to give an account of the very act of decision, of creative choice, of action choice which is not mere response; is not, because the pressures to which the choice might respond are not in themselves coherent and intelligible. The Keynesian gap must be filled more effectively than by the mere footnote on page 24 of *The General Theory*.

I have been suggesting to you that the economic theoretician must be content to know many things and not seek to know one big thing. Economics in its orthodox form is concerned rather with the surface of things (I do not in the least intend this as a derogatory remark). It has renounced the endeavour to reach down to the deep roots of human conduct. Thus it is from the outset precluded from the search for any unifying principle in that conduct. What can be done? If we cannot have a *system*, we can have a *scheme*, an orderly array of theories differently grounded in basic assumptions, some assuming perfect knowledge, some acknowledging uncertainty, some concerned with progressive, irreversible evolution, some with mechanical, insulated, deterministic repetition: an outfit of tools, not an ultimate philosophy.

# 3

# KEYNES AND THE NATURE OF HUMAN AFFAIRS

The first of John Maynard Keynes's principal works was *A Treatise on Probability*, and the second was *A Treatise on Money*.* A casual reader of these titles might suppose them to represent two unrelated aspects of the work of a man who, the son of a distinguished economist, was himself trained in mathematics and was later drawn back into economic concerns by his early career as a civil servant. In reality, these two books are outward manifestations of the two elements which Keynes fused into his final vision of men's economic life. *Probability* was a bad title for the earlier book, since it suggested the essentially arithmetical procedures by which knowledge and certainty can be attained in such matters as insurance. Instead, that book is concerned with the bases, the meaning and the proper scope of *judgement* in human affairs; and the scope of judgement is precisely that area which excludes the kind of arithmetical certainty attained by actuaries in their proper concerns. No doubt Keynes thought when he wrote the *Treatise on Probability* that it would prove possible to formulate a logic of judgement, so that *uncertain judgements* could claim to be as well founded as the conclusion of a syllogism. Later, perhaps, he came to regard any such 'certainty in uncertainty'† as illusory. For in the last of his central works, a mere article in length‡ and yet in power and fundamental challenge certainly the apotheosis of his thought, Keynes tried to exhibit the evasions, the conventional modes of refusal to recognize the nature of life, by which business

* John Maynard Keynes, *A Treatise on Probability* (London, 1921, reprinted London, 1952); *A Treatise on Money* (London, 1930, 2 vols; reprinted London, 1952).

† I venture, by this phrase, to try to express the paradoxical, will-o'-the-wisp nature of the goal which Keynes, and others since, seem to me to have dreamed of, necessarily in vain.

‡ J. M. Keynes, 'The General Theory of Employment', *The Quarterly Journal of Economics*, vol. LI (Cambridge, Mass., 1936/37), pp. 209 seqq. Reprinted in *The New Economics, Keynes's Influence on Theory and Public Policy*, ed. with introd. by Seymour E. Harris (New York, 1948), pp. 181 et seqq.

men pretend to themselves that their acts are based upon sufficient reason.

What, then, has *money* to do with this inherent ignorance concerning the outcomes of our acts, in which we make our choice of those acts? At those times when we are more than usually aware of this ignorance, we are strongly tempted to postpone decision, to wait until we feel less unsure. But how can we wait? In what sense can we wait? Do not the events of life press upon us all the time, calling for response on our part, calling for choice and for action? In particular, how can there be postponement of choice in the market-place? When a producer wishes to exchange his own product for another man's product, must he not decide, there and then, what other product he will seek and accept? No. For he can take money. Money, traditionally called a medium of exchange, is indeed a medium of postponement, a means of separating in time the act of sale and the act of purchase. This is so obvious that it may be thought scarcely worth putting into words. And yet it is this which, in a money economy, destroys the validity of Say's Law, the proposition that supply creates its own demand; it is this which makes possible an insufficiency of effective demand, so that not everyone can get employment who offers his labour for the going wage.

Keynes's vision of the nature of money, as something which enables the individual person or firm to *save* without committing himself to specialized, concrete, vulnerable forms of wealth, and his understanding that the source of the desire to do so is a part of the inescapable human condition, the conscious inability to know for sure the consequences of our far-reaching actions, are beyond the reach of fashionable attempts to find fault with details of what is supposed to be his 'system'. To build an economic 'model' or abstract deductive scheme, in which it is assumed that all economic variable quantities, such as prices and the quantity of money existing in the economy, and the money balances which individuals wish to hold, attain a final and perfect mutual adjustment without friction or lapse of time, or alternatively that all the time in the world (Alfred Marshall's *long period*) is available for them to find this adjustment; to seek plausibility for this model by bestowing upon the persons in it a guarantee that all their expectations will prove uniquely correct; and to proceed to a demonstration that this model is different from the world of human limitations and fallibilities which Keynes was studying, and that therefore his theory can be dismissed, is to tear the pages out of the history books and declare that the 1930's never happened.

I have referred to the first, the second and the fourth of what it seems to me proper to regard as Keynes's central works. The third in the series is by far the most famous of them all, a book which exploded into the world of liberal economic thought in 1936 and obtained for itself, overnight, bitterly outraged opponents and also converts who saw in it practical and theoretical salvation. *The General Theory of Employment, Interest and Money** is something of a paradox. In it the equilibrium method is made the vessel of a theory which emphasizes the insecurity of the human mind in its business affairs to explain the failure, as earlier economists would have regarded it, of the economy to attain its optimum in the full and best use of its available resources. For the 'classical' economists, by which term Keynes meant the subjective value theorists of the period from 1870 until the date of his own writing, an equilibrium was an *optimum* state of affairs, either within a particular part of the economic system or throughout every part and aspect of that system. For those economists, moreover, it would have been inconceivable that the economy as a whole could fail, except through friction and slowness of adaptation to change, to use to the utmost the resources available to it. Was not economics the study of how men deal, or can best deal, with *scarcity*? How can they be said to be overcoming the parsimony of nature if they do not at least bring into service all that she offers them? Anything that could be called an 'unemployment equilibrium' would have seemed to them impossible, and the expression itself a contradiction in terms. It was this view which Keynes contested, and which, in the opening pages of his book, he rejected with a scornful intransigeance which offended some of his earlier readers.

Keynes found a science whose central idea was that of scarcity; he left one in which scarcity had been joined by a second idea of equal importance, that of *insecurity*. *The General Theory of*

* J. M. Keynes, *The General Theory of Employment, Interest and Money* (London, 1936). German ed.: *Allgemeine Theorie der Beschäftigung, des Zinses und des Geldes.* Ins Deutsche übers. von Fritz Waeger (Munich and Leipzig, 1936).

*Employment, Interest and Money* shows in detail how insecurity kills the enterprising spirit which, in the Western economy of free enterprise, is the driving-force that gives employment. Its use of the equilibrium method was natural and justifiable, for equilibrium is that state of affairs which results from the free play and interplay of self-interest. Self-interest, when oppressed by a conscious ignorance of the future, may take refuge in a defensive policy, a policy of avoiding the risks of enterprise and the dangers of committing one's wealth to concrete and specialized forms that depend for their success, and the maintenance of their value, on fortunate guesses about that future. It is *rational*, in some circumstances, for individual firms and persons to desire money rather than machines; but the creation of money gives no employment, the making of machines gives much employment, and so *liquidity preference* can lead to a state of affairs where particular self-interest has defeated general prosperity and has led to an under-employment equilibrium.

*Production* consists in making things more useful, and so more valuable. By bringing up coal from the seams, by tanning skins, by fabricating steel into ships' plates, by fashioning clay into pottery, by gathering crops from the fields, we increase the power of all these things to serve men's needs. When allowance has been made for the fact that, in making some things more useful, others are made less useful (so that a gain in the usefulness of iron is obtained at the cost of a loss in the usefulness of the coal which is burnt in the smelting process), the market value of the total gain in usefulness achieved in one week or one year is the aggregate *income* for that week or year of all the people who have helped, by working, by allowing the use of their property, by organizing and by bearing the risks of commerce, to effect this gain in usefulness. This income is paid out to them in the form of money, and by spending this money they can claim their shares of the various things which embody the results of their productive efforts. They are then free to *use up* these things, by eating them, wearing them as apparel, burning them as fuel, or, in general, by *consuming* them.

Suppose, however, they do not wish to consume all that they have produced. Or, at any rate, suppose they do not wish to consume all of it *now*, but prefer to hold in reserve the right and power to consume some of it at a later date, when they may need it more acutely. So far as these income-earners, who thus wish to *save*, are concerned, the matter is simple: they merely refrain from spending, within a week or a year, some of the money they have earned in that week or year.

From the would-be savers' point of view, the matter is simple. But what will now happen to the goods whose production gave rise to the money income, only part of which has been spent on these goods? The value of these goods is equal to the *whole* of the money income earned in producing them; the *whole* of the money income will need to be spent on them, if all of them are to be bought. Who will buy that part of a year's total production, which corresponds to that part of the year's total income which the income-earners wish to save? There are, in broad headings, three kinds of people who may buy it. First, there are business men themselves, the heads of firms, who may wish to extend and improve the machinery and buildings which they use in production. To do this is, in the economist's language, to *invest*. Secondly, there are the people of other countries, who may be willing to buy more from our country than they sell to it. When they sell goods to us, they use up some of our income, which we might otherwise spend on our own products. But when we sell to them, our products are bought without the use of any of our income. So any *export surplus*, any excess of the total value of our exports over that of our imports, is an outlet for some of our products which we, as *consumers*, are not willing to buy. And thirdly, there is the Government itself, which needs masses of goods and services of all sorts, to provide medical care, education, justice, defence and even housing and transport, and which taxes away part of the people's income in order to pay those individuals who actually supply these services. By annually buying goods worth more, in total, than the income which the Government annually collects in taxation, the Government also helps to provide an outlet for goods which cannot be sold to consumers.

There were two ideas which Keynes had at the outset to impress upon the readers of his *General Theory of Employment, Interest and Money*. First, the act of *saving*, that is, of not spending on consumption part of the income earned in producing goods, is in itself a destroyer of employment. By buying goods a person encourages others to produce further goods of the same kind. But by refusing to buy goods, a person makes it appear unprofitable to produce such goods, and to give employment in order to supply them. Secondly, in contrast to what the 'classical' economists had assumed, there is no mechanism or link by which acts of saving encourage investment. The fact that private income-earners wish to save does not, of itself, in any way encourage business men to wish to extend or improve their equipment. On the contrary: saving in itself implies a reduction of the annual quantities of goods which can be sold; why should it be expected to encourage business men to prepare to produce larger annual quantities of goods for sale?

The 'classical' answer to his latter question was the next of the fallacies which seemed to Keynes to need refutation. That classical answer rested on the idea that the rate of interest (which business men must pay when they borrow money to buy machines) was determined by a tug-of-war between this desire to borrow for the purchase of machines, and the reluctance of income-earners to save and lend because they wished, instead, to consume their income at once. This reluctance to save and lend, the classicists thought, had to be overcome by the offer of interest; but plainly business men would only offer such interest as they could hope to recoup from the profits of using machines. Thus the interest rate would settle at a level which would balance the demand for and the supply of saving. Keynes pointed out, in criticism of this view, that many people who have saved or acquired in some other way a stock of wealth which they are free to consume, do in fact neither consume nor lend it but hold it in the form of money. Moreover, he said, only if aggregate income were constant could we ascribe the determination of the amount annually saved to the working of the interest rate; while in fact aggregate income varies very greatly.

In supposing that the variability of income destroyed the classical case, Keynes's logic was unsound. He sought to overthrow the classical belief that the interest rate equilibrates saving and investment, and has its level in that way determined, by pointing out that large changes in aggregate income, such as we are bound, by the very nature of the problem of massive unemployment, to recognize as possible, would themselves imply large changes in the amount annually saved, even if the interest rate remained constant. A man who saves £200 a year out of an income of £1000 will not be able to save £200 if his income drops to £500. From the fact that the aggregate amount annually saved plainly depends upon aggregate income among other things (and might, for example, quite reasonably be assumed to be a constant proportion of aggregate income, the other things being given, over some ranges of that income), Keynes deduced unjustifiably that the interest rate is not influenced by the 'propensity to save' of the people all taken together. To make this inference was to out-Marshall Marshall in his method of considering only two variables at a time. For let us accept Keynes's own assertion that interest is the price of *money*, and is received by those who lend their money and foregone by those who insist on retaining money itself rather than interest-bearing bonds. Now when income is less, a smaller quantity of money, changing hands a given number of times a year, can mediate the transactions and thus, if instead of shrinking with income the quantity of money in the economy stays constant, there will be more spare money available to satisfy people's desire for a reserve. Thus the price of money, that is, the interest rate, will be lower when income is lower; and income *will* be lower, Keynes had shown, when people wish to save a larger proportion of each given possible level of income. Since the lowering of the interest rate will encourage investment, and investment means the creation of income, a new equilibrium may be attained when for any reason the propensity to save has become stronger. The propensity to save, or the general level of thriftiness, does, it seems, influence the interest rate, and the latter could, if we treated money merely as a medium of exchange and a reserve against contingencies, be looked upon as determined by thriftiness and the profitability of machines.

Keynes had, we have to admit, an even cruder argument to show that the interest rate is not the equilibrator of saving and investment. For, he said, saving and investment are necessarily equal. In the language of mathematics they are *identically* equal, being but two names for the same thing. For investment is the excess of what is produced over what is concurrently consumed; and saving is the excess of what is earned by production over what is spent on consumption. But to argue thus is like arguing that because, in the market for some commodity, the quantity bought is necessarily equal to the quantity sold, price cannot equilibrate the supply and demand for that commodity. If we assume that the annual amount people are willing to save is a function of the interest rate, and that the annual value of equipment they are willing to buy is another function of the interest rate, all we need further assume is that some market or mechanism exists where agreement can be reached between potential saver-lenders and potential borrower-investors as to the interest rate which will satisfy both parties at some determinate level of annual lending–borrowing. Keynes was here less excusably wrong, for warnings were available from two distinct sources. A consideration of the meaning of Marshallian demand-and-supply analysis would really have supplied one. But there is an alternative, more illuminating and more realistic approach. When we speak of *potential* savers and investors, we are really speaking of people's intentions or plans for action in some, still future, interval. It is difficult to imagine in reality any arrangement for organizing compatibility between the plans of different people in regard to saving and investing, for unlike their purchases on a commodity market, these plans are not instantly put in execution but look forward over a stretch of time. When the attempt is made to execute incompatible plans, some plans will necessarily fail to be realized and will have to be revised. Thus we may think of a particular time-interval as looked at first from its beginning, when the actions and quantities related to it are intentions or expectations and everything in this interval is seen *ex ante facto*; and secondly from its end, when the interval has passed into history with its actions and quantities necessarily made consistent with each other, and all these things are seen *ex post facto*. The essential distinction between the *ex ante* and the *ex post*, due to the Swedish school, would greatly have clarified Keynes's thought had he been familiar with it.

We shall touch below upon the antagonism that the *General Theory* roused, and was, one might say, intended to rouse, amongst those who thought of economics as the science of being economical. The theory of interest rates was, perhaps, the focus of this antagonism. For the traditional theory declared that it was morally right and practically expedient to *save*, and that the act of saving, of abstaining from consumption, was the way to build up wealth. Now Keynes appeared to be saying that saving, in itself, would do harm, that it did not encourage but merely *permitted* investment and the augmentation of wealth, and that in particular it did nothing to reduce the interest rate. What, then, did Keynes put in place of the older theory?

Whereas income, saving and investment are quantities of the kind which economists call a *flow*, that is, something whose size is stated as so and so many tons, gallons, dollars, etc. *per unit of time*, Keynes directed attention to quantities of a different kind, namely, a *stock*, the size of which is stated as so and so many tons, dollars, or dollars' worth, *simpliciter*, without any division of the number of dollars by the number of weeks or years. Thus £1,000 *per annum* is a flow, but £1,000 itself is a stock. Two particular quantities of the 'stock' type seemed to Keynes especially relevant to the problem of interest rates, the stock of money and the stock of bonds, that is, of acknowledgements of debt. The whole quantity of money, existing at some instant in an economy, we may think of as made up of the number of money units owed by all the commercial banks to their customers, plus the bank-notes and coins in the pockets of people and in the tills of shops, plus the still unused amounts which banks have given permission to their customers to borrow from them. If, in other words, we ask 'What is the total value of payments which could be *simultaneously* made, at some one instant, by all persons, firms, etc., taken together?', this is the quantity of money.

Now it is convenient and necessary for several reasons for each person and firm to have his own stock of money; to possess at all times some portion of the nation's total stock of money. He needs it in order to make payments in the interval between his receipts of money from other people; for example, in the intervals between the payments to him of his wages or salary. He may also wish for a reserve against contingencies. But, especially, he may wish simply to hold money as a form of wealth, because by doing so he is guarded against any fall in the money values of *other* forms of wealth. Now amongst these other forms there is *bonds*, each bond being a promise given by a borrower to make payments to a lender according to some stated schedule. One type of such schedule specifies equal payments at equal time-intervals in perpetuity. The ratio of each such payment to the sum initially lent is then the 'coupon' rate of interest. But it is only the genuine rate of interest received by the lender, so long as the bond can be sold on the Stock Exchange for a price equal to the sum originally lent. If that price falls, for example, to half the sum originally lent, the genuine interest rate, called the yield, has doubled. The essential fact about lending on such terms is that the lender acquires the right to receive payments of stated amounts at *stated deferred dates*, and if, when he makes a loan, he cannot feel sure that he will not want his money before these dates, he exposes himself to the possibility that he will need to sell his bond on the Stock Exchange *at a price which he cannot know in advance*.

Naturally, a prospective lender needs both a safeguard against loss in such an event, and a reward for bearing the insecurity of mind which the making of a loan will place him in. This, Keynes said, is the most important reason why interest is paid. Is it not, however, just as possible, in general, for the price of bonds to rise as to fall? Is there not in the mind of a prospective lender the idea that he may make a capital gain, and be able after a time to sell his bond for more than he now gives for it? For most people, uncertainty is in itself a disutility, and the bearing of it requires a reward, so that lenders broadly require compensation. But there is a very important consequence of the fact that bond prices can, in general, move either way. For if all or the great majority of actual or potential owners of bonds believe that these prices are about, say, to rise, all of them will wish to be bond-holders and will buy bonds or refuse to sell those they have, and the generally expected rise of bond prices will follow *as a consequence* of this attitude and expectation. Again if all or most potential bond-holders believe in an imminent fall, all will sell or refuse to buy and the fall will occur. How far will such movements go? Any such movement must go far enough to change the beliefs of some of the wealth-owners so that there are at all times enough believers in an imminent bond-price *rise* to hold all outstanding bonds, and enough believers in an imminent *fall* to hold all the existing stock of money or, at any rate, such part of that stock as is not held for the 'transaction motive', the need to be ready to make payments.

To offer an explanation of interest which divorced it from the equilibrium mechanism was an essential part of Keynes's task. For suppose he had made interest to depend merely on the transactions and precautionary motives for holding money. Then, when unemployment rose, the pressure of job-seekers upon money wages, and of the poverty of the unemployed upon money prices of goods, and the general lack of effective demand, must so have reduced the total need for money to mediate the process of production, exchange and distribution that eventually the stock of money would have become so ample for these needs as to lower the interest rate and thus encourage investment to the point where full employment would have been restored. Instead, Keynes showed that the interest rate depends upon expectations, and thus that the whole demon-world of uncertainty enters in to baffle the calculator of nice margins of profit and prevent price flexibility from restoring full-employment equilibrium.

Uncertainty, however, has a far vaster channel than the interest rate through which to act upon investment decisions. For investment is action in search of profit, and profit is a mere figment of imagination. Not, of course, the accountant's profit, which has been realized and recorded and is a thing of the past. Investment is not undertaken in pursuit of a past, but of a *future* profit, and this in the last analysis is mere guesswork and hope, however carefully all available evidence is assembled and sifted. Who can know what the market for a new product will be like in a year or five years' time? Who can know what inventions and discoveries, between now and then, will make today's machinery obsolete? Who can know how the costs of the labour and the materials needed to operate this machinery will have changed? Who can know how the business man brings orderly simplicity and consistency out of the arrays of diverse and conflicting notions he may have on these matters? Yet simplicity and consistency must somehow be supposed to be attained, if we are to have a theory within the traditional equilibrium or maximizing frame of thought which Keynes used. For something has to be maximized, and one cannot maximize a bundle of contradictions. The formula he used, typical of the maximizing method, has an air of precision and certainty which sorts ill with its subject-matter. The profit which an investor seeks, this formula says, is the excess of the value of product over the operating costs of the equipment, considered separately for each year of the supposed useful life of the equipment, and discounted to the 'present' or moment of decision at the appropriate market rate of interest. The sum of such discounted profits is the investor's demand price for the equipment, and equipment will be ordered in such annual quantity, at a supply price per unit increasing with this quantity, as to make the supply price equal to the demand price for the *marginal units* of equipment which are ordered. Alternatively, we can discover what uniform percentage per annum, used in discounting the profits, would equate their discounted value to the supply price, and call this the *marginal efficiency of capital*.

The marginal efficiency of capital must of course be thought of as a schedule, having a different numerical value for each different annual amount of investment. In a Cartesian diagram with annual total value invested in equipment on one axis, and a scale of percentages per annum on the other, the marginal efficiency schedule will be represented by a curve falling from left to right, and thus intersecting, at some particular level of annual investment, a horizontal or rising interest curve. Thus we may formally suppose investment to be determined.

This conception of an equilibrium does not of itself at all suggest the part which investment plays in Keynes's scheme of thought. Some of his expositors, and those who, for example, have built theories of the trade cycle upon his ideas, have wanted to make a closed 'dynamic' system in which investment would depend on other variables within the system, so that, given the numerical values of some variables at a few different dates, the behaviour of income, consumption and investment through time could be calculated indefinitely. An example of such a self-contained dynamic system is Professor Hicks's *Contribution to a Theory of the Trade Cycle*,* where investment depends on the speed of growth of output as a whole. Such theories are alien (let me say with all respect to such writers as Harrod, Kalecki, Kaldor and Hicks who have most ingeniously exploited these possibilities of Keynesian economics) to the spirit of the *General Theory*. For Keynes, investment was highly capricious, autonomous and unpredictable. It was a *source* of the things which happened to the system, rather than a mere transmitter of circular impulses from one part of the system to another. The *accelerator*, the supposed dependence of the *speed* of investment on the *acceleration* of output as a whole, is notably absent from the *General Theory*. Investment could, indeed, be influenced and organized by the Government, and it was the possibility and the great unappreciated power of such action to cure unemploy-

* J. R. Hicks, *A Contribution to the Theory of the Trade Cycle* (Oxford, 1950).

ment which was the theme of Professor Richard Kahn's classic article on 'The Relation of Home Investment to Unemployment'.* This article established in economics the famous conception of the *multiplier*, which is one of the chief structural members of the *General Theory* and which we are now ready to consider and to use as the keystone of our discussion of that book.

We showed, above, that saving in itself creates a gap which has to be filled, in order that output as a whole, or income, may reach any predetermined level, such as that corresponding to full employment. But the annual amount that people will try to save depends pre-eminently, Kahn and Keynes said, upon the level of the income which they count upon receiving. This will be true for each individual in regard to his own income, and unless the shares of aggregate income going to various income brackets change very markedly as the aggregate increases, it will be true of the saving and income of people all taken together. Regarding the specific form of this functional dependence of aggregate saving, or of aggregate consumption, upon aggregate income, it is difficult to think of any milder or less special assumption which anyone could in any circumstances have made. He suggested, merely, that when a person receives extra income he will, out of this increment, spend some and save some. Keynes's thesis does not make or require any assumption whatever about the *proportions* in which larger or smaller individual or aggregate income will be divided between expenditure on consumption and non-expenditure on consumption. The belief, totally unfounded, that Keynes's basic scheme assumes for the economy an *average* propensity to consume, defined as total consumption divided by total income, which decreases as income increases, has now for twenty-four years enabled his critics to confound themselves. As I write in 1960, the current issue of a famous journal of mathematical economics renews this misconception. It might have been supposed that mathematical economists could formulate for themselves the distinction between

$$0 < \frac{dy}{dx} < 1 \quad \text{and} \quad \frac{d(y/x)}{dx} < 0,$$

where $y$ is total consumption and $x$ is total income.

* Richard Kahn, 'The Relation of Home Investment to Unemployment', *The Economic Journal*, vol. XLI (London, 1931), pp. 173 et seqq.

When we ask: what *directly* determines income? the answer plainly is: the production plans to which firms commit themselves. (We may here allow ourselves to include the Government as a firm.) For we may think of each business man as deciding at the beginning of each month or week how much of his own product he will arrange for his factory to turn out during that time-interval, and we may think of him then as engaging the necessary labour and contracting to pay it such and such incomes; and we may think of him also as telling himself that he can reasonably count on such and such a profit for himself out of the sale of the intended output. Thus when we take all the firms together, and think of them in this way, it is plain that the phrase 'the aggregate expected income' means something which in principle could be calculated. For we would merely have to ask every worker who engaged himself to work for a stated wage, and every business man who looked forward to profits from his enterprise of production, how much they expected to receive. Now whatever happens during this particular, immediately future month or week, we can take the outputs of goods, and the corresponding employment, during this interval, as given. But we cannot take the *sales* of goods as given. If some of the goods which are going to be produced have in the end, *contrary to plan*, to be added to the stockpile, then at the beginning of the *following* month, surely, business men will plan to produce smaller outputs, and the level of employment will fall. We cannot, however, easily investigate a 'dynamic' process whose steps consist in over-production, or under-demand, in one month followed by lessened production in the next month, with, very probably, a corresponding reduction of demand and a second emergence of unsold stocks of goods, and so on. Our understanding will best be served by referring to an *equilibrium* consisting in the equality, in any month, of the value of goods *successfully sold* as intended, with the value of those produced, so that, if employment is determined on the basis of such experience, the level of employment can be kept unchanged from month to month.

As to the conditions whose fulfilment will ensure such an equilibrium we have seen two things: first, that the saving gap must be filled by investment or some other component of the multiplicand consisting of goods bought otherwise than for consumption in the home country; and, secondly, that the saving gap will be bigger when aggregate income is bigger. It follows that for a bigger *equilibrium* income we must have a bigger planned and intended multiplicand, e.g. a bigger monthly or annual purchase of machinery for augmenting the productive power of firms, or for some other non-consumption purpose.

Let us now turn the matter round, and ask what, with a given marginal propensity to consume, will happen if the business men's plans for investment (for purchase of machinery, ships, buildings, roads, etc.) are bigger in total value for the immediately future month than they were for the just elapsed month. Looking back on that past month we know that the value of the net additions made during that month to the economy's stockpile of wealth must, by the meanings we give to our terms, be equal to the difference between what was earned by productive activity, and what was spent on buying goods for consumption, during that month: realized or *ex post* investment is identically equal to realized or *ex post* saving. Just as the saving gap must be filled by investment, so investment must be made room for by saving. Now we are supposing that business men intend to do a larger value of investment per month in future than in the past. Where can the extra saving come from, to make room for this extra investment? It cannot, under our suppositions, come from a willingness of income-earners to spend less out of a *given* income, for we have assumed the marginal propensity to consume to remain unchanged when investment increases. It must arise then, if at all, from an *increase* in the economy's aggregate income. Some increase there will certainly be, for the production of the extra flow of goods for investment will generate an extra flow of income. Will this be sufficient to provide the necessary extra saving? No, for this necessary extra saving is precisely equal to the *whole* of the extra income arising *directly* from the extra investment, and we have assumed a marginal propensity to save of *less than unity*; that is, we have assumed that *less than the whole* of any extra income will be saved. What, then, must happen?

When those who perform the extra work, or otherwise provide the extra productive services, called for by the production of the extra output of investment goods, receive their extra incomes for so doing, they will, according to our assumption, spend part of this extra income on consumption. The makers of consumption goods will thus be induced to increase their output of consumption goods, and for this purpose they will pay out yet another stream of extra income, *additional* to that being paid out for the extra investment goods. Out of this second extra stream, some will be saved, some will be spent, and this will induce a third increment of general output of goods and a third extra stream of income, out of which some will be saved and some spent.... Each extra income stream will be smaller than the last, and we shall have what the mathematicians call a *convergent series* of terms, which though infinite in *number* are finite in *sum*. The *total* extra income will be just sufficient to allow a total extra saving equal to what is required to match the intended extra investment.

It is even possible to work out just how large this total extra income will have to be. For let us take a marginal propensity to consume of $\frac{3}{4}$. This means that out of any increment of income, $\frac{3}{4}$ will be consumed and $\frac{1}{4}$ saved. It follows that if the extra saving required is an annual amount of £*A*, the extra income, out of which this saving will arise naturally, is £4*A*.

Here, then, is the great lever which Kahn and Keynes showed could be applied to the elimination of unemployment. If, when there is massive general unemployment, the Government starts an extra stream of annual purchases of machinery, buildings, roads or anything which cannot *directly* satisfy consumers, of, say, £100 million, and if the marginal propensity to consume is, say, $\frac{3}{4}$, then £400 million a year of extra income, and the corresponding extra employment, will be generated.

The resistance which the *General Theory* encountered amongst economists was only superficially due to the manner of its presentation. For it seemed to be cutting deep at the roots of an essentially *moralistic* discipline. Keynes (they thought) was being irreverent, not only to his predecessors and elder contemporaries, but to the very meaning of the 'dismal science', which was dismal in the sense that it taught man his limitations and showed him the place to which he had been called in the scheme of things. Man had lost Eden and must toil. Nature is parsimonious and man must be parsimonious also, in order to repair as well as he may, by abstention and thrift and plain living, and by careful accumulation of wealth, the plight in which he finds himself. It was not for nothing that economics was invented by a Professor of Moral Philosophy and a Scotsman to boot. In this seventh decade of the twentieth century, it is mainly in the United States that Keynes's theory is rejected and what is supposed to be his philosophy meets with odium and distrust. This surely is to be expected, for America is still profoundly puritanical. Yet what did Keynes say? Only that at those times when things are *not scarce* it is absurd and suicidal to reduce consumption and curtail investment and so throw still more people out of work. When, as in 1932, millions in England and tens of millions in America are unemployed, is labour scarce? When hundreds of fine ships are lying idle in remote lochs and estuaries, is transport scarce? Does it make sense at such times to *save*, to refuse to make use of real resources which are, for the time being, superabundant? Had he been listened to, Keynes might have saved the world from war.

# 4
# THE RUIN OF ECONOMY

A case can be made out for saying that economics, as a discipline intended to satisfy the mind in part of its curiosity about life, has steadily disintegrated for the last third of a century. In that time we have seen the beautiful, complete, unified explanation of the economic world, representing it as a self-regulating mechanism for continuously pursuing the best that was currently possible for every one, eroded and undermined from several directions. That picture was based, in the first place, on the concept of perfect competition, and my choice of thirty-four years as the period of gradual debacle looks back to a classic article by Mr Piero Sraffa in the *Economic Journal*, in which he pointed out that the economic theory of that day only studied the two extremes of the range of diverse market conditions under which things can be sold. It recognized pure monopoly, and had done so since Adam Smith; moreover, the great French mathematical economist Augustin Cournot had given in 1838, in his book called *Recherches sur les principes mathématiques de la théorie des richesses*, an account of monopoly which underlies all later treatments. It recognized also the exact antithesis of monopoly, namely perfect competition, the latter being the sale of a good by an indefinitely large number of similarly sized firms, and the former being the sale of a good by one sole and unique firm with no competitors. In 1926 Mr Sraffa called for the study of all the area between these extremes, which area, he said, really embraced much the greater part of all business in the real world. How right he was! There is, of course, no such thing as perfect competition, for this is defined as requiring the commodity in question to be perfectly homogeneous, not only in those matters which could be tested by a chemist or an engineer, not only in the absence of any advantage whatever in the place of sale of some specimens of it compared with others, but actually by being free even of imaginary differences in the mind of any single consumer. There has also to be in the perfectly competitive market instantaneous communication of every price offered or asked to every buyer and seller in it. Indeed, that is not really enough. Léon Walras, whose *Eléments d'économie politique pure* sought to picture the economic world as a unity and an organism where everything influences everything else, invented the notion of *tâtonnements*, of provisional bargains not ratified until a final price had been discovered which would clear the market and satisfy all buyers and all sellers. What real market, then, can meet all these requirements? Again, the monopolist is supposed in strictness to have no competitors. If there is only one television company, is it not a monopolist? Not quite. I can always spend my money on books instead.

Perfect competition is more than a description of the market for each commodity separately. Amongst the markets where it is assumed to prevail we can include the factor markets where firms obtain their means of production. And we can even add to our definition of perfect competition and say that it means costless mobility of all these factors, so that when everything in the economic system has reached its ultimate adjustment with everything else, in a *general equilibrium*, the price per unit of any one factor will be the same everywhere; each firm will be just and only just able to cover its costs of production at that output which makes these costs a minimum; and the community as a whole will be getting a set of outputs of the various commodities and services which, *given the corresponding income distribution*, is the best attainable for everyone.

This conception of general equilibrium was the great achievement of the last third of the nineteenth century. It was formulated by Walras in 1874, contributed to, as regards its theory of the sharing of aggregate income, by Philip Wicksteed in 1894, refined by Vilfredo Pareto in the early years of this century. It asserted a natural, impersonal, self-regulating harmony of interests in the whole economic world. It showed how available resources would be allocated to this industry and that, how income would be shared and how spent to the best individual advantage, how saving would ensure progress and how even profit had its part to play in ensuring the general optimum.

It is this picture which the events and the theorizing of the last thirty years have overthrown. It is the ruin of this great edifice that I had in mind when I said that a case can be made out for the progressive dissolution of economics. For in these days we no longer believe that perfect competition is natural; we no longer think that there is anything in perfect competition to guarantee the best, or even a fairly just and desirable, sharing of income; we see that this destroys any basis for claiming that competitive general equilibrium is a general optimum in any fundamental sense; we have even learned that, although the whole purpose of economic theory is to explain how men *rationally* behave in face of all-pervading scarcity, what they sometimes do *in fact* is not even to make full use of the resources that *are* available, but on the contrary they endure massive unemployment. And when they are not enduring unemployment, they cannot abjure the buying of each other's votes with inflationary finance which makes nonsense of the pricing system, the very nerve system of equilibrium.

When, in the early 1930's, Sir Roy Harrod (as he now is) produced his classic articles on imperfect competition with the new tool of marginal revenue, and Mrs Joan Robinson wrote *The Economics of Imperfect Competition*, and Professor Edward Chamberlin *The Theory of Monopolistic Competition*, they believed themselves no doubt to be repairing and improving the temple, not blowing it up with gunpowder. It was left to Professor Hicks in his *Value and Capital* to state the policy to which he has adhered: once we abandon competition *as a basis for theory* there is little theory left.

Imperfect competition was a family matter for economists; no scandal leaked to the outside world. Not so with unemployment. When millions in Britain and tens of millions in America were unemployed in 1930 and the following years, and when the national income of the United States fell, in money terms, by half, orthodox economic theory could not explain what had happened. A few men outside the Establishment, in particular J. A. Hobson, were struggling to hold in focus a vision of the truth. But only one was ready with a complete explanation. J. M. Keynes had already published his *Treatise on Money*, and now he was rewriting it as *The General Theory of Employment, Interest and Money*. By its provocative brilliance, its grounding of the new in the accepted and familiar, its aggressive confident sounding of a trumpet of salvation, and by its unmistakable classic importance, this book was a sensation from the moment it appeared, and before. I may be permitted to record the feelings of a student who, by a marvellous stroke of fortune, happened to have begun his postgraduate work a year before it appeared, and so was ready to receive its impact with every sense alert and a mind already, for personal intellectual reasons, desperately needing some new illumination.

Rumours of what Keynes was doing filtered out, of course, and reached the London School of Economics, where a galaxy of brilliant teachers and researchers included F. A. Hayek, J. R. Hicks, A. P. Lerner, and Miss Ursula Webb. Hicks was at that time, I believe, strongly Hayekian in outlook although he was working on lines of his own which led in the end to *Value and Capital*. Lerner, however, was the spy who brought in news of the coming revolution. He had a Leon Fellowship at Cambridge, and I suppose it was his tidings which led to the planning of a larger expedition. The Joint Seminar of research students from London, Oxford and Cambridge was formed, quite *ad hoc*, for the express purpose of finding out about Keynes or disseminating his ideas, according to which University you happened to belong to. It assembled at Cambridge, in King's College, one famous Sunday afternoon in October 1935, and one member of it, at least, underwent almost a spiritual conversion. We heard first a paper by Mrs Joan Robinson, and no other discourse has ever released upon my mind so staggering and thrilling a flood of light. At last I understood. I was released from the torments of my thesis, which struggled to explain unemployment in terms of a model of inflation. I tore it up. I began again. I joined the elect, for I understood Keynes. (And this, at first, put one in rather the position that understanding Einstein had done a decade earlier.) After Mrs Robinson we heard Mr Richard Kahn, Professor Kahn as he now is. He, as Keynes acknowledged, was almost a co-author of the *General Theory*. His quiet and deadly provocation of those who were not ready to abandon orthodoxy provided me with my first examination in Keynesian economics. Could I follow an argument *intended* to be baffling to those resolved to be baffled? Yes. I saw the flash of each bomb as it exploded.

There are countless explanations of Keynesian economics and I shall not add to them here. The best of all is a book called *The General Theory of Employment, Interest and Money*, by J. M. Keynes.

The ideal would be never to let your students read potted versions until they had read the original. A short and deceptively titled book by Mrs Robinson called *An Introduction to the Theory of Employment* is not a potted version at all, nor a text-book: it is part of the canon. You can read also Lawrence Klein's *The Keynesian Revolution* which is also difficult and also excellent.

Keynes seemed to many of his contemporaries to be attacking ideas which they valued and venerated. One of these was freedom, and here I feel sure they did Keynes a great injustice. Having followed where logic led, he had concluded that there is not, in a so-called *laisser faire* economic system, anything which ensures that full employment will be maintained at all times or even restored when it has been lost. This is because all that is produced must be sold, if the business men are to go on producing it and thereby giving employment. It must be sold for what it has cost, that is, the total income of all the people in the economy. But if they refuse, as they do, to spend 100 per cent of this income on buying goods for *consumption*, the rest of the goods, not bought for consumption, must be bought for *investment*, that is, as additions to the economy's total stock of buildings, machines, roads and so forth. The business men can buy goods for investment by borrowing, in their capacity as business men, the spare income, the saving, which income-earners, including themselves, have refrained from spending on consumption. But it is only in so far as they do order extra machinery and buildings and get them produced, and so fill the 'saving gap', that there will be any saving. The larger the annual value of investment, the larger the saving gap which can be filled, and the larger the economy's employment and real income, up to the point of full employment. Now suppose that because the business men see no hope of profit, they will not do enough investment. Then the Government must step in and do it instead. But (the other economists thought) when the Government does things this is waste of public money, this is interference with freedom, this is against the liberal spirit of English institutions. So Keynes was distrusted in England and even more in America.

Keynes seemed to be undermining morality and freedom. He was decrying the virtue of thrift, and he was advocating

Government interference in the field sacred to private business. Moreover, he was helping to break up the image of the self-regulating, optimum-seeking automatic economy that had only to be left alone to do the best for everybody. Now that the things he advocated are accepted as a matter of course, it is difficult to realize what a dark menace some economists saw in his argument.

I have tried to describe the Keynesian impact on some research students of the London School of Economics in the later 'thirties. From what did it convert them? From Hayekism. Was this the antithesis of Keynesism? Not at all, it only seemed to be. Hayek was describing what happens when easy credit in a time of full employment leads to over-ambitious schemes of equipment-building, to consequent shortage of consumers' goods and to rising consumers' goods prices, which finally defeat the equipment schemes by bidding factors of production away from them, so that they are left half finished and stranded. It is strange that this theory gained adherents in the 'thirties, when it was scarcely being illustrated anywhere in the Western world. It is not surprising that it was readily abandoned in favour of Keynes. But it has made a dramatic come-back. For since the Second World War we have seen in many countries just that steady rise of the general price level which comes of trying to do too much with given resources. The question has been posed by no less a Keynesian than Sir Roy Harrod, whether, after all, industrialization can be effectively carried through by means of inflation and the 'forced saving' which accompanies it, and he has referred to Hayek's position in this matter. We may say that the Hayek–Keynes debate of 1932 was unnecessary, for Keynes was discussing deflation and Hayek was describing inflation.

So we come to growth economics, which examines how the industrial equipment of a country can be built up, perhaps, from almost nothing, and how in this and related ways the standard of living can be raised even in the face of rapid increase of population. This question is being passionately studied in Western countries, partly from genuine goodwill towards the poorer nations of the world, but mainly perhaps because if these countries do not get help from the West they will get it from elsewhere, and with it an indoctrination that seems to threaten our own freedom. If we ask when this or that branch of economics was invented, there is never a completely clear-cut answer. But there is usually one writer who, with some touch of genius, has seen lying about the workshop of his subject a variety of odd component parts, seemingly with nothing to connect them with each other, and has had a sudden vision of how they can be fitted together. This is what happened when Newton or Leibniz invented the differential calculus and perceived its intimate unity with the integral calculus which Archimedes had invented thousands of years before. In our humbler and immeasurably more confused and fog-bound subject, we cannot hope for such superb visions of principles stretching through all heaven and earth and uniting everything. But there can be great inventions, and one of these, I would myself say, was Sir Roy Harrod's discovery of the regularly progressive economy. I can only guess how this came about. But perhaps Harrod may have been struck by the fact that in the Keynesian multiplier we have one functional connection between the pace of equipment-building and the size of the flow of consumption, and that in the accelerator, introduced into economic theory fifty or more years ago, we have a second, quite different, functional connection, namely between the pace of equipment-building and the speed of *increase* of the consumption flow. Is it not necessary to reconcile these? And to ask what happens if they are for the time being in conflict with each other? Out of such questions Harrod drew some conditions for the successful, steady growth of wealth without violent ups and downs of prosperity and employment. These ideas he first proposed in his book *The Trade Cycle* in 1936, then in the *Economic Journal* in March 1939, and further developed in his *Towards a Dynamic Economics* in 1948. Another name which is famous in growth economics of this rather abstract type is that of Professor Evsey Domar in America. Growth economics 'in the flesh' has been studied by a host of writers since the war, some of them, like Professor Arthur Lewis and Professor W. W. Rostow, with a vast historical perspective, others in a more contemporary setting.

Let us go back to 1930. That year saw the proclamation of a movement which, in its broader interpretation, has changed the face of economics and raised an acute crisis within it. The application of mathematics to economics goes back as far as economics itself. In 1711 Ceva published a treatise on the subject in Latin. The first of the famous mathematical economists was von Thünen whose great work *Der isolierte Staat* began to be published in 1826. He described a self-contained agricultural community and proposed an algebraic wage-rate formula which is inscribed upon his tomb. Augustin Cournot was a professional mathematician who turned his attention to economics and became, by his *Recherches sur les principes mathématiques de la théorie des richesses* of 1838, one of the acknowledged masters of our subject. Alfred Marshall himself was in the first place a Cambridge mathematician, one of the famous Second Wranglers who became more famous, sometimes, than their Senior Wranglers. The great Swedish economist Wicksell and the majestic Pareto in Italy both brought a knowledge of mathematics to bear upon economic theory. So, of course, did Maynard Keynes. Yet all this while there were great economists with no formal knowledge of mathematics, and in Cambridge there had grown up a tradition and unwritten law that algebra must be confined to an Appendix. Subscribers to this law were Marshall, Keynes and Hicks, to name only a few of the best known. In 1930, however, the revolution was proclaimed. The Econometric Society was formed to encourage and to publish the work of those who were prepared to make mathematics and mathematical statistics the main, overt tools of their endeavour. The tools they have used have been far removed from the 'little potted calculus' which Marshall said was all you needed.

The Econometric Society was, of course, a symptom and not a cause. Whether it was wholly a good thing for some economists with competence in mathematics to segregate their work in a separate journal and even to risk a charge of thinking themselves holier than others, is, I think, just possibly debatable. But just as mathematics was an immense and all but indispensable help to the 'marginal revolution' of the 1870's, so in our time it has afforded some insights, some means of proof and of calculation, which verbal logic would have been hard put to it to attain. Examples are the Leontief matrix which does for us quantitatively what the Austrian theory of capital in its day sought to do qualitatively; the Theory of Games with its proliferant techniques and applications, only a little of which is, as yet, plainly relevant to economics; and Linear Programming, the modern version of Wieser's method of analysis which varies the relative outputs of goods each made with fixed proportions of factors but each differing in these proportions from other goods.

So much, then, for the decline and fall of economics, which has descended from being a fit pursuit for a gentleman in his study, something expressible in civilized verbal language and describing a world where all is for the best, to being the output of a computing factory seeking to show how best the harsh economic strains and distresses of the world can be relieved. Now in what time remains, let me try to make out for you a list of the sorts of questions which, in my view, any student of economics ought to feel himself in some degree on terms with if his economics course, however short, has been a success:

1. Since we cannot have as much as we should like of everything, and to have more of one thing means ultimately that we must have less of another, how does it come about that different goods are produced each week or year in this quantity and that, rather than in some different set of quantities?

2. How does it come about that things exchange for each other in such and such ratios?

3. How does it come about that the total value of what is produced in a year is shared out in such and such proportions amongst different people, or groups of people, who have contributed to making it?

These first three questions belong to the theory of *value and distribution.* They beg one fundamental question:

4. Is there any guarantee that the ultimate limitation of our economic real resources, of land and labour and machines, will always be translated into a full use of such resources as we have? If, in a society whose basic method is free enterprise, there is no such guarantee, what is it that can sometimes inhibit full employment? If belief in profit opportunities fails, what can re-establish or replace it?

5. If it is *money* which destroys Say's Law and divorces demand from supply, so that there can at times be supply without sufficient demand, cannot this negation of Say's Law work in reverse, so that there can at times be demand without sufficient supply? If so, is this all we need to account for *inflation,* the loss of purchasing power by each unit of money?

Questions 4 and 5 belong to the unified subject of *money and employment*. Money, however, has institutional as well as theoretical aspects:

6. What are banks, and how do they work? If *money* is part of the fabric of the state, how is it that private firms are allowed to make a profit by manufacturing it? If some citizens can be enriched at the expense of others, if some can be impoverished to the benefit of others, by changes in the value or purchasing power of money, and if this purchasing power is governed in turn by the quantity of money in existence, ought that quantity itself to be governed by the mechanism of private profit, and changeable at the will of private profit-seeking interests?

7. But does not the Bank of England control these interests? Can it do so effectively? It is the agent of the Government and acts at the Government's direction. But is the Government itself to be trusted in this matter? A Government is a political party, itself a kind of private interest. It wishes to secure votes and retain power. Is it not tempted to buy these votes by means of expensive schemes of public welfare which can be paid for by inflationary finance? Ought not the Bank of England to be as independent of the Executive as the Judiciary is?

Questions 6 and 7 belong to a branch of economics to which I would like to give a separate identity under the name of *money and politics*. This subject would evidently include far more than the institutional aspects of money, and would embrace public finance itself:

8. By taxation, borrowing and creation or expunging of money on one hand, and by expenditure on the other, the State can direct resources to produce this pattern of services and goods rather than that; and can strongly influence the sharing of the national income amongst different groups of citizens. What principles ought to be the foundation of policy on these matters?

9. The world contains rich nations each with growing total wealth and a stable population, and poor nations each with stationary total wealth and growing population. Does not this endanger the peace and stability of the world? What can be done about it?

Question 9 is, of course, yet one more link between politics and economics, and leads us finally to the question of international economic relations:

10. Specialization gives the same sort of benefits between nations or regions as between individuals and firms. Free trade is best for the world as a whole. In case it is less advantageous for some individual nations than a protective policy might be, can some system be devised for compensating those who gain least in a policy of universal free trade?

These ten questions cover, I believe, by some relevant suggestion or glimpse, every main aspect of economics as a subject of insistent practical concern to all of us. To present the matter in a more orthodox way, these ten questions touch by implication on the following recognized divisions of economics:

### I. *Value and distribution* (questions 1–3)

This branch of theory discusses the supply, allocation and reward of the factors of production, and the sharing of their product. In the atomistic or free enterprise economy, the explanation of all these things rests on the *price system*, and the power of the price system to regulate the free economy (such a juxtaposition of words is paradoxical but not self-contradictory) depends in turn on the ideas of *diminishing marginal utility* of commodities and of *diminishing marginal productivity* of factors. What is the intimate connection of the marginal idea with automatic regulation? It is, that automatic regulation depends on the notion that each individual person or firm seeks to maximize his own satisfaction, or profit, within a frame of law which guarantees equal rights to everyone else to do the same. The consequence is *balance* or equilibrium; and the marginal idea provides the *test* to tell whether maximization has been achieved. It is merely the principle, used in mathematics, of putting the first derivative equal to zero, to find out at which values of the independent variable a function can have a maximum.

### II. *Money and employment* (questions 4, 5)

Here we have the total general output (of goods of all kinds) divided into those goods which do or those which do not directly meet the needs of consumers. Those which do not, namely, investment goods, Government purchases, and the export surplus, nevertheless generate income when they are produced. They are thus able to fill the *potential gap* between a given level of general output and the *corresponding* level of consumers' off-take. The bigger this *multiplicand* of non-consumption goods, the larger the propensity to save which is compatible with a given level of employment and general output (e.g. *full* employment); and the smaller the propensity to save, the larger the level of employment attainable with a given multiplicand. Unless the multiplicand and the propensity to save have such a pair of respective numerical values as to give full employment, we cannot apply the whole of the theory of value and distribution to explain fully what is done *within* the available resources.

III. *Money, banking and public finance* (questions 6–8)

It is quite unorthodox to lump together 'Money and banking' and 'Public Finance', yet the events and discussions of the last few years and weeks will surely have convinced us that this is the logic of the matter. The actions of the Bank of England are nowadays the actions of the Chancellor of the Exchequer, who publicly accepts responsibility for them. The purposes in pursuit of which these actions are taken are the very same ones which are envisaged in the Budget, namely, to steer a middle course between unemployment and inflation, to keep our foreign payments and receipts in equilibrium and conserve our stock of gold and foreign currencies, and to encourage the building up of our national equipment, both privately and publicly owned, at some speed which is for the time being regarded as desirable. The Budget, of course, has additional aims, especially the redistribution of the national income by progressive taxation and the provision thereby of 'welfare' in such forms as education and medical care; and the securing of law and order, justice and defence. Not only because of this, but for invincible practical reasons, it will still be necessary to give separate courses on the technical and institutional details of the banking system, on the one hand, and of the national Exchequer and its supervision by Parliament, on the other. But there ought surely nowadays, in all comprehensive syllabuses of economics, to be a course called 'Political finance and monetary management', with stress on the word 'political' and all it means. The decision to stop inflation is one of the most courageous *political* decisions that any *Government* could take.

IV. *Growth economics* (question 9)

Growth economics, like economics as a whole, is a bipolar subject, containing writers like Sir Roy Harrod and Professor Domar who evolve abstract theoretical models by exact inference from assumptions, and writers like Professor W. W. Rostow, who apply a Toynbeean technique to the historical record and produce inductive models typifying what, in their vision, has been observed frequently, or always, to happen in fact. Between these extremes we find economists such as Professor B. S. Keirstead, whose reach of mind embraces both types of procedure and offers a synthesis.

How do poor countries ever attain a level of saving which can do more than just keep pace with the growth of their population? How can rich countries help them to make this 'take-off into sustained growth'? What do we mean by 'balanced growth' and what setbacks will occur if care is not taken to maintain it? These are, unquestionably, the most vital current questions for the Western economic world as well as for the less developed countries themselves.

V. *International trade* (question 10)

International trade has been until the last year or two the most fashionable subject amongst British economists. Its reign has, perhaps, been ended for the time being by the sudden apparent ending of the dollar crisis. By one of those dramatic turns which econometrics has not yet demonstrated its ability to foresee, the flow of gold to the United States from the rest of the world has been reversed, and the recent outflow from the United States has even been causing some concern there. It is far too early for Britain to be complacent. Our long-term import and export problem is a quite different matter from our immediate position. When all the present 'primary producing' countries are equipped to make their own manufactured goods, and are rich enough and populous enough to absorb most of their own output of raw materials and food, where are we going to find markets for our factories' output and sources whence we can buy with that output the food we cannot grow for ourselves? This island cannot by present farming techniques support a population of 50 millions from its own soil, except at starvation level. International trade will be always with us, a pressing practical anxiety and a subject for thought and theory.

With a very thick crayon and with sweeping strokes I have tried to outline for you the course, as I see it, which economic thought has taken in Western countries during the last ninety years, and the shape which it presents today. I called this sketch 'the ruin of economy'. In those ninety years there have been two high winds of change in economic thought, that of the 1870's and that of the 1930's, each of which has bent but not broken off the tree of our subject. Another ninety years will carry us to the exact middle of the twenty-first century. There will be more high winds, and we need not be so foolish as to try and guess what direction they will take. I will stick out my neck with just one remark. Surely the attitude of aloof self-sufficiency with which economics has in the past avoided contact with psychology, anthropology, sociology and political theory must now end, as it has, indeed, been plainly ending through the work, for example, of those who have been fortunate enough to spend time at Nuffield or the Behavioral Sciences Center at Palo Alto. Much recent work in economics has treated man as a computer. Let us also study him as an artist, a poet, a mystic, a dreamer, in some degree, even in his economic activity.

# 5
# THE 'GREAT THEORY' IN ECLIPSE

If we ask at what epoch economic theory attained its greatest beauty, there can be no doubt of the answer. Its age of Periclean glory lies in the last decade of the nineteenth century and the first of the twentieth. At the beginning of those twenty years, Marshall's *Principles of Economics* founded the modern English school, a school which, *per impossibile*, includes its harshest critic, Maynard Keynes; for Keynes's thought was Marshallian in all its methods, differing only in its premisses and its conclusions, as though an old-established railway line had been lifted bodily from the land between London and Bristol, and made to run between York and Edinburgh. At the end of them, Pareto's *Manuel*, at the opposite extreme from the *Principles* in basic philosophy and outlook, established the conception of *general equilibrium* like the crowning temple of the economic acropolis, splendid in symmetry and timeless grace. Pareto's work was the full and final blossoming of the great tree planted by Walras. Between Walras, Jevons, Menger and Wieser in the early 'seventies (and they, had they but known it, were in some respects anticipated by Gossen) and Pareto in 1910, came in procession Böhm-Bawerk, Wicksell, Wicksteed and John Bates Clark. The last three of these completed the Great Theory, the demonstration that a single principle (the self-interested seeking of maximum result from given expenditure whether by producers or consumers) could explain the whole structure and metabolism of economic life, by applying to the factor market that marginal analysis which had in the 'seventies been applied to the product market. The theory had a wholeness, an inclusive unity and a severity and simplicity of logic which are scarcely matched in science save by classical astronomy and by the table of atomic weights in chemistry.

All this depended on the concept of perfect competition. It is under perfect competition that goods are produced in just those outputs at which their cost per unit is a minimum, and that they sell at a price per unit equal to this minimum, so that the revenue obtained by each firm is just and only just sufficient for that firm to pay each of its employed units of each factor of production a weekly or monthly reward equal to the addition made to the value of the firm's weekly or monthly output by the presence of the marginal unit of that factor; including amongst the factors the services of the entrepreneur himself, so that he has no reason to quit this industry for another, where, in the nature of perfectly competitive equilibrium, he would be no better off. When perfect competition prevails throughout the economy, that economy may be said to be meeting, in the most efficient way that its technology allows, the needs of its people, given their distribution of wealth. If this distribution of wealth, including the intangible wealth of exceptional ability, is satisfactorily distributed, the perfectly competitive system yields an *optimum* position.

Yet Marshall himself saw a difficulty. Marshall's economy was no abstract and petrified state but the living British nation itself, carefully observed in its time-requiring reactions to autonomous shifts of taste or other historical events not explicable by the economist as such. In 'the short period' a strengthening of demand would encounter obstacles on the supply side expressing themselves in a rising supply curve. But if this stronger demand seemed likely to persist, firms would reorganize their production with more powerful equipment and thus gain *economies of large scale* which would actually cheapen the product. In perfect competition, the firm can sell any practicable output at a market price independent of its output. How can a *falling* supply curve ever intersect a horizontal demand curve? The firm would expand until it had swallowed the industry and competition was destroyed.

Marshall himself proposed the solution. The firm's own market is not unlimited. It has a circle of established customers and to gain others it will have to make a special effort, reducing its price sharply if it desires to expand rapidly. There can still be competition amongst firms, but this is not *perfect* competition. Yet the basis of the perfect, general equilibrium of maximum efficiency *is* perfect competition. Marshall's greatest theoretical contribution is his picture of the time-process of expansion, reorganization and cheapening of production, and this conception undermines the Great Theory completely.

The massive challenge inherent in Marshall's work was not taken up for nearly forty years. In the *Economic Journal* in 1926 Mr Piero Sraffa looked back to Marshall's dilemma and called for the great no-man's-land between Cournot's monopoly and Smithian competition to be filled in. But it was left for Sir Roy Harrod, in the same journal in 1929, to take the decisive step by solving an *inner* problem of Marshall's dilemma. Marshall saw that *increasing returns* and *perfect* competition were incompatible. He also saw that it was only *perfect* competition which validated a central proposition of the Great Theory, namely, that the firm's most profitable output is the one which makes marginal cost equal to *price*. With what, if not with price, can marginal cost be equalized? Strangely for a mathematician, it was here that Marshall faltered. He concluded that marginal cost is inapplicable in other than perfectly competitive conditions, whereas in fact all that was needed was the invention of marginal revenue.

Harrod, believing that continuing debate should precede any final formulation of a canon, elected not to gather his articles into a book. After consulting him as to his plans in this respect, Mrs Joan Robinson wrote the classic treatise which, together with Professor Edward Chamberlin's independent volume, established *Imperfect Competition* as a major department of economic theory. All three of these great pioneers, it may be supposed, believed themselves to be completing or repairing the Marshallian city, not planting a new one in incongruous style upon its ruins. Yet the upshot of their efforts seemed to Professor Hicks to be 'the threatened wreckage of the greater part of economic theory'.

'Imperfect competition' was a mere wind of change compared with the volcanic upheaval which was preparing itself at the same time. Economics was the science of human reaction to scarcity. Because means of need-satisfaction are limited, they are husbanded with anxious attention by people of all conditions in their capacity of consumers and in that of producers. Much of human conduct can be thus explained. One thing that cannot be thus explained is the leaving of available resources unused, the existence, in some historical conjunctures, of mass unemployment. The Great Theory seemed in this respect, far more fundamentally than with imperfect competition, to have failed. A cavernous gulf, unparalleled since Adam Smith became the mentor of statesmen, had opened between the world of academic economics and the world of political action and business enterprise. John Maynard Keynes bridged this gulf with a strange and unparalleled book, *The General Theory of Employment, Interest and Money*, and across his bridge the academic economists have ever since been pouring into the world of administrative power and political influence. Keynes's book was strange, for it was the rigorous and exacting work of a man trained in mathematics, yet such was its author's charismatic power that politicians and business men who could not follow the logic of the book followed the magic of the man, and accepted his conclusions. What were they? That, overshadowing all the material scarcities, there is a profounder and more ineluctable scarcity, that of the means of judging the consequences of actions. In their ignorance of the future men are sometimes afraid to act; afraid to invest, to produce, to give employment, for fear of losing their resources. In these circumstances, the Government itself, and better still, all the governments of the nations together, must show a collective audacity which it may be too much to ask of the individual, and embark on great public schemes of investment in the *equipment of society*; for such action will of itself cause private industries to prosper and to give extra employment on their own account.

A greater difference in problems and conditions than that which separates the 'thirties from the 'sixties is hard to imagine. Each generation must cope with its own troubles for itself. Economics has its fashions and re-orientations, sometimes becoming apparently contemptuous of problems that once engrossed it. The wheel will come round again. The Great Theory seems today remote and academic, yet some of our insight still flows from it and our knowledge looks back to it. *Vixere fortes ante Agamemnona multi*, and they did not live in vain.

# II
# DECISION VERSUS DETERMINISM

# 6
# TIME, NATURE AND DECISION

## I

Theories of human action represent men as having ends which they seek to attain by acting in conformity with nature. Nature is assumed, by the men to whom these theories refer, to be orderly; that is, to have a structure which constrains or places limitations on the kinds of sequence in which one set of circumstances can follow another in time. Thus in order to attain a desired set of circumstances, it is necessary to proceed from the existing set to that desired set by a path prescribed by this structure, by these laws of nature. One must set off along that path by taking the correct first step or action, and theories of human action are mainly concerned to show, in very general terms, how the character of that step is exactly determined by the logic of the individual's position: a given end, a given existing situation, given laws of nature. When we express the matter thus, it appears that he has *no choice.* He must either act in the way dictated by this position, or else act in defiance of the laws of nature or of his own ambitions, either of which courses would mark him as a madman. Are we then driven to conclude that in spite of all human intuition and everyday linguistic usage *decision*, the act of thought by which a man brings himself face to face with his next action, is *not choice*?

This is only the beginning of the paradox of decision. You may feel that the escape is obvious. Men choose their ends. The end once chosen, the laws of nature prescribe how it must be pursued. But when we speak here about nature and its laws, we are evidently including the whole of human concerns as well as the world of non-conscious, of inanimate, or of merely biological nature. In order to have recipes of action for attaining his ends, a man must know not only what effect this or that act of his own will have within the world of non-conscious nature and what the laws of physics, chemistry and physiology are; he must also know what actions of other people his own act will accompany. For the effect of a man's actions will plainly be entirely different according as other people are, *at the same moment*, acting in manner *A* or manner *B* or what not. And if we claim that men can choose their ends, in some substantial meaning of the word 'choose', how can any man know what ends, and therefore what actions, others are *simultaneously* choosing when he is faced, as he may be at each moment, with the need to make his own decision? The paradox is this. If there is choice of ends, there are no complete laws prescribing the means of attaining ends. There is no complete rationality. If decision is choice, it is not choice of means which will *certainly* attain the chosen ends.

There is an alternative assumption. We can suppose that history is a book already written, whose pages the hand of time is merely *turning*, not composing. The age-old question whose conventional formulation is in the words 'determinism or free will' may never be answered. All we can do is to discuss what consequences logically follow from each of the two suppositions, that the world we live in is, or is not, predetermined as to its whole course and pattern of events. Now if we opt for a determinist world, this plainly implies an altogether different meaning for 'decision' from the meaning it would have in a non-determinist world. Is decision in the former case even an interesting object of study? It is then a part of physiology, the operation of a neural mechanism which may, indeed, be fascinating, but which belongs to a conceptual world where morality, ethics, wisdom and, above all, creative thought have no place. To try to study such a world with the techniques of the economist, the political theorist, the philosopher, the moralist, would be absurd. Let us therefore opt for a non-determinist world and see what kind of thing we are thereby choosing.

Let us come back to the paradox from a slightly different point of view. When we elect to study a non-determinist world, we elect to study one in which a man seems to need *laws* according to which this or that action of his will have knowable, determinate consequences. He seems to need these laws, in order that he may know what action will give him the consequences which, out of all within his reach, he most desires. Yet when we suppose that *everyone* has this same freedom to choose his actions, the possibility of such laws seems to dissolve. For the consequences of my act depend upon the character of the simultaneous acts of others, and those acts, by our explicit assumption, are not determinate, are not the unique inevitable consequences of past history, and therefore cannot, even in principle, be known by me when I am deciding on my own action. This is the paradox again. If laws of consequence are needed, they are not there. They are available only if they are perfectly otiose, in a world where all is predetermined.

## II

The paradox of decision, in whichever of its many guises we look at it, presents us with this problem: How to find a scheme of thought about the basic nature of human affairs, which will include *decision* in the meaning we give to this word in our unself-conscious, intuitive, instinctive attitude to life, where without examination or heart-searching we take it for granted that a responsibility lies upon us for our acts; that these acts are in a profound sense *creative*, *inceptive*, the source of *historical novelty*; that each such act is, as it were, the unconnected starting-point of a new thread in the tapestry which time is weaving. Let us seek in yet a third manner to pin down the dilemma of decision. In a determinist world a human decision is an item in a mere stage in a process or sequence of stages fixed in advance, fixed in a manner, or by an agency, which is part of the nature of such a world, a world where human beings are entirely non-creative, where they act according to inescapable necessity in just such and such a predetermined manner. In such a world they only *seem* to themselves to be the source of any current of events; everything that happens is the necessary consequence of what has gone before. In such a world, I shall say, decision is *illusory*.

Let us then make a somewhat different assumption, and suppose (disregarding for the moment any internal logical contradictions of this supposition) that the decision-maker we are concerned with assumes himself to have perfect foresight, that is, that he has in mind what he accepts as a complete list of all the relevantly distinct actions open to him, and that for each of these available actions he sees one and only one possible sequel differing from that of every other of the available actions. We may then say that he specifies and takes as true a one-one correspondence between his available acts and their sequels. If we now further assume that these sequels can be completely ordered by him so that when he compares any two of them, one is preferred to the other, it is plain that his available actions will be similarly ordered, and that the question 'Which action shall I take?' will call for nothing which can be called judgement and will involve nothing which is amenable to any further analysis. I shall say that, in such a case, decision is *empty*.

Lastly, let us indulge in the fantasy that, so far from feeling himself able to set up a one-one correspondence between his available acts and their consequences, he can discern no pattern of association between act and sequel, so that it appears to him that any sequel (out of a finite or an infinite list or altogether without limitation) can follow any act. Then if in the *sequel* of an act we include every subsequent event or situation which is of any concern to him, it follows that he will see no purpose to be served by choosing amongst acts. In such a case I shall say that decision is *powerless*.

## III

We have concluded that in a determinist world, decision is illusory; that in a world of certainty, it is empty; that in a world without discernible order, it is powerless. What kind of world can we find, wherein decision will be none of these things, but where, instead, decision will appear as the source of history, creating essential novelty from moment to moment? These three propositions by themselves yield the answer. We must assume a world where there is action and not merely the illusion of action; a world where history *comes into* being, not a world where the whole of history is complete and is merely revealed in successive stages to the human consciousness; a world where there are constraints upon the ways in which events can follow each other, yet where even a complete and perfect knowledge of these constraints would leave us ignorant of 'what will happen next'; a world where, in short, events are only partly shaped by what has gone before. In such a world a man cannot know what *will* happen, as the sequel to this or that act of his own; but he feels able to form judgements about the sorts of things that *can* happen, he can set bounds to the range and diversity of the consequences that he can conceive for each act amongst those open to him. In face of this bounded uncertainty his choice of act is not empty and automatic, but calls for thought and something more, and matches the meaning implied, by the thoughts by which we seem to ourselves to conduct our lives, for the word 'decision'. I define *decision* as *choice in face of bounded uncertainty.*

Bounded uncertainty leaves room for non-empty decision. But if by calling it bounded we mean that a man can list for himself the distinct sequences of situations or events, the distinct paths of history, that *can* flow from, let us say, act *A* of his own, and that he can do the same for act *B*, and for act *C*, and so on; and if further, letting *U*, *V*, *Z*, *S*, *T*, ... stand each for one such distinct bundle of possibilities corresponding to one and only one of his available acts, we suppose him able to order these bundles amongst themselves just as we might suppose him to order the *certain* consequences of this act or that in a world without uncertainty; then are we not back in a world of determinism, where decision avoids emptiness only by requiring a listing of possibilities such as might be done by a computer? Where in this world of listable possibilities is there room for *creation*?

There is evidently one, and perhaps only one, escape from this second dilemma of decision: the 'possible' consequences of an act are *not* listable. In a game with stated rules, the outcomes (each specified in those respects only which are relevant for the game) which can follow any act are in effect listed by implication of these rules. But do we know that such a set of rules, making possible, in principle, the listing of all relevantly distinct outcomes, exists for the game of human conduct in general? Do we know that the 'laws of nature', including the laws of genetics and psychology, by postulating which we make it reasonable to suppose that a man feels his uncertainties to be bounded, are sufficient to render the outcomes, each specified in all respects which are of concern to the individual, of each of his available acts listable? The way to examine this question is to examine first the nature, in the most general and basic sense, of the 'outcomes' it refers to.

## IV

*Where*, let us ask, are to be sought the outcomes in hope of which a man elects one act rather than another? These outcomes must exist in his own mind. For surely, if they are to be of any interest or concern to him, they must be, or must at the very least entail, *experiences of his own*? What does he care about, except experiences of his own? What else is there, that he can call *actual*? Now if these experiences, in hope of which he acts in one way rather than another, are to be in his own mind, where are they *in time*? They must, we may claim without argument, be in his *now*. For there *is* no other place in *time as he experiences it*.

Time there is, indeed, of an altogether different kind from *time lived in*. For time lived in, the time of actuality, of experience, the time in which we receive impressions from outside our minds, the time in which thoughts take place and everything which makes up consciousness goes on, is but a single moment. It is not always the same moment, for it surely *consists* in events, that is, in transitions from one instantaneous state of affairs to another, and such events, having happened, have led us into a different moment. But the present is solitary. Standing in contrast with this notion of the *solitary present* there is the idea, sophisticated and yet familiar through all our training as 'detached observers', of time as a space, or a dimension of a space. Perhaps we may not claim that this is quite an abstraction. For memory, working in each new 'present', presents to us the images of former 'present moments' and suggests that these images can be mentally arranged in a sequence, forming 'a stretch of time'. This stretch of time is, let me again insist, something imagined or constructed, and it *exists* in each new, solitary, present moment. Its *content* is an extension, and the very picture we make in our mind's eye of a 'stretch of time' is in fact a 'stretch of space' in the ordinary sense of 'space' or length.

Each solitary present moment turns into a new present before our eyes, and there seems no reason to suppose that this will not continue. So we construct time in the other direction from that presented to us by memory, and have a 'calendar axis' along which we imagine the present to move like a variable point on a geometrical line. The variation of its place on the line is, of course, not under our control, and when we think about time in this fashion we have to imagine our *viewpoint* or present moment as moving along the line under a rule of 'one-way traffic'.

## V

Corresponding to the two conceptions of time which we have just considered, there are perhaps two points of view which each of us can adopt. One of these is the natural, unsophisticated, childlike attitude which would, I suppose, be our only attitude to time if we had received no education. This is to see time from inside, to be aware only of the time of actual experiences and thoughts, the time *in* which we seem to live. This attitude accepts the *solitary present*. The other point of view is that of the mathematician or historian who stands *outside* the time which provides a 'space' for the events he studies. Thus the scientist makes, in effect, a list of distinct points of time, and to each of these points there corresponds for him some definite state of the affairs he is studying. For the scientist, time thus listed or turned into a space or endowed with extension is a time in which all moments have equal and, by a seeming paradox, *simultaneous* validity. How can different points of time have simultaneous validity? This is possible because we are talking about two different views of time. The points of the mathematician's or the historian's extended time all exist together in his own mind and imagination, they all exist at once in his solitary present, in a single thought.

Sense-perception, feeling, thought, all take place in and are part of the solitary moment of actuality. Memory is a thought, and that, too, occurs in the present, though the *content* of it is labelled with dates of the past. And, lastly, imagination is a thought, and here we have several different possibilities about its content. Imagination can be free untrammelled fancy, linked with 'reality' only by having perhaps to use materials ultimately furnished by experiences which come from outside the mind. But these materials need be no more than 'fundamental particles', sounds, shapes and colours, and their arrangement need not be subject to any law of nature or logic. If the patterns that free imagination makes of these materials are more interesting, more able to communicate something to other minds, when they are subject to some laws, the constraints which constitute some art, still they are fictions and are fundamentally exempt from being questioned as to whether they are 'possible'. They have no relevance for decision. But suppose that imagination sometimes does concern itself with the question of what is possible; suppose that there are figments which, still existing only as thoughts in the present moment of the mind of some individual, are subjected by him to the test of congruence with reality as he apprehends it. Suppose that one feature of that reality, which he must himself supply before he can test any such figment in relation to it, is his own next action. Then such figments, when tested and accepted as in certain senses congruous with reality, become statements of *possible outcomes* of the act in question. They are what we shall call *expectations*.

To be congruous with reality means two things. There must be conformity with general natural laws; and there must be a discernible path by which the expected state of affairs, labelled with a future date, could, without breach of those laws, be attained from the existing situation within 'the available time'.

## VI

Now for our questions, when and what are the experiences, the pursuit of which guides decision? The occurrence, the existence of these experiences is in the now, for this is true of all experiences. But the totality of a moment's experience is of two kinds. On one hand there are the experiences seeming to come from without and to reflect happenings in the world external to the mind. In these perceptions or apprehensions the mind is partly passive, the inceptive stimulus is something unique which, when it arrives, is beyond choice. When sights and sounds and the feelings or thoughts to which they *immediately* give rise are occurring, it is too late to choose different ones. For *choice* to be possible, there must be a *multiple* experience amongst whose components choice is made. Each of these components is the set of imagined outcomes of one of the acts available to the decision-maker. For, on the other hand, there are in the totality of a moment's experiences those which seem to come from within, those in which the mind is non-passive, those which can consist in creative thought and in imagination. Only by imagination can thoughts of those kinds occur which make possible comparison of outcomes.

Only imagination can present the *stopped*, the *multiple*, the *telescoped* picture of sequences of events or situations, making choice amongst these sequences possible. For choice requires comparison, and comparison means, at least, that the things being compared must exist together, in some sense, in the mind or that they must exist in swift sequence so that memory can tell which made, as it were, the highest score. If 'reference back' is required, only a product of imagination can be precisely reproduced. For choice to be possible, then, there must be an array of seemingly available alternatives, and these must be accessible for re-examination. These conditions, we claim, can be fulfilled only by things imagined. But further, each of these alternatives comprises *sequences* of situations, that is, events strung out along the 'calendar axis'. That axis, we have claimed, is itself a construct merely, a figment and mode of thought. But experiences from without, sensations or perceptions, thoughts and feelings arising directly from external stimulus, must be those which all belong to the same single, solitary present, they cannot belong to 'different moments'. Experiences which we associate, or label, with different calendar dates are necessarily, some of them, imagined or remembered experiences, they cannot all be actual together. Thus the alternatives of choice, when these alternatives are sequences of experiences, must each be presented as a telescoped picture, *existing* in the solitary present though referred by the mind to a series of different dates. Only imagination can present the *stopped*, that is, the *repeatable*, picture; the *multiple* picture allowing choice amongst its components; and the *telescoped* picture rendering in a simultaneous actuality the events of a 'stretch of time'.

For there to be choice, we have been saying, there must be presented to the mind an array of alternatives. Since 'the external world' presents only an experience which, though complex and many-sided, is unique and not multiple, the external world cannot present an array of alternatives. Such an array can be presented only by the imagination. But an imaginative product that forms part of any one such alternative belongs to the second of our kinds. It is a product of imagination constrained to be in conformity with general laws of nature and the existing situation, it is what we have called an expectation, it is one of many *possible* outcomes of one of many *available* acts.

What then, is the experience itself in whose pursuit the choice amongst the alternatives is made? It is yet a third type of imagination, where what is pictured is the supposed sequel to an act to which the individual is *committed*. This is no longer expectation, the picturing of what could happen if the decision-maker did this or that, but it is the picturing of what can happen now that he is, psychically speaking, past the point of no return. I shall call the imaginative experience of consequences of an act upon which the individual *has decided*, experience by *anticipation*.

## VII

We were led to discuss time because we had asked whether the distinct things which a decision-maker will look upon as rival possible sequels to a given act of his own, can in principle be listed completely by an outside observer from a knowledge of the decision-maker's history. Let that knowledge be never so complete, we are saying, still, Will the detached observer know what list of possible sequels the decision-maker will assign to each available act? In trying to get light on this question, we concluded that the consequences, in pursuit of which a man chooses one act rather than another, are figments of imagination. By this conclusion we have turned our original question into a different one. We can now ask: are we to suppose that the work of the imagination is determined by the individual's past?

We can no more answer this question than any of those we have been posing. We can only point out the array of things amongst which our choice of assumption must lie. Is there anything in common experience which forbids us to include, amongst this list of rival assumptions, the idea that the imagination has a source of ideas *outside* of what the individual's past experience provides? Or let us put it in a single word: can there be inspiration? Can things happen in the mind which are not the inevitable sequels of the mind's previous operations? It is in supposing that there can be inspiration that there seems to me to be an escape from the dilemma of decision, the dilemma that if a man's tastes determine his choice of ends and if the laws of nature determine his choice of means to those ends, his action is determinate and we can find, in the meaning to which we are thus driven for the word *decision*, no satisfaction of our intuitive assurance of interior power of our own to help in the making of history.

## VIII

I want to turn now to two consequences of our electing to give to decision the meaning I have proposed. If decision is the pursuit of imaginative experience, and if also it is choice in face of uncertainty, how can we reconcile the plurality of the imagined consequences of an act with the need which I think a decision-maker will feel, to have a comparatively simple picture as the basis of his experience by anticipation? Secondly, what becomes of those schemes, now more than ever in fashion in economics, by which it is proposed to calculate the future from the past?

We need now a more exact conception of uncertainty. Suppose first that in answer to some question a man has in mind a hypothesis which he thinks could be true, and that he can discover no other hypothesis which he thinks can be true. Of the answers that he can think of, all but one seem to him impossible. Then if some action, whose character depends on the answer to this question, is to be taken immediately, he will not, effectively, be in any uncertainty about the practical answer to the question. He will assume that he knows the answer. If this be accepted we have already, by implication, defined uncertainty as the entertaining of plural rival hypotheses all of which seem possible. By rival hypotheses we mean mutually exclusive hypotheses all referring to the same question. Now it is plain that a man may conceive of any number of different answers to a question, seeing plainly that many of them are false or absurd. To make the plurality of rival answers meaningful, we therefore need some test which they must pass to be included in his list, and this test is possibility in a personal and subjective sense. Finally, what do we mean by a 'conflict' between a hypothesis and his general notions about the world or his notions about its particular momentary state? Do we suppose that there is in his mind a simple dichotomy between the congruous and the incongruous, or are there *degrees of possibility*?

If we suppose that, without distinguishing degrees of possibility, he divides the answers which have suggested themselves to any question merely into the possible and the impossible, there appears a way of reconciling the decision-maker's uncertainty, that is, the plurality of his 'possible' hypotheses, with his need for an unconfusing picture as the basis of experience by anticipation. For when the rival hypotheses concern the outcome of some act of his own, they will not all seem equally desirable. The most desirable one of all, we may be tempted to say, will also be the most *interesting* of all, the one with the greatest power to claim the decision-maker's attention. For if a good outcome and a superlative outcome both seem possible, and if 'possible' means one and only one thing and is not subject to distinction into greater or less, then why trouble one's mind with a good outcome which seems possible when there is offered the pleasure of contemplating a superlative outcome which seems equally possible? This would reduce the basis of anticipative experience to the greatest possible simplicity, presenting for it a single picture. But this is not a defensible attitude, for it does not 'count the cost'. If there are good, and very good, outcomes all seeming possible, there may be (and if we properly interpret the words 'good' and 'bad' as implying a comparison with the decision-maker's existing circumstances as he sees them, there will be) also bad, and very bad, possible outcomes. Amongst these, also, there will be a 'most interesting' one, and it will be the *worst*, the most undesirable. For the price of contemplating and experiencing by anticipation, by imagination, the best of the possible outcomes is the necessity, imposed by the human instinct for survival, to contemplate also the worst of the possible outcomes.

## IX

There is no room here to give more than this hint of a solution of the problem of reconciling uncertainty and imaginative experience. This solution I have elsewhere called the focus-hypotheses solution. We must now turn to the question whether those who may accept the meaning we have suggested for the word *decision* can at the same time believe in the possibility of what economists call a *dynamics*, a scheme of calculation of the future from the past.

To be scientific, it is sometimes said, an account of any branch of human experience must be able to predict. This is the test and the purpose of a science. Let us, however, distinguish between prediction and prophecy. A prophecy is an *unconditional* statement of what is going to happen. By making a prophecy a man is either claiming omniscience or else making an unashamed guess. Such a claim conflicts with the whole character of science which looks forward to continual discovery, test, amplification and revision. What the scientist or the engineer does is to state that, given the fulfilment of specified conditions, such and such will happen. This is conditional prediction. If this be accepted, the admission that a theory of human action cannot make prophecies does not condemn it as unscientific. The proponent of such a theory can make the same sort of reservation as the natural scientist. The economist, for example, can suggest what the course of events will be, given that people have resolved at a particular moment on certain plans and that no new *decision*, in our sense, is taken within the time-interval to which his prediction applies.

If we are to take a strict view, the constraints on the proponent of a theory of human action are very severe. For what we have been claiming for him is the right to make what I will call a *ceteris paribus* prediction. Now the things which he has to take as given are the plans of all individuals in force at some instant. Should any individual subsequently make a non-empty decision, the *ceteris paribus* condition will no longer be fulfilled as regards the prediction made at the earlier instant, and that prediction ceases to claim validity. Yet how, in the nature of *decision* as we have elected to understand that word, can the predictor know when a decision will be taken? If any meaning can be given to our idea of inspiration, that meaning must surely include the notion that it is not only the *content* of an inspired decision but the moment of its occurrence which cannot be predicted. It follows that in making a *ceteris paribus* prediction the predictor can give no indication of how long the interval is for which his prediction claims validity. That interval may be zero.

However, the economist at any rate will not allow himself to be entirely inhibited by these thoughts. The inherent imprecision of economics has taught him to be satisfied with broad statements. He will claim the right to make short-term forecasts on the ground that change takes time, that there is a momentum in human affairs arising from the difficulty of changing people's beliefs or of conveying an understanding of news; from the time taken by mere physical processes; and from the effect of habit and settled institutions, which justifies the projection of recent tendencies into the near future. I propose to call a dynamic system, justified on these grounds, an *inertial dynamics*. The proponent of sciences of human action, the economist, the sociologist or the political scientist, can make use, I think, of a *ceteris paribus* dynamics or of an inertial dynamics. To concede this does not preclude us from maintaining that if *decision* is non-illusory, non-empty and non-powerless, it is also non-predictable, and the non-predictability of decision inevitably entails that of history itself.

# 7
# THE DESCRIPTION OF UNCERTAINTY

A model or scheme of the psychic act of decision requires amongst its elements something called uncertainty, and must give a meaning to this element. If we look upon future history as in every respect determinate, human decisions have plainly no creative part to play in the unfolding of this history. If on the contrary future history is not determinate, each decision-maker may be conceived to create history by each of his decisions. If, in that case, there is a plurality of decision-makers, none can know at any moment what are the simultaneous decisions which others are then taking, and since the outcome of his own decision will be partly shaped by the effects of those decisions of others, he cannot know exactly and for certain what will be the outcome of his own decision. We therefore claim that if human decision contributes to history, injecting into the stream of events something that was not implicit in the past of that stream, uncertainty is part of the essence of decision, and it is, indeed, in the strictest sense meaningless and self-contradictory to speak as though decision could be both creative and free from uncertainty. This conclusion, surely, is intuitively obvious without argument. If we wish to analyse, and for this purpose to schematize, decision, we have therefore no escape from uncertainty and must bond it into our fabric from the start. Those who discuss 'decisions' made with 'complete information' are not discussing creative and contributive decision but, at best, merely a passive link mechanism and human obedience to 'necessity' or Fate. Creative decision may be illusory; but if real, it is performed in face of uncertainty, it is inconceivable except on condition of the non-existence of a determinate future. If there is no objective, determinate future to be known, how can there be knowledge of it?

We turn now to propose a formal interpretation of the word 'uncertainty'. Uncertainty is a state of the decision-maker's thoughts, and it will be absent from those thoughts if he can describe, in all respects which matter to him, some one future course of events or future sequence of situations, and if all other courses or sequences seem to him impossible. Thus uncertainty, in our view, consists in the plurality of those descriptions of the future which the decision-maker looks upon as in some degree possible. We thus define uncertainty as a state of mind and as subjective. Is it not then possible that a man might *mistakenly* feel sure that one particular course of future history and one only was all he need reckon with? It is evidently possible, but, except for a solipsist, such a view would be self-contradictory, for it would deny the creative freedom of others. We say, then, that consistency in a man's thoughts requires him either to regard history as determinate or recognize that he acts always without full knowledge of the outcome of what he does.

But he is not entirely without knowledge, for this would mean that choice of one act out of many available acts would be pointless and useless. If a man can set no bounds to what may follow upon any act of his own, he evidently looks upon himself as powerless to affect the course of events. There are, indeed, two views of history which would compel him to acknowledge his own powerlessness. If history is determinate, he cannot alter its predestinate course. If history is anarchy and randomness, he cannot modify this randomness nor mitigate the orderlessness of events. It is only a *bounded* uncertainty that will permit him to act creatively.

Uncertainty is bounded, for the decision-maker, when some courses of history, which he can imagine *formally*, seem to him impossible as sequels to some act of his own available to him. Enclosed, as it were, between such bounds there are, for each available act of his own, a number of distinct courses of history which seem to him possible. It is natural, we therefore claim, for the decision-maker (and ourselves, as outside, detached observer) to look upon *possible* and *impossible* as the two fundamental categories, in relation to some given present action, into which statements about future history should be distributed.

In this distribution there is already a basis for choice amongst available acts. For let the decision-maker order according to his preference and advantage those sequels which, in relation to some one act, he classes as possible; and let him do this for each of his available acts. Then amongst the possible outcomes of any act there will be a best and a worst; and if an outcome is either possible or not possible, and nothing more of this kind can be said about it, these two outcomes of each act are the only ones which bear upon the question of which act to choose. For if a given bad outcome is possible, and nothing more or other than possibility can be ascribed to any other outcome, no other outcome can stand as a barrier between the decision-maker and the given bad outcome, should he elect the act concerned. Thus the worst outcome shoulders aside all other bad outcomes. Likewise the best outcome eclipses all other good outcomes and claims for itself all the attention that the decision-maker can spare for good outcomes. All the comparisons we have just discussed take place in the decision-maker's mind in his 'present moment', and the outcomes in question are figments of that mind, figments in regard to which, in that moment of decision, the question, asked by an outside observer, whether they are true or not is meaningless.

Do we, in this construction, require to suppose that the decision-maker can distribute his imagined outcomes of any act into those which are in some absolute sense good and those which are absolutely bad, as well as being able to order them according to his preference? We think not. For even if all the hypothetical outcomes were regarded as in some degree bad (even if, that is to say, the decision-maker declined to draw a frontier between 'good' and 'bad' outcomes) there would still be a *worst* which on that account would claim special attention. And, similarly, there would be a *best* outcome which on that account would claim special attention. However, there is another solution to the problem implied by our question. For there is, indeed, a natural frontier between those outcomes which are good, and those which are bad, compared with the decision-maker's *existing situation*. That 'existing situation' will itself be constituted partly by the hopes and possibilities which the decision-maker entertains at that moment, and thus it will depend on the whole list of acts available to him at that moment and the outcomes which he considers possible in relation to each of them. But this does not render it inapt as a means of dividing hypothetical outcomes into 'good' and 'bad'.

To the criticism, then, that goodness and badness of outcomes is only relative, the criticism that, while one outcome may be thought by the decision-maker better or worse than another, outcomes cannot be divided into sheep and goats, we answer that such division is indeed meaningless in a vacuum, that is, if it is supposed to be absolute without regard to the circumstances of the individual. For if it were absolute in this sense for one individual, why should not the very same criterion apply for all individuals? The notion of absolute goodness or badness of outcomes is plainly absurd. But from a given starting-point, an outcome may be an improvement or the reverse. It is, of course, only in the circumstances of the individual, as assessed by himself, at some particular moment of the calendar, that the question arises for him whether a given outcome is good or bad, and this question is the same as the question whether the outcome is an improvement or otherwise compared with these initial circumstances. Thus if the notion of *focal outcomes* that we have indicated, at one level of refinement, in the preceding paragraph does, as some think, depend upon the possibility of dividing outcomes into those which are desired and those which are disliked, we claim that this division is possible. But we also suggest that the conception of focal outcomes could subsist without this division.

If the conception of focus values, established as we have above suggested, is accepted, we have still to show by what formal process the decision-maker could be supposed to select one out of a number of available acts when each of these acts is represented by such a pair of focus outcomes. For how would he compare two acts, $A$ and $B$, if the best outcome of $A$ was preferred to the best outcome of $B$, but the worst outcome of $A$ was worse than the worst outcome of $B$? This problem is analogous to that of the consumer faced with a choice amongst various sets of quantities of goods, and we shall suggest below that an indifference map can picture his mode of choice. Meanwhile we wish to consider another question. The basic assumption, on which the idea of focus values is primarily founded, is that the decision-maker can distribute all the outcomes he conceives for any act into one or other of the two classes 'possible' and 'impossible'. What, then, of a state of mind describable as doubt? In this first construction, we have made the whole meaning of uncertainty to reside in the *plurality* of the hypotheses which are looked on as possible. May not the decision-maker have in mind hypotheses which he feels unable to class as 'impossible' and yet cannot admit to the same status as other hypotheses to whose realization he can see no distinct obstacle? What of *impeded* but not *impossible* outcomes? Do we need a category, or a large number of categories, of imperfect possibility?

This matter may be approached by a different route. The statement that a man has in mind a *plurality* of hypotheses about the outcome of some act or experiment (about the sequence of states of the world which would follow the performance of that act or experiment) is very easily taken, without the slightest warrant, to mean that he has in mind a list which he assumes to be complete of all contingencies which could possibly result from this act or experiment. Why is it taken for granted that the list is known, or assumed, by the decision-maker to be complete? Because the whole probability calculus is founded on this assumption. This calculus assumes that one or other contingency out of some fully specified set must occur whenever a certain *type* of trial or experiment is made. When one such trial is contemplated, the assertion that its outcome will belong to this set has the status of certainty, and this is represented by unity. The status of an assertion that the outcome will be some particular member of the complete set must then be represented by some proper fraction, and since all members of the set, taken together, compose the set, so the corresponding proper fractions must sum to unity. The probability *unity* attaching to the complete set of contingent outcomes is thus *distributed* over the component outcomes, and we may therefore call probability a *distributive uncertainty variable*. What now happens if the decision-maker cannot assume that his list of contingencies is complete? Probability fractions cannot be assigned to outcomes if the number and character of these are unknown. Thus the use of a distributive uncertainty variable depends entirely upon the possibility of assuming completeness in the list of outcomes. But this assumption is wholly inappropriate to the case of creative decision.

The man who throws a die or draws cards at random from a pack cannot by resort to creative imagination alter the 'rules of the game', the physical features of the die or other mechanical apparatus. He cannot, therefore, alter the number of outcomes or their character. But the man who tries to imagine the paths of future history as it will evolve after some given act of his own has been injected into its stream, must acknowledge his helplessness to attain or approach completeness. The ineffable diversity and complexity of the conceivable states of the world and their sequence, the fact that this sequence is, for all practical human purposes, endless and eternal, preclude any but a sketchy sampling by the human mind of an unimaginably complex 'phase space'. It follows that a distributive uncertainty variable cannot serve to express the decision-maker's judgements about hypothetical outcomes of an act of his own, as to whether some particular outcome will or will not, may or may not happen. What, then, can be the nature of a *non-distributive uncertainty variable*?

Probability must be abandoned in favour of *possibility*, and a means must be sought of defining and expressing degrees of possibility. For possibility is not a limited total which must be shared, but can on the contrary be ascribed to any number of distinct and mutually exclusive outcomes without limit. The *possibility* of an outcome is a purely subjective, judgemental and *ex ante* concept, and to ascribe possibility to any outcome does not preclude its ascription to a rival outcome. It is plain that the degree of possibility, thus understood, ascribed to this and to that outcome cannot meaningfully be added together, for since in principle there can be infinitely many distinct outcomes, and since the possibility assigned to one outcome need not reduce that assigned to another, we might have an infinite 'total' of possibility. The temptation to add together the respective degrees of possibility ascribed to rival outcomes can be avoided by using a scale in which *perfect* possibility will be represented by zero while some arbitrary number is assigned to mean perfect impossibility. This scheme is specially well adapted to the means we shall propose for giving the notion of degrees of possibility a psychological content. If any event is looked on by a particular person as perfectly possible, its actual occurrence will cause him no surprise. If it has been regarded as perfectly *im*possible, its occurrence in fact would cause him the most intense surprise conceivable. Between these two extremes, occurrences whose practicability and realism he had regarded sceptically without quite dismissing them, and others which he had thought possible except for some slight incongruity with the current situation, and so on, will have an intermediate power to surprise him by their actual occurrence. The debate concerning the possibility of setting up, for any one individual, a cardinal scale of the intensity of his feelings has resulted, amongst economists, in some recognition of the practicability of a scale 'cardinal up to a linear transformation'. If this be accepted, we have in the notion of *potential surprise* a means of expressing *degrees of subjective, adjudged possibility*. The potential surprise assigned by the decision-maker to any hypothetical outcome is that degree of surprise which he would feel if, without there having been in the meantime any change in his knowledge or his interpretation of the facts, the hypothetical outcome should be realized.

The conception of degrees of subjective possibility, or of potential surprise, enables us to refine the notion of focus outcomes. For now we can consider the influence, not only of desirability or undesirability of hypothetical outcomes, but also of their degrees of possibility, on the power of such hypotheses to command attention from the decision-maker. This power we shall call *ascendancy*, to be treated as a function $\varphi = \varphi\ (G, y)$ of the 'face value' or pure desiredness-undesiredness, $G$, and of the possibility, $y$, of each *expectation element* $(G, y)$. There are now two technical methods open to us. We can treat each of $G$ and $y$ as a stepping-stone variable consisting of discrete values, so that these variables together form a lattice whose points will be expectation elements as defined in the foregoing. These points can evidently, if we wish, be stated as a matrix or rectangular array. Corresponding to each such point there will be a value of $\varphi$. Alternatively we can treat $G$ and $y$ as continuous and consider a surface $\varphi\ (G, y)$. The latter method, if perhaps less close to the nature of our psychic subject-matter, allows us to use the familiar differential calculus notation and its corresponding geometrical symbolism. We argue as above that there will be some value of $G$, close to what the decision-maker considers his 'present position', for which $\varphi$ will be a minimum for all $y$. Circumstances are conceivable in which we might wish to take a more general view and suppose the value of $G$ giving a minimum of $\varphi$ to depend also on $y$, but we have no present need of such a refinement. By definition, let $G = 0$ be the value of $G$ for which $\varphi$ is a minimum. Then, as we scan numerically increasing $G$ whether positive or negative, $\varphi$ will increase. The argument is more commanding in concrete terms. Let values of $G$, then, be hypotheses of money profit from a business investment. It seems realistic to say that, when the question of possibility is disregarded, hypotheses of large profit will seize the decision-maker's mind more powerfully than those of small profit. But likewise hypotheses of numerically large *loss* will be of more concern to him, if we again disregard the question of possibility, than those of small loss. However, the question of possibility is, of course, of the essence of the matter. A hypothesis will, we think, be less interesting the less the possibility accorded to it, and so $\varphi$ will be a decreasing function of $y$. Lastly, if the hypothesis is rejected as impossible, we shall assume that $\varphi = 0$.

The shape of the surface $\varphi = \varphi\,(G, y)$ which arises from these assumptions can best be pictured by means of curves $u = u(G)$ in the $Gy$-plane given implicitly by $\varphi =$ constant $> 0$. We have

$$\frac{\partial\varphi}{\partial G} > 0 \quad \text{for} \quad G > 0,$$

$$\frac{\partial\varphi}{\partial G} < 0 \quad \text{for} \quad G < 0,$$

$$\frac{\partial\varphi}{\partial y} < 0 \quad \text{for} \quad 0 < y < \bar{y},$$

where $\bar{y}$ is the absolute maximum of $y$ representing adjudged impossibility. Substituting $u(G)$ for $y$ in $\varphi = \varphi(G, y) =$ constant, we have

$$d\varphi = 0 = \frac{\partial\varphi}{\partial G}\,dG + \frac{\partial\varphi}{\partial u}\,du,$$

or

$$\frac{du}{dG} = -\frac{\partial\varphi}{\partial G}\bigg/\frac{\partial\varphi}{\partial u}.$$

Since $\partial\varphi/\partial G$ and $\partial\varphi/\partial u$ are of opposite sign where $G > 0$ and of the same sign where $G < 0$, we have, where $G$ is positive, a family of curves sloping upwards (that is, towards increasing values of $u$) with increase of $G$ and, where $G$ is negative, sloping upwards with *numerical* increase of the negative values of $G$. Since $\varphi$ is zero everywhere on the line $y = \bar{y}$, that is, where hypotheses are rejected as impossible, none of the lines $u = u(G)$ implied by $\varphi =$ constant $> 0$ can anywhere attain the line

$y = \bar{y}$. If each such curve always approaches but never reaches this line, it may be said to approach it asymptotically. The picture thus presented will broadly resemble Fig. 1.

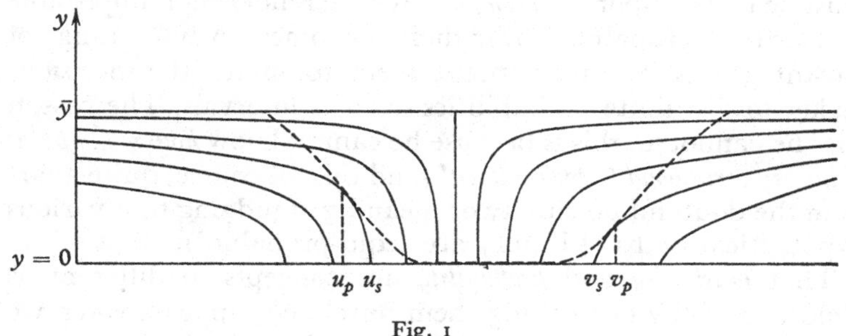


Fig. 1

The general conception of a surface $\varphi = \varphi(G, y)$ of the type we have described is a means of specifying, in those respects which bear on his assessment of actions available to him, the psyche of an individual decision-maker. Not his intellect only but his whole temperament must be thought of as reflected somewhat in its shape. Each particular specimen of such a surface will be peculiar to one individual, and will be unique in the details of its shape as he is unique. The $\varphi$-surface is a far cry from the attempt to characterize an individual's 'attitude to risk' by a single ratio, and is a tool which should offer possibilities to a refined empirical psychology.*

Having found a means to describe the individual, we next need one to describe the sheaf of possibilities which some available action stands for in his mind. A careful distinction is here necessary between the set of distinct paths of history which seem rival possible sequels to his acting in a particular way, and the range of different degrees of advantage (e.g. money profit) which corresponds in a complex way to that set of paths of history (set of sequences of states of the world). For in claiming that his uncertainty must be *bounded* if he is to decide meaningfully amongst mutually exclusive available actions, we are requiring

* The author has been exceedingly gratified and encouraged by the interest which has been shown in this conception by Professor G. Patrick Meredith and Professor John Cohen, very eminent psychologists who have referred to it in their published work. See Professor Meredith's contributions to *Uncertainty and Business Decisions* (Liverpool University Press, England, 2nd ed. 1957) and Professor Cohen's luminous book, *Chance, Skill, and Luck* (Pelican Books, 1960).

that the range of advantage–disadvantage or of desirability–undesirability should itself be bounded. But in saying that if decision is history-creating the list of possible outcomes of an act must be looked upon as *incomplete*, we are rendering it impossible to distribute probability over these outcomes. A finite range of advantage–disadvantage might seem to invite the decision-maker to distribute probabilities over its intervals. The reason why he cannot do this is because he cannot know *how many paths of history correspond to each interval* (and this, of course, quite apart from the doubtful possibility or meaning of judging that various hypothetical paths of history are 'equi-probable').

That *possibility* and *probability* are concepts so different as almost to justify our calling them unrelated, appears when we consider what the decision-maker can do instead of assigning probabilities. For if he can find, for any interval on the advantage–disadvantage axis, a hypothetical path of history which seems to him to be free of fatally disabling present circumstances or inherent characteristics, he can regard that path of history, and hence that advantage interval, as possible in some degree. That degree will be perfect (potential surprise zero) if there is nothing which inhibits or makes difficult his imagining the coming-true of that hypothesis. Such inhibition could arise from two kinds of source. A specific path of future history, or what we may call a sequence of states of the world, might seem to conflict with natural laws in the widest sense, including those of human nature and political institutions, so that such a path of history would seem *inherently* difficult to imagine as real. Or this path might seem unreal, not *in vacuo* but considered as the immediate sequel to the decision-maker's current situation. Otherwise expressed, the supposed course of events might seem to the decision-maker to be impossible, even in a remote future, no matter how the interval between his present moment and the initial date of that sequence of events were filled in. Or it might merely seem impossible as a picture of the immediate future itself. This impossibility being a matter of the individual's own judgement, based on an immense diversity of ideas, some clear and some vague, about how the world works and about its current state, we cannot suppose that he will always be able to divide hypotheses unequivocally into the two classes, possible and impossible, but will need categories of *imperfect* possibility.

We have supposed, above, that the possibility variable $y$ will be continuous from perfect possibility to perfect impossibility.

For each available action, each of those actions amongst which he sees himself free to choose, the decision-maker, we suppose, will have in mind a *possibility curve* or function $y = y(G)$ connecting points on the desirability–undesirability axis $G$ with degrees of possibility $y$. Great success and great misfortune are such by comparison with the decision-maker's present situation. The time available to him is limited by human impatience and ultimately by the human life-span. The greater the success, we may broadly say, the swifter, more dramatic and more radical must be the changes away from his present situation. Small effects can be achieved by a multitude of paths of history, and only when great effects are sought need he look for surprising events and sequences of events. Thus it seems reasonable to suppose that for most actions which are *prima facie* worth considering there will be some range of the desirability–undesirability variable, $G$, within which any value seems perfectly non-surprising, perfectly possible. For all this range of $G$ the decision-maker will assign $y(G) = 0$. Beyond the extremities of this 'inner range' at either end there will be outcomes which he looks on as less than perfectly possible, as potentially surprising in some degree, as requiring some 'stretch of the imagination' to see them coming true. The further these outcomes are beyond one end or the other of the inner range, the higher the value of $y$ which will usually be assigned to them. Eventually outcomes will be reached which are 'too good to be true' or 'too bad to be true' and for these $y = \bar{y}$, they are rejected as impossible. From these considerations the *shape-type* of the possibility curve $y = y(G)$ emerges as resembling a vertical section through a diameter of a flat-bottomed basin. Such a curve is illustrated by a broken line in Fig. 1.

In this Fig. 1 we have now two classes of curves. The curves of one of these classes are specimens of the family of curves given implicitly by $\varphi = \text{constant} > 0$, which we write explicitly $u = u(G)$ and which, for simplicity of reference, we shall in future call *contour lines*. These contour lines fall into two groups belonging respectively to the positive and the negative ranges of $G$, and represent two sheets of the surface $\varphi = \varphi(G, y)$. The other class of curves in the figure has only one member, which is the *possibility curve* $y = y(G)$ representing the degree of possibility adjudged by the decision-maker to various hypothetical degrees of advantage from some one available action. It is convenient to consider the positive and the negative half of the diagram each by itself, and we shall accordingly take the positive half first. Because each of the contour lines $u = u(G)$ must broadly approach the line $y = \bar{y}$ asymptotically, they are here taken to be everywhere convex to that line. If we take the relevant branch of the possibility curve $y = y(G)$ to be either straight or else convex to the $G$-axis this curve will have a point of tangency with some one or other of the contour lines and, as is easily shown and intuitively clear, such a point of tangency will be a maximum of $\varphi(G, y)$ subject to the constraint $y = y(G)$. For if we imagine a wall, perpendicular to the $Gy$-plane, to be erected along the possibility curve, this wall will cut the surface $\varphi(G, y)$ in a twisted curve or space curve $\varphi = \varphi(G, y(G))$.

$$\frac{d\varphi}{dG} = 0 = \frac{\partial\varphi}{\partial G} + \frac{\partial\varphi}{\partial y}\frac{dy}{dG}$$

gives us

$$\frac{dy}{dG} = -\frac{\partial\varphi}{\partial G}\bigg/\frac{\partial\varphi}{\partial y},$$

and this latter expression is the same, when $y$ is renamed $u$, as that obtained from the differential of every curve

$$\varphi = \varphi(G, u(G)) = \text{constant}.$$

By a parallel argument, there will be a point of tangency between the other branch of the possibility curve and the other group of contour lines on the negative side of the diagram.

The two constrained maxima of the space-curve

$$\varphi = \varphi(G, y(G))$$

are, in this more sophisticated model, the two expectation elements $(G, y)$ which, we claim, will concentrate the decision-maker's attention and interest upon themselves. They do not, however, lend themselves to the use we proposed for the focus outcomes of our more primitive model. For these focus outcomes were simply values of the variable $G$, scalar quantities which could be used as co-ordinates on an indifference map, while the constrained maxima of the space curve are points or vectors $(G, y)$. We wish therefore to eliminate $y$ in each of them, and for this purpose we seek *equivalent* expectation elements which, like the focus outcomes of our primitive model, are simply scalar quantities $G$. Since these equivalents are to be mere values of $G$, they will lie on the $G$-axis, and since the sense in which they are to be equivalent is evidently that of leaving unchanged the value of $\varphi$, each will lie on the same equal-$\varphi$ curve or contour line as its corresponding constrained maximum point $(G, y)$. All we need do, therefore, is to follow the particular contour line on which the constrained maximum lies, down to its meeting with the $G$-axis. Thus for each *primary* focus element, say $(G_p, y_p)$, we shall find a *standardized* focus point $(G_s, 0)$ such that $\varphi(G_s, 0) = \varphi(G_p, y_p)$. In Fig. 1 we have relabelled the standardized focus *gain* as $v_s$ and the standardized focus *loss* as $u_s$, while the corresponding primary values of $G$ are labelled $v_p$ and $u_p$ respectively.

Our final tool is an indifference map on which the coordinates are standardized focus gains and losses. 'Gain' and 'loss' can of course stand for desired or undesired outcomes of any character, but these words are suggested by the application of our scheme of thought to a particular field, that of economic *investment* or purchase of industrial equipment. For this reason also, we shall refer to the map as an investment indifference map.

Every action available, at some moment, to the decision-maker will be assigned by him its own special form of possibility curve, and by that psychic operation which we have sought to illustrate by means of the surface $\varphi = \varphi(G, y)$, he can thus determine for each of these actions a pair of standardized focus outcomes, values of $G$. Any such pair will yield a point on the indifference map, and, correspondingly, every point of the positive–positive quadrant of the map will represent some conceivable pair of standardized focus outcomes. For any such point, chosen at random, there can in principle be found an infinity of other points which, to our particular decision-maker, seem neither better nor worse. If our individual is reasonable and consistent, all these points will lie on a continuous curve. Since a greater possible loss will need to be compensated by a greater possible gain, each such curve will have a positive slope. In the particular context of investment decisions we can go further. In this case the decision-maker will have available some particular amount of money, a 'disposable fortune', which he is free to use wholly or partly for the purchase of industrial equipment. The use of this equipment will require the co-operation of other means of production such as labour services, materials and power, the cost of which in each year or other interval will have to be deducted from the sale proceeds of the goods made by the equipment in that year to determine that year's *trading profit*. At the moment of deciding whether or not to buy this equipment, the trading profit of any year will be both hypothetical and deferred. The fact that it is hypothetical can be subsumed in the status of any calculation based on it, the result of which calculation will itself be a hypothesis. But the *deferment* of the assumed amount of trading profit of any year must be allowed for by multiplying this amount by a discounting factor $1/(1+r)^N$, where $r$ is the market interest rate and $N$ is the number of years' deferment. The sum of such discounted amounts for all the years of the equipment's assumed operating life will be the money value indicated for the equipment by the series of assumed future trading profits. Since the owner of such equipment is not bound to operate it at a trading loss, we shall suppose that no estimate, thus arrived at, of the value of the equipment will be negative. A *zero* assumed value would imply the loss of the whole price to be paid for the equipment. The difference, positive or negative, between any hypothesis or assumption of the value of the equipment, and the purchase price which would have to be paid for the equipment, is an algebraic value of $G$ in the meaning we have given to this variable.

According to these assumptions, the greatest sum of money which the decision-maker could lose through buying the equipment would be its purchase price. However, if the price is less than the whole 'disposable fortune' available for investment, we must consider the consequences of his investing the remainder in various ways. If he spends it on other equipment, the consequence might be a loss of part or all of this remainder. For simplicity, therefore, we shall here assume that he retains in the form of money any part of the 'disposable fortune' not needed for the purchase of the equipment we are concerned with. Thus it will be the case that the loss of the whole purchase price of this equipment is the largest loss he need fear out of the 'disposable fortune', and we can accordingly erect a 'barrier' at a point on the 'loss' axis of the investment indifference map corresponding to this amount of loss. Let the loss axis be the horizontal one. Then the indifference curves will rise towards the barrier, but, if they reach it, they will there terminate and can have no meaning beyond it. However, will they in fact reach this barrier?

Any point on this barrier stands for the loss of the whole of the 'disposable fortune', and the choice of an investment (a piece of equipment) represented, for the investor, by such a point would imply his willingness to expose himself to the total loss of his invested sum, for the sake of putting himself also within reach of a finite gain. Surely it is a question of temperament whether a decision-maker will ever accept such a position. If he does not, then the indifference curves can never attain the 'total loss' barrier but must rise ever more steeply and approach it asymptotically. Can we not infer also that the indifference curves will rise with increasing steepness even when the individual concerned does not reject positions on the barrier itself? By these arguments we arrive at the two types of indifference map illustrated in Fig. 2.

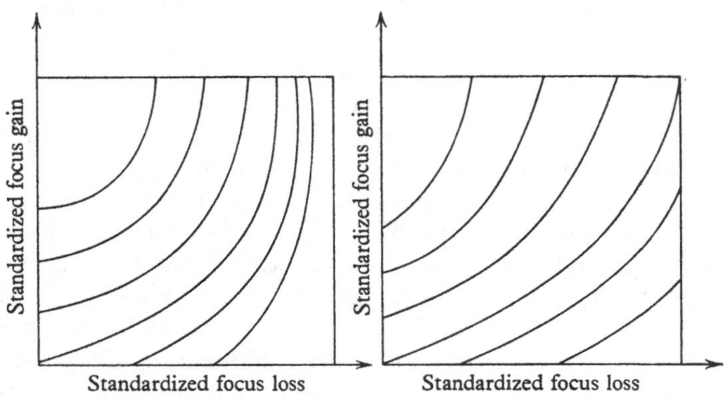


Fig. 2

The human psyche and the source and nature of its thought remain a profound mystery which may never be understood. The insight we can hope to gain by means of such a scheme as we have outlined consists merely in discerning some of the logical implications of our choice, if such it is, when we assume that *decision*, an event occurring in that solitary present which is our whole experience of time, is *creative* and not merely a symptom or meaningless accompaniment of the working of a machine.

# 8
# DECISION AND UNCERTAINTY

If the act of decision is no more than a response to circumstances, and if each such act can be wholly explained in all its particulars as necessitated by the circumstances and the personal character of the decision-maker, then plainly such an act makes no contribution of its own to the course of affairs. It is passive, mechanical, non-creative and, in principle, predictable. This conclusion is not altered by an appeal to human proneness to make 'mistakes'. 'The circumstances' can of course never be completely or precisely known; the impossibility for the individual to know all that concerns him about the state of affairs existing at any moment is itself part of his circumstances or of himself. If we say that a decision is a response to circumstances, we mean that it is determined by the individual's conception of his circumstances.

If each decision can be fully analysed and explained in terms of its antecedents, it is hardly interesting, and we may as well argue from one visible external situation to the next. Moreover, it is only on condition of this passiveness, this *sterility* of the act of decision, that it is logically possible for us to argue from the past to the future. We cannot predict the course of human affairs if the sequel to each present moment is partly created within that moment, by decisions which generate essential novelty. In the derivation of one historical moment from another, are there genetic mutations? To give to *decision* the meaning of a creative act, a *source* of history, we have to assert the non-existence of the future: if a decision can contribute a new strand to the self-weaving tapestry of history, there must be a gap for this strand to fill. If there is a gap, the conditions for determinateness are not there. If the future must wait for the completion of its conditions, must wait for determinateness, it does not yet exist.

Let the philosopher, then, abandon for a time his professional attachment to determinacy, and take sides with the unthinking ordinary man, the man who feels a weight upon his spirit when it appears that he has freedom to choose amongst rival available actions. Must this man act in one way and one way only, or face a charge of being 'irrational'? Is there always one best act in face of circumstances as he knows them, and does his freedom consist merely in the two alternatives, either to choose this one best act or else to act arbitrarily, that is, foolishly and against his own interest?

We say that his circumstances are not given, but partly created by himself. The meaning, the nature, of each available act depends upon its consequences. Those consequences, in the moment of decision, do not exist, they are created in the *imagination* of the decision-maker; created, who shall say how? It is in this act of imagining the possible consequences of each available rival course that the door is open for essential novelty to be injected into the stream of history. The decision maker is not constrained to follow the one rational course in face of *given* circumstances, for the circumstances are not *wholly* given. By this route, we think, the philosopher, if he wishes, may find himself on the side of man in his unsophisticated and natural moments of endeavour and crisis, when, living within the solitary present and not observing the fiction of extensive time from without, he seems to himself to be helping to *make history*.

If we elect to escape by this route from the barrenness, passivity and emptiness of determinate 'decision', we are depriving the decision-maker of the power to make a list, which he can logically look upon as 'known to be complete', of all the possible eventualities of any one of the acts amongst which he can choose. How, then, can he meaningfully 'distribute' amongst these hypotheses a fixed total representing the *certainty* that the true event will select itself from them? There is no such certainty, for there is no list which, at any moment, is accepted as complete. It is of the essence of non-empty decision that it *interrupts a process of imaginative creation of hypothetical outcomes.* When such interruption occurs, there is no sense in looking on any such list of hypotheses, so far as it has gone, as a complete statement of everything that the decision-maker thinks could be the sequel to some act of his own. For each of his available acts he entertains a number of more or less precisely specified hypotheses, and *also a residual hypothesis*: 'If I did this, such or such or such might be the consequence, *or something else*.' But how can a *probability* be allotted to this Pandora's box of a residual hypothesis? The number and nature of its distinct, specific contents is not only *unknown* but *unknowable in principle*, since it is endless, the upsurge from the creative well of inspiration.

When we throw a die, we accept it as certain that the result will be one or other of the numbers 1, 2, 3, 4, 5, 6. These six contingencies taken together make up a whole. If we think of this whole as a target, our throw of the die will hit this target *for a certainty*, and we represent this certainty, which arises from the comprehensive completeness of our target-list of contingencies, its all-inclusive and unified wholeness, by the number *one*. This whole is composed of the separate contingencies, and if we can find some suitable and defensible scheme for doing so, we may *share out* the number one in fractions amongst the contingencies. What is the purpose of doing so? To refine our judgement of whether the bet we are proposing to make, on the basis of this particular throw of the die, is attractive or not. We are not here concerned to validate or to reject any particular scheme on which this sharing could be performed, but simply to point out that *no scheme* could have validity if it were not for the accepted completeness of the list of contingencies. Only this completeness allows us to use a *distributive uncertainty variable*.

Subjective probability is neither more nor less than a distributive uncertainty variable, a means, that is to say, of expressing the decision-maker's judgement as to how near a given hypothesis is to 'certainly right' or 'certainly wrong' or how remote it is from one or other of these. From being called 'probability', this means of quantifying the distillation of evidence, experience, and temperament gains a spurious prestige, for we are led by this name carelessly to think of it as a *source* and not merely an *expression* of such judgements. It steals, in our thoughts, the diadem by which *objective* probability rules a totally different realm. In their nature and role the two 'probabilities' are fundamentally and radically different, for objective probability is a means to knowledge and subjective probability an acknowledgement of the absence of knowledge. What question does objective probability answer? It tells us the proportion of instances in which some type of performance, many times repeated, has had this and that result out of an explicit and complete list of possible distinct results. If what the decision-maker contemplates is a further large number of this same type of performance, and if he can promise himself that the circumstances of this further series will be constrained within precisely the same limits as those which circumscribed the past series, the counting of cases offers him, not a means of expressing ignorance but a means of obtaining *knowledge*. For objective probability is knowledge and eliminates, not expresses, uncertainty. It thus eliminates the need and possibility of *decision*, for in those contexts where the outcomes can be known there is no freedom of imagination and no judgement, and 'decision' is empty. Objective probabilities, however, can be obtained, and applied, only in such operations as those of an insurance company. In the vast areas of politics, diplomacy, enterprise and investment it can serve only as one of the possible bases, and seldom the most relevant, on which judgements *expressible* by means of an uncertainty variable can be based. For the decision-maker is concerned (it cannot be too strongly emphasized) with a *single whole*. A decision is the act of committing oneself and one's resources, at one particular historical moment, to some one experiment out of many available. That experiment may consist in what is naturally thought of as a single act, such as the signing of a contract for the purchase of some system of industrial equipment as a whole; it may, that is to say, be *non-divisible*; or it may consist in the *totality* of a series of performances all in many respects similar and all circumscribed by the same set of conditions: it may be a divisible experiment. But in this latter case it is the *total* result of the entire series of performances which is relevant, and a divisible experiment is precisely that sort of act whose outcome can be known by means of objective probability.

When a counting of past cases serves as the basis of judgement about the outcome of a single, specific, individual, named and particularized act, what precisely is the train of thought leading from the evidence to the conclusion? The theory of probability, applied to a *single* impending performance for which the results of a series of similar past performances are known, conceives some listed contingencies as possible, all others as impossible. The only handicap under which a particular contingency of the list suffers, in its efforts to realize itself, is that of being *jostled* by a number of other contingencies, all of them, in Bernoulli's phrase 'equi-possible'. But if the number of these other contingencies (without necessarily being infinite) is unreckonable, the measure of such jostling cannot be determined. The whole approach must therefore be different. Attention must be directed, not to the numbers of the competing contingencies but to the relation of the particular contingency, in its precise and essential character, to the whole circumstances in their depth and fullness. The decision-maker must ask himself whether such knowledge as he has, of nature and human nature in general, of the particular current state of affairs, of the plans and intentions of other people, makes this contingency seem to him 'possible'. He may even ask what degree of possibility he can assign it. Then he must weigh against each other those contingencies, both good and bad, to which, by his contemplated act, he would expose himself.

If we cannot know what *will* happen, we must concern ourselves with what *can* happen. The uncertainty variable appropriate to decision is an indicator of adjudged *possibility*. Such an uncertainty variable is by its nature non-distributive, for a particular hypothetical outcome can seem perfectly possible regardless of the number and even of the diversity of its rivals. That which we had deemed to be somewhat inhibited by nature or circumstances will surprise us if it occurs, in just that measure by which we had found difficulty in imagining its occurrence. If, examining hypothetical outcomes, we can assign to each the degree of surprise its actuality would cause us in our present state of knowledge and interpretation, this *potential surprise* can serve as the measure of subjective possibility that we require. It has the advantage of resulting, in a sense, from an inversion of our problem, for it answers the question, not what is our degree of belief in each hypothesis (how, indeed, can one believe *positively*, even in a less than wholehearted manner, in each of several mutually contradictory hypotheses at once?) but what is the degree of our *disbelief* in each hypothesis? *Zero* disbelief thus corresponds to, and means the same as, perfect subjective possibility; and so we are saved from any temptation of adding together the degrees of possibility of different hypotheses, or of distributing some 'total' of possibility amongst them.

A hypothesis concerning the outcome of some act, when this hypothesis has been assigned a degree of possibility or of potential surprise, may be called an *element* of the decision-maker's expectation scheme concerning that act. Thus by an expectation element we mean a vector of two entries, one of which represents the decision-maker's *valuation* of a hypothesis regardless of its capacity to become actual, while the other entry represents a measure of this adjudged capacity. Such elements will, we think, possess in differing degrees the power to engage the decision-maker's attention. This *ascendancy* or attention-arresting power will, we think, be an increasing function of the numerical valuation of the hypothesis, whether that valuation be positive or negative, and a decreasing function of its possibility. Thus it becomes possible to define, in a manner whose details it would be out of place to describe here, two *focus elements* for each act available to the decision-maker. These focus elements will, according to our conception, be his basis of comparison of the different acts.

My concept of focus elements has been sometimes referred to as a means whereby the decision-maker can *simplify*, that is, *manipulate*, his thoughts. It is, instead, in my view, a natural psychic entity, the fusion of thought and feeling at the core of the act of decision.

# 9
# THE DILEMMA OF HISTORY

Let us suppose that men imagine and desire particular states of affairs, or the events each of which would carry one such state into another. A number of different actions appearing to each man at each moment to be open to him, let us suppose that he is conscious of selecting, amongst these available actions, that one which offers to realize his desired states or events. Given something, a source or mechanism, which feeds his imagination, we have in the foregoing a hypothesis of how history is created. This hypothesis confronts us with a dilemma. If men are to be successful in choosing those actions which will realize their ends, there must be a consistency in nature, including human nature, such that imagined outcomes can be linked, in some manner and degree, with given actions. The effect of any man's given action, however, will be different according as other people's contemporary actions are *A*, *B*, *C* or .... Unless each man's action is completely determined by circumstances and unless these circumstances are known to each other man so that every man can deduce every other man's action, the knowledge necessary for the existence of a discernible link between action and outcome will be lacking. It seems, therefore, that choice of action must be either *illusory*, in the sense that the answer to the question what to do is unambiguously supplied by circumstance, or else *ineffective* in the sense that desired results cannot be secured by considered selection of acts. To suppose that the trouble of choosing is worth while is to suppose that the general course of events is *structured*, so that we may form ideas of what will follow what. Yet to suppose that this structuring is *complete* is to leave no room for choice. How, then, can there be a non-determinist theory of history? How can we assign to human beings anything but a purely passive role? What sense can there be in studying *decisions* as though these were *sources*, not mere stages in a determinate reactive chain, of the past that continually emerges from the future? This is what I mean by the dilemma of non-determinist history; it is for this dilemma that I wish to seek some solution other than mere surrender to the determinist view.

To ask for a non-determinist theory of history is to ask for a history which is *not completely structured*, a history, that is to say, in which we need not regard every situation or event as the inevitable, sole and necessary consequence of antecedent situations or events, a history in which, therefore, a situation or event can be essentially and inherently not fully explainable, not fully analysable, not fully assignable to conditions or causes which are sufficient to guarantee the occurrence of it and it alone. A fully structured history leaves nothing to be created, nothing to be done by human decision, no room for the truly and strictly inceptive thought. A fully structured history denies imagination except as a distorting mirror of the past. History may, indeed, be fully structured, but if so it is not interesting to talk about decision: we should refer instead to the computational patterns of the brain, with perhaps their capacity for 'error'. Complete structure, if it be the truth, makes of decision the passive vehicle of the commands of circumstance passed on to compose fresh circumstances.

Yet a total absence of structure is equally incompatible with the idea that history originates with men and not merely employs or manipulates them. Absence of all structure, the complete divorce of a sequel from its antecedents, an entire lack of consistency and orderliness in nature, would render decision powerless and worthless, would restrict it to being a thought in a vacuum, with no effect outside the mind of the decision-maker. What, then, if we elect to follow intuition and the universal tacit assumption of ordinary discourse and practical life, and take for granted that decision can be *inceptive*, are we to suppose about the nature of history?

To release men from determinism it is not sufficient to suppose that they are ill informed about the circumstances with which they have to cope. It is, indeed, scarcely conceivable that they could be other than ill informed, for the mass of detail arising every second could not conceivably be noted, digested and interpreted by any man before he was overwhelmed with the equal flood of news arising in the very next second. Thus men act in the dark. But it is none the less conceivable that the precise *dossier* of information reaching their minds in every moment might be determinate, their interpretation of it and response to it likewise determinate, and that thus, by-passing their conscious strivings to understand and grapple with circumstance, history might push them in helpless hordes along the road of her choosing. 'Blind Fate' we say, but if history is Fate, it is we, perhaps, who are blind. Human error is not an escape from determinism.

In order to suppose that men create events rather than merely act them out as players following the script of a play, must we suppose them to act in defiance of reason and self-interest? Let us suppose that every man knows an algorithm or procedure for transforming the set of data, no matter whether true or false, sufficient or insufficient, that at any moment he possesses, into a policy or plan of action which in some sense gives him his best hope or best chance of attaining his desire. Then if all men follow the indications, each of his own data, we can suppose without internal contradiction in our argument that, unconscious nature being herself determinate, the set of data presented at each moment to each man will be determinate and so the whole course of history in its most general aspect will be determinate. But if men act in defiance of the indications and in conflict with their own interest, if, that is, they act as madmen, this determinacy will vanish. Must we, then, say with Locke that only madmen are free to act otherwise, in any instance, than in that single way which the rational pursuit of their ends dictates?

Instead of ends, let us speak of success. The word *end* suggests something final, complete, once for all, something which is either attained or not attained. But men's imagination shows them more often, not places to get to, but directions in which to travel. Success can be lesser or greater, and the same feeling of success can be secured by a variety, perhaps an infinite variety, of distinct specific courses of personal history. Men do not know what results they can achieve with the means at their disposal. The things they desire to achieve may be of a very general kind: wealth, power, fame, the creation of beauty, the relief of mankind's unhappiness, the solace of personal conscience, sainthood itself. These are matters of greater or less degree, their potential extent is in human terms unlimited, the technical routes of approach not given but to be endlessly imagined. It is in the imagining of these routes, each man's *technical* objectives, that men can be freely creative, that they can be inspired.

If acceptable at all, such a view as I am trying to sketch involves semantic questions of the greatest difficulty. There is one concept in particular which so far I can define only by stating its logical consequence. This is the idea of *essential novelty* in history. What do we mean by saying that 'a new strand' has been introduced into the pattern of events? I can define it only by saying that in such a case something has happened which, even with all conceivable information about the antecedents of this happening, could not have been predicted. One cannot avoid a wish for a more positive account of the nature of the *enlargement* of history by the imaginative invention of new supposed outcomes of available acts.

Let us suppose, then, that history is made by the interplay of men's actions; that at some moments a man sees open to him a number of distinct actions, and that he chooses amongst these according to the outcomes which he assigns to them. If to each action he assigns one and only one outcome, his problem of choice will be solved by arranging the outcomes in order of his desire for them. But these outcomes are thoughts, and our escape from determinism is to suppose that, in the most essential and the strictest sense, these thoughts *originate* in the decision-maker's mind, that, with no matter how complete a knowledge of his antecedents, it would be impossible to foretell these thoughts. If so, on what ground could we suppose that he will invent only one hypothesis about the outcome of each action? Let us suppose, instead, that the need to decide (in order that the fleeting moment may not impose its own decision by default) *interrupts* a process of continuing invention, that is, of imaginative creation. Two consequences follow. First, there will be for each of the rival available actions a plurality of already devised hypothetical outcomes; and secondly, the list of these already devised hypotheses cannot be looked on by the decision-maker as in any basic sense exhaustive or complete.

The decision-maker has now to choose, not amongst actions each of which offers its own single outcome, but amongst actions each offering a set of outcomes, some good and some bad. Within each such set, the members are rivals only one of which at most could prove true. How is the choice now to be made?

This problem has usually been mistaken for a different one, the problem of calculating the total outcome of a large number of trials all conducted under some set of known rules. From these rules a list is deducible of all the distinct possible results amongst which the result of any particular trial is bound to be found. Thus the rules may be that a die is to be thrown, a coin spun by hand, or a pack of cards shuffled and cut. In such circumstances it is found that, as the number of trials is increased, the proportion of them which yields any one of the possible results settles down into what we can regard as a fluctuation round some notional number. This number can thus be statistically estimated and is the objective or statistical probability of the particular result. When all the possible distinct results are taken together, the sum of their probabilities ought in logic to be unity, for according to the known rules of the game it is *certain* that in every individual trial the result will be one of those in the list, and in assigning probabilities we are merely treating the whole collection of trials as a single thing to be divided up into fractions representing the relative frequencies of occurrence of the various possible results. If, in some way, the desirability of each result can be represented by a number, each of these numbers can be multiplied by the corresponding probability and the results all added together to give the so-called 'mathematical expectation' as a measure of the attractiveness of the action in question.

For the comparison of actions, the hypothetical outcomes of each of which are not a known and static list but a stream of imaginative improvisation, the procedure of assigning probabilities seems essentially out of place. *Statistical* probabilities, when obtainable and when applicable, constitute *knowledge* of the outcome of the 'action' in question, which must in this case consist of the totality of many performances all bounded by the same conditions, and this brings us back to the case of 'one action, one outcome'. When statistical probabilities are not applicable, or not obtainable, we may resort to 'subjective' probabilities. But there remains the most basic objection of all. How can we *distribute* a total probability of unity over outcomes of which we have not a *list known to be complete*?

The proposal to escape from determinism by the supposition of imaginative creation of outcomes for each action, in a stream whose ending cannot be discerned at the moment when the necessity of deciding cuts off the process, thus requires a new means of representing the degree of *uncertainty* with which hypothetical outcomes are entertained. Such a means must be *non-distributive*: its values or numbers respectively assigned to various hypotheses must not be required to add up to unity or to any other pre-assigned total. Probability, even in its subjective meaning, is essentially and inherently distributional, for we cannot assign probability to a *residual hypothesis*. If we feel the necessity of saying 'The outcome of such and such an action may be *A*, or *B*, or *C*, *or something else*', the lack of any idea of what 'something else' means, or of how many distinct things it may embrace, prevents us from assigning it a *share* of the total probability which is to be shared amongst all hypotheses. Thus we do not know how much should be left for these other, specific, hypotheses, and cannot determine their shares either.

An uncertainty variable having a radically different meaning and nature suggested itself to me. It consists in a scheme for rendering *possibility* discriminable into a scale of degrees, by pointing to the connection between the degree of *surprise* felt at a given event and the 'degree of possibility' or of *difficulty*, *unfeasibility*, *implausibility* we had previously assigned to this event. This is not the occasion for an elaborate account of this suggestion. It seems to provide us with a *non-distributive* measure of the uncertainty of any hypothesis concerning the future outcome of any contemplated action, and thus to fill the non-determinist need. For *possibility* can be assigned in *any* degrees simultaneously to any number of hypotheses whether their number and characters are known or not, and thus allows the outcomes imagined for each action to be regarded as a continuing and essentially unpredictable stream rather than as a finite and known list.

## 10

# MODELS OF CONJECTURE

The prime tool of social science is the *model*. It organizes our intuitions and impressions, suggests interesting questions, offers testable conclusions, maps in advance the empiricist's or the statistician's procedure and finds a place for hypotheses and gives them exact expression. The invention of a new model is the most difficult and, I think, the most valuable form which a contribution to any one of the social sciences can take. This is the contribution which Monsieur de Jouvenel in his first lecture has given us.*

The concepts which distinguish this model are, first, the imagined and desired state of affairs and the imagined action-path leading to it from the subject's existing state; and secondly, the recognition, which efficient action calls for, of two types of possible frustration of the plan, namely, first, the *casuel* and secondly the *deformation of the social space*. The *casuel* is an event of a kind which, when it has occurred, is acknowledged by the acting subject as perfectly congruous with his personal world-picture, but nevertheless unforeseeable in its specific detail. *The deformation of the social space* is an event or process which renders the subject's world-picture obsolete in some vital respect, and thus destroys the basis or meaning of his plan. Let us examine first the concept of the social space itself.

The social space is simply the rules and apparatus of the game. When a footballer in his dash for the goal is tackled by an opposing player and loses control of the ball, that is a *casuel*. But if, *per impossibile*, the referee interrupts the game to announce that, henceforth, the ball may be *carried* and not merely kicked, this change of rules devalues the skill of those who have practised foot-control of the ball, and ruins any strategy based on the supposition that handling the ball is not allowed. It is a *deformation of the space* or 'receptacle'† of the game. In a game

* Monsieur Bertrand de Jouvenel's three lectures on *Prévision* were given in the summer of 1962 at the Institut Universitaire de Hautes Etudes Internationales at Geneva, to an invited audience from many countries and disciplines.

† ὑποδοχή.

(save for that famous occasion when Rugby football was invented by the spontaneous revolt of a frustrated schoolboy in the midst of the struggle) such a deformation does not happen except by long and explicit deliberation and public advance announcement. But in the general arena of life it can happen abruptly in a manner unforeseen, unplanned and perhaps almost universally undesired. How can this be?

Deformation of the social space, however various the fields of human action which it may affect and however diverse the time-patterns which it may follow, could perhaps itself be represented by models or stereotypes, and these could be looked on as sub-models of Monsieur de Jouvenel's more general scheme of ideas. Here I want to suggest just one such stereotype, to which, however, I think a large class of highly important cases may in some degree conform and which, while explaining the origin of some deformations, may also offer an answer to the question: In what respects and within what limits can impending political or social upheavals be foreseen?

By the *rig* of a society I mean the set of tensions or pressures existing at some moment in that society. In the individual mind, such a tension arises from a divergence of that individual's image of what his situation could be from his sense of what it is. His imagination has outstripped the performance of his nation, his party, his firm or himself. It is only when a great number of people experience such a tension, and all are consciously or unconsciously agreed upon the kind of action or policy which would relieve it, that there is social pressure. Such a social pressure may take many years, decades or generations to build up, and may remain ineffective or silent even after it has become potentially powerful. Some spark, some slight incident or some breaking of a circuit or of a linkage, in a system where divergent forces have hitherto been resolved in a mutual balance, can release them with tremendous effect. Examples are the perhaps banal ones of the French Revolution and the First World War. If we could always recognize the specific character of the rig at any time in some society, we should have a basis of judgement as to *what this society was preparing to do*.

To have sufficient insight and data to formulate such a judgement is very far indeed from having *foresight* of the course of history. Any given discernible rig could explode in very diverse ways, so far as one could ever tell in advance. The shape of its explosion would doubtless be partly governed by the exact nature of the impact which set it off. The world is divided into many societies and subsocieties, into races, regions and religions, linguistic groups, industries, parties and classes, each perhaps with its own rig. Who can say which of these precariously balanced systems of forces will first be de-balanced, which rig will first be released and have its incalculable effect in releasing the others by detonating or absorbing and superseding them? In short, we do not, and in my own belief we cannot, know what event, at what moment, will release the rig which exists in a given society at that moment. All we can do is to study as best we may what unsatisfied desires and discontents have come into being, through the spread of knowledge and ideas and of acquaintance with varied ways of life, or by the experienced worsening of economic or political conditions, in each society at each succeeding epoch, and to imagine the possible outcomes of a release of that rig. We may, that is, be able to guess what sort of thing can happen, we cannot guess when it will happen. This kind of exercise scarcely deserves the name of prediction, and by Professor Oskar Morgenstern's test it is disqualified by its refusal to name the day. But I believe it is the most we can do and that it is not altogether useless if it enables us to be ready for each of the rival, mutually exclusive possibilities which seem implicit in the rig itself, so that we are as little liable as may be to be taken by surprise. The most searching and continuous examination of contemporary social history will never tell us for sure that our list of contingencies is complete, but we may be able to feel that we have an insight and coherent understanding of this social flux which gives us some assurance of that sort.

I should like to propose some analogical models of the concept of the rig. We may compare it, I think, with the conformation of a set of ninepins (or tenpins) which, *because* they are arranged in a certain stance or pattern relatively to each other, must fall down in one or other of a comparatively few different sequences. What we cannot tell is at what angle the ball will strike them, and which sequel, of those which the stance of the pins makes possible in general, will accordingly result from this impact. Or we may say the rig is like a complex system of stretched wires bearing irregularly distributed weights, like a *téléférique*. If one of these wires is cut, let us say by an aircraft, the consequences can be roughly known to lie within a certain range of patterns of events. If an electrical transmission grid is overloaded, the sequence of failures of elements of the system, by which its total breakdown will occur, can perhaps be visualized by the engineers. But who can tell when that excess load will be brought into being?

This impossibility of identifying in advance the nature and the date of the event which will release the forces whose combined pattern I have called the rig can be treated on two distinct levels. The first is the merely practical one: we appeal to common experience and a mere survey of the superficial human scene. The complexity, diversity and seething multiplicity of what goes on doubtless yield some statistical regularities, but these are apt for discovering, not the crucial, dramatic, and unique event which *happens to happen* in just those precise circumstances where it will detonate an explosion or touch off an avalanche, but rather the character of the rig itself. In fact, it is plainly impossible to have even brief warning of the spark that fires the powder-train that blows up the keg that detonates the magazine entire.

For the central notion is the self-reinforcing process, where every stage generates a sequel larger than itself. Minute or invisible beginnings emerge as gigantic consequences, because they are amplified by the stored energy which they release. We have spoken of one rig triggering another and possibly larger one, and such a series of detonations is surely realistic. Even in mechanical or electrical systems total collapse or disaster can stem from the slightest causes, even when we look no further back than the internal functioning of these systems themselves, and do not seek to trace or account for the human error which may lie behind it. A jetliner was destroyed not long ago through the absence of a split-pin which would have prevented the working loose of a nut which retained a bolt which, by falling out, broke the linkage between the pilot's hand and the control surfaces. This jetliner turned on its back and plunged to earth, because a mechanic had forgotten to fit a split-pin. How do we know when a mechanic will forget to fit a split-pin in an aircraft which is about to carry one of the world's rulers, a man whose policy would affect the lives of everyone if he survived to execute it?

The foregoing is a rather literal example of what the historians call 'accident', that is, a decisive or influential event which cannot itself be explained as part of the visible drift of history, or which may in fact divert or run counter to that drift. But we need not appeal to rare and violent 'accidents'. There is a kind of event whose occurrence is totally invisible to any but a single individual, which by its nature is unpredictable even by him, and yet is the focal point where, if at all, a human being contributes to the making of history. I mean the act of *decision*.

There are, I suppose, two possible and opposite views of the nature of such an act of mind. We may believe that any such act is completely analysable, that it is completely explicable by reference to the decision-maker's desires and information at the moment of deciding, at any rate if we include his subconscious as well as his conscious drives. But if we believe this, in what sense can we regard him as a *source*, an originator, or if I may venture upon another new term, an *inceptor* of new trains or streams of consequences which will flow *from his decision* and *not* from antecedents of that decision, antecedents which, in an infinite regress, fully account for that decision and so render it mechanical, passive and sterile? If decision is not to be looked on as a mere clicking of the history machine as it goes robot-like through its pre-ordained drill, or as the whisper of the pages of the book of history as they are turned for us to read, not *written* by us, then decision must have some element of 'uncause', perhaps in some parallel sense to that in which the disintegration of the individual atom of radium is so far as we know uncaused, or as the character of the biological 'sport' is the result of powerful 'uncaused' genetical mutations. But if so, where is the possibility of predicting what a man will decide? Such prediction is essentially and logically impossible by the meaning of decision, if the meaning we elect is of the kind suggested above.

It is needless to say that the range of actions amongst which at any moment a man can effectively choose is bounded. What I decide to do must be something which can be done with my own voice or hand; if its medium is language, it must suggest or require of others some actions which they have the power to perform. In short, it must be action within the existing circumstances, and if it is action meant to release forces composing what I have called the rig, the events which a powerful individual can expect to flow from his decision will be partly shaped and constrained by the character of the rig itself. Insight into the rig is insight into the future, and except perhaps in astronomy, this insight into the present is the only insight into the future that we can have.

It may, I think, be claimed that the notion of the 'rig' provides a basis for empirical work. If it be accepted that some social drives or political ambitions need to gather force or definition over a stretch of time before they can effect anything outside people's thoughts and feelings, how can we account for this? By what psychic and social mechanism is this force stored and built up? What is the nature of an 'accumulator of social energy'? Is the lack of power in the early stages due to imperfect communication, so that feelings, which in fact are shared by many, remain unvoiced because each individual fears to speak alone? Do vague desires and pressures need to be focused by a prophetic utterance, by public discussion, by example from other fields of action, other geographical areas or social strata? What is the psychic nature and role of conservatism in providing a friction, so that the landslide remains poised for a long time instead of trickling continually down the slope?

It may be that there are branches of organized knowledge already equipped to answer these questions. It is certain that any investigation based upon a clear-cut model will in the end obscure that model's initial simplicity and sharpness of outline, perhaps to the extent of its entire abandonment. This does not mean that the investigation could ever have begun without the model. Columbus's model was 'The earth is round; sailing westward will therefore bring me to the Indies'. It did not; but he would never have started if his model had been 'Sailing westward does not bring you to the Indies'. The social or psychic model, like the explorer's vague notion which gives a general direction or visionary purpose to his expedition, even when ultimately abandoned may still have served a purpose. A model is an abstraction, a map, an idealization, a dramatic heightening of supposed essentials; while an empirical procedure is in a sense the opposite of this, a procedure of gathering facts in their confused mass and continuously shading diversity, facts many of which will qualify, blur or deviate from the model, and suggest a modified or a new one. Without a model, however, we cannot even discern a fact or classify it. Let me return briefly, therefore, to Monsieur de Jouvenel's basic suggestion.

From the argument we have sketched there emerges a remarkable paradox: that of the two types of event or evolution which can frustrate an action plan, the one which is radical and comprehensive, and which undermines and renders meaningless the whole aim and method of the plan, may in a partial sense be somewhat foreseeable, whereas the minor and 'casuel' obstruction, so aptly named by Monsieur de Jouvenel in describing his model, cannot in its particularity be foreseen at all. The possibility of a deformation of the social space we can investigate and prepare for, the 'casuel' eludes all but the most general, blunt-edged and routine precautions. Such distinctions as that between the 'casuel' and the 'deformation', and the insights which they yield, are impossible until a suitable frame of ideas, an apt model, has been invented. It is this kind of service which Monsieur de Jouvenel's invention has rendered us in our endeavour to trace the boundaries of the possible in the business of conjecture.

# II

# BRIEF TESTAMENT

## COMMENTS ON 'WAHRSCHEINLICHKEITSTHEORIE UND INVESTITIONSTHEORIE' AND 'KRITISCHE BETRACHTUNGEN ZU G. MERKS AUFSATZ'*

May I first express the warm pleasure I had in reading the articles by Dr Gerhard Merk and Dipl.-Volkswirt H. G. Krüsselberg on the place of notions of uncertainty in the theory of investment. Dr Zottmann having very kindly invited me to comment on these articles, I should like to try to make clear the frame of more general ideas within which my own proposals about uncertainty were put forward.

I start with the conception of the *solitary moment of actuality*, an 'atom of time' within which all reality is, for the human individual, confined. The life and death of this moment, in a sense, are one, since its very existence is an *event* by which it is changed into another and different 'solitary moment'. The evolving moment is the locus of all the psychic events which make up the individual's life. No two moments are actual together, and there is no 'stretch of time', no time-dimension, otherwise than in the individual's own thought and imagination. He has to choose amongst a number of available immediate actions, and it follows from what we have said (if that be accepted) that his choice in so far as it is made in view of its consequences, must depend upon *imagined* consequences. The objective consequences belong to a different moment, one which cannot co-exist with the moment in which the decision is made. It is the characteristics of the *imagined* consequences of this or that action which will influence the decision-maker.

Uncertainty is ignorance. It is a gap which cannot be filled by the finding of additional knowledge, since if such knowledge

* Cf. Gerhard Merk, 'Wahrscheinlichkeitstheorie und Investitionstheorie', *Weltwirtschaftliches Archiv*, Bd. LXXXI (1958), II, pp. 66 et seqq.—H. G. Krüsselberg, 'Kritische Betrachtungen zu G. Merks Aufsatz: 'Wahrscheinlichkeitstheorie und Investitionstheorie', *ibid.* Bd. LXXXII (1959), I, pp. 122 et seqq.

were available (in the moment of decision) there would be no uncertainty. This gap must, therefore, be creatively filled by the individual. He fills the uncertainty gap concerning the outcome of any action by asking himself, not what *will* happen (this question is unanswerable, since if it were answerable, there would be no uncertainty) but what *can* happen, within the bounds afforded by his conception of the 'nature of things' and of the existing situation. Amongst the things that can happen, two will be of especial concern to him: the best and the worst. What do we mean by 'can happen'? The individual's measure of the *possibility* of an outcome is the degree to which that outcome would surprise him if it did occur, an outcome regarded as 'perfectly possible' having no power at all to surprise. If we suppose the decision-maker to divide all the distinct outcomes, which he imagines for any available action, simply into the possible and the impossible, then he is concerned simply with the best and worst among the possible outcomes. But if he recognizes degrees of possibility of outcomes, measured by degrees of the *potential surprise* which he associates with their occurrence, then it may be that an outcome regarded as less than perfectly possible will occupy the focus of his attention, since its 'face value' (the attractiveness of the tale it tells regardless of the plausibility of that tale) may compensate some degree of difficulty in imagining it to come true. Then the two 'focus outcomes' which will claim his attention, when he considers a particular available action, will be the best and the worst amongst the not too implausible imagined outcomes.

Expectation, I would say, is imaginative creation within a freedom conferred by uncertainty; a *bounded* freedom, however, confined to the 'possible' according to the laws of nature and of human nature as the individual decision-maker conceives them.

# III

# BUSINESS AND PSYCHOLOGY

# 12
# THE ECONOMIST'S MODEL OF MAN

The economist's chief model of man has, on the one hand, needs and tastes, and on the other, exact, complete and infallible knowledge of the degree to which any pattern of disposal of his resources would satisfy each of those desires. His intellectual attainments are mathematical only: he can integrate the small increments of want-satisfaction which are yielded by small increments of any one resource devoted to the satisfaction of one want. In this way he arrives at a total of satisfactions of all kinds, and this total is maximized, he also knows, when equal small increments of any one resource yield the same amount of extra satisfaction no matter which want they are devoted to, and when this is true simultaneously of every resource. Many economists today would think shame to talk of satisfaction in this way, and instead of 'equi-marginal satisfactions' they speak of 'equi-marginal rates of substitution'. They also, however, admit that the economic man must be supposed to be maximizing something, and indeed they often agree that economics is the logic of maximizing behaviour. But they do not explain what he is maximizing, if it be not satisfaction, utility, comfort or some other thing that can go equally well under any of those names.

There are some other queer things about economic man. He is utterly free from all feelings of emulation, and the sight of someone riding in a Rolls-Royce or drinking champagne does not put any ideas into his head. His tastes do not change, he learns nothing and forgets nothing. This means, of course, that the world he lives in is a little queer also, since advertising is useless and the introduction of new products is impossible. Since he already knows all he wants to know, there is for him no such thing as uncertainty or curiosity, no such thing as information, news, discovery or invention. It is realized nowadays that money, too, has no place in his world, since he can arrange all his affairs so that simultaneous exchanges of equal values precisely clear the account and leave him owed and owing nothing.

I spoke of this creature as the economist's *chief* model of man.

He is, perhaps, a sort of Model T economic man, and a few gadgets fitted on here and there during the last hundred years have made him a little more subtle. But let us not be unjust. Economic man can answer some questions, which economists have put to him, in a clear, forthright and intelligible manner that might, were he to become more human, be changed into a doubtful and inhibited mumbling. He wielded the sword of Alexander and cut a Gordian knot. We must also recognize that economists on the whole are proud of his incisive methods. The conception of static equilibrium, of comprehensive, instantaneous and perfect adjustment of everything to everything else, which is embodied in him, is a miracle of economy in two senses: its very inhumanity, the list of human attributes which it can ignore, as well as of institutional and social complications which it can short-circuit, is a recommendation in the eyes of those economists, at any rate, who are ancient enough to regard the theory of 'value and distribution', that is, the theory which explains relative prices, the sizes of outputs of particular commodities and the allocation of resources to making this good and that, and the prices of the factors of production and hence the incomes of those who supply them, as still the core of economic theory.

These ancients we may call, as a matter of chronology, the Marshallians, though in fact Marshall bullied his economic man a good deal and made him run to and fro through long and short periods and along 'historic' and 'irreversible' curves and made him grow to maturity and then decline, and so on, in a way that makes Marshall seem perennially young. The middle-aged group of today's economists we may call the depression economists, since they were at their prime of ardour and receptivity in the dreadful and glorious 'thirties, when actual events were tragic and economic theory was driven by the anguish of those days to discover and annex a new continent of thought. Keynesian economics, the economics of unemployment and depression, found the Model T economic man quite useless. He had to be redesigned with a new high-power but very erratic and unreliable engine called expectation and a new set of brakes called liquidity preference, and a petrol tank called income with a carburation system called consumption which had a very large leak called saving, which, if too large, slowed the machine down until it could no longer carry its proper load of full employment, unless expectation could be tuned up to a very high marginal efficiency of capital.

Now all these new design features involved activities of the mind and spirit of real-flesh-and-blood man which go altogether beyond the mere automatic response to an environment under the pressure of bodily needs. Model T had only tastes; the new model had the power to look out to distant horizons, he had hopes, doubts and fears and an eagerness for news and too sensitive and unstable a responsiveness to it. Keynesian man was a subject for the psychologist, in a way that I will try in a moment to elaborate a little. It should be said in justice that a close relative to Keynesian man, Lindahlian or Myrdalian man, was found in Sweden.

And lastly we come to the young economists, young in the sense of not yet having grey hairs, and they are interested in still another kind of problem, that of growth or attempted growth with insufficient resources, and the resulting inflation. This problem of how a people can lift itself from a mere subsistence economy and 'take off into sustained growth', or how an advanced nation can achieve, simultaneously, fast growth of wealth, full employment and nevertheless stable prices, is perhaps more a sociological than a psychological one. The purely economic aspects of inflation are well understood, it is the political and sociological ones which are nowadays the more important and the more obscure.

You will now appreciate, I think, why I believe that it is Keynesian man who most urgently invites attention from the psychologists. His day is by no means done, indeed the newspapers every day carry reports of his return to Europe via America and Britain. So I will try to outline to you my conception of Keynesian man's psychic constitution and the special insights that we, as economists, would like you, as psychologists, to give us.

What makes Keynesian man utterly different from Model T man is in greatest measure the supreme gift of imagination. I do not mean only or chiefly visual imagination, though this is to me one of life's most profound mysteries. How is it that a scene, complete in all the details that the bodily eye would see if the scene were real, can rise unbidden in a moment before the mind's eye, and yet be a scene that the bodily eye has never dwelt on, an original composition, a pattern of trees, walls, roofs, stream and sunlit ripples that is pure fantasy, except for the perfect realism of its atomistic detail? Is man's imagination a kaleidoscope of little pieces of visual impression, stored up and continually added to through life, little pieces each in itself a *memory*, each in itself fixed, but able by some means to be shaken into a new pattern, one of a literally unlimited number of possible patterns? If so, what does the shaking? May we allow ourselves to call the untraceable faint quiver of the mind, which does this, *inspiration*? And if so, if there is no knowing when will come this protean unheralded mental flash and no possibility of reckoning the infinite range and diversity of possible patterns from which it can select, what possibility is there of prediction?

I hope you will not think that I mean this crude analogy of the kaleidoscope to be more than a vehicle for suggestion, for an enquiry, and the expression of the nature of the mystery as it presents itself to an utterly uninstructed mind. These speculations, too, may appear wildly irrelevant to the concerns of economists, but I do not think they are. It is patent that men's *decisions* are not choices amongst *actual* but amongst *imagined* consequences. Actual experiences, events and situations which the bodily senses can apprehend, are beyond the reach of decision; they exist, they cannot now be changed or prevented. It is only future experiences, events and situations which can be chosen, and where is the future? It is only inside man's mind, it is imagined. Thus to decide is to make a choice amongst fantasies and figments of the mind. Yet not altogether fantasies, for there is a constraint. We require our vistas of the future to pass a test before we treat them as a basis of choice between this available course of action and that, the test of seeming to be *possible* consequences of the act in question. When they pass this test, in some degree whose measure is, perhaps, another of our problems, they rank as *expectations*.

Expectations is a word which has made a certain showing in the literature of economics, yet not so great a one as we might expect. It seems to me that insight into how expectations are formed, how rival and mutually contradictory expectations about the outcome of any one course of action are made use of so as to compare the merits of this course with another, and the conditions under which expectations of given kinds stimulate or inhibit positive action, must be one of the foundations of an understanding of economic life. Yet such foundations are still a matter of mere speculative construction. So I would like, above all, to equip economic man with an expectation-forming faculty, and this must surely be done by psychologists.

A sketch for its design has, I believe, already begun to be drawn. In his chapter called 'A Modular Theory of Expectation'* Professor G. P. Meredith has chosen as his key idea (if I have rightly understood him) the conception of what I would like to call the current geometry of a man's mind. This does not mean merely the stock of conscious and unconscious knowledge, beliefs and habits of thought which his experience and formal education have piled up in his mind, but the *configuration* of those ideas, the lines of magnetic force, as it were, which have been built up in him, so that when the compass-needle of suggested action comes within their influence, it swings in a particular direction. (I hope Professor Meredith will forgive me if I am misrepresenting him.)

A more homely illustration perhaps suggests better what I understand to be the essence of the idea. In a skittle alley, the skittles are set up in a particular pattern, and the dynamic pattern of their various movements, which results when the player bowls at them, depends in part on that initial, static configuration. If they were differently arranged, their movements when the ball strikes them would be different even if the ball's own movement were identically the same. What we seem to need is some means of describing the mental set-up on which news and fresh impressions impinge; some means of classifying different types of this pattern; and some means of visualizing, as it were, the manner in which any such impact elicits, from this pattern or *modulus*, a vista of expectations from which decisions will arise; and finally, some understanding of how such an impact modifies the modulus itself and leaves the individual's *potential* expectations somewhat different from what they were before. Professor Meredith has drawn the boundaries of the study of *epistemics*, which he has made so much his own, so as to include the study of expectation-forming along these lines.

* G. P. Meredith, *Uncertainty and Business Decisions*, 2nd ed. (Liverpool University Press, 1957).

A contribution very sympathetic to this line of thought has come from an economist. Professor Kenneth Boulding's fascinatingly suggestive book *The Image** is (again if I have rightly understood what I have read) a proposal to apply somewhat related ideas on an immense canvas embracing all forms of life and all human conduct. *Eiconics* is the name he wishes to give to this vastly (too vastly) comprehensive unifying science. I do not find it easy to believe in the *concrete* usefulness of so ambitious a scheme, but his sketch of the idea shakes the mind out of its too familiar courses.

Interfused with the problem of how expectations come into being there are the problems of their structure and their role. *What like* is the system of expectations that a man entertains at any moment? Is it a single, self-consistent picture of the consequences that would flow, early and late, from such and such a scheme of action on his own part, with another such picture for every other action open to him? Or does he see for each such scheme of action a complex diversity of possible outcomes ranging from glittering success and glory down to the pit of disaster? And if this latter version is the truth, how then does he choose between schemes of action? For it is not simply expectation but *uncertain expectation* that poses for the economist his most intractable and most basic problems. We saw that that austere Victorian, Model T economic man, has no use for money. Why not? Because like a good Victorian he does not suffer from uncertainty. Money is dope, a tranquillizer against the effects of not knowing what to do. Money it is which saves you from having to make up your mind what to buy. In a barter economy, which is the one where Model T man is really at home, you cannot sell anything without at the same instant and in the same act acquiring some other specific object *wanted for its own sake*, useful in itself. But in a money economy you can sell a thing for money (do not be surprised at my putting this into words, economics is largely made up of these flashes of revelation), and nothing compels you to spend that money again at any particular time. You can wait for the fog to lift, you can wait for one of those moments when unanswered questions and contradictory answers and confusing signs are at a minimum, before you de-

* K. E. Boulding, *The Image* (*Knowledge in Life and Society*) (Ann Arbor: University of Michigan Press, 1956).

cide what to do with your money. This very great convenience, conferred by money, is called *liquidity*, and when preference for liquidity over more specific schemes of gain becomes very widespread and very strong, we have unemployment and business depression, because, of course, merely *holding* money rather than investing it in the purchase of plant, equipment, buildings, livestock and so on employs nobody. Money and its liquidity, the very essence of its nature, are then *psychic* phenomena which must be investigated as such. They are poles asunder from the mechanical behaviourism of Model T man.

Can our model of expectational man be cast in a mathematical mould? I should have liked to say something on this question, which is more than a merely formal and technical matter. The model will be different, and will give a different sort of answers to the questions proposed to it, and will encourage a different attitude towards action of this sort or that, according as it is built up in the language of words or the language of mathematical symbols, for a technical notation once devised carves its own way through problems and powerfully aids as well as constrains its user. But the presence with us of Dr Lawrence Klein, one of the most internationally distinguished of the still small band of mathematical *virtuosi* who are devoting themselves to economics, would make it out of place for me to do more than merely refer to this extremely important question.

Those I have mentioned, with some few companions, have been hacking their way through the jungle for some years already. So far they have been lone pioneers. But I hear the drums of advancing reinforcements. Not all of big business, I am afraid, will be able to throw such a searching and brilliant light on our problem as Sir Geoffrey Vickers. But the presence here of Mr J. C. Kenna is to me an immense portent. If the real, deep-dyed, clinical psychologist can be induced to join us, things will begin to happen. I must not give the impression that Mr Kenna is a professional clinician purely. An hour's conversation with him is enough to reveal a breadth of interest and erudition which goes far, no doubt, to explain his part in promoting this symposium. But clinician he is, and greatly to be prized.

How accidental are the particular lines on which economics

itself has developed was brought home to me three or four years ago, when the convener of this symposium, Mr David Duncan, read to a gathering of economists, psychologists and philosophers a paper on 'The Psychological Analysis of Economic Behaviour'. While I listened to that paper, the centuries seemed to pass before my mind's eye in strangely altered guise. Instead of Adam Smith, Ricardo and Marshall I seemed to see a procession of moral philosophers who became, not students of markets and money or of incomes and prices, but psychologists, students, in the first place, of human nature *direct*, proceeding thence to an understanding of the business manifestations of human nature. And the kinds of explanation of human business conduct, which might have emerged from this discipline of *economic psychics*, would perhaps, as it then seemed to me, have been just as satisfying and fruitful as our own actual ones. It is not too late. We can still swing part of the great stream of general economic research into a new and exciting channel.

# 13
# THEORY AND THE BUSINESS MAN

Decision-making is the act which marks out the business man from all those who collaborate with him in production. In this statement the word decision has a quite special and exact meaning. It means choice of action in face of uncertainty about the outcome of each available course. The man who blindly applies a complete set of rules, which prescribe his action in every set of circumstances that can arise, is not making any decision. His work can be taken over by a machine, even though it may consist in solving problems. Some problems, such as the arithmetical sums we do at school, have been provided with an algorithm that always, if properly followed out, gives a uniquely correct answer. To solve such problems, we do not need to invent, to evolve something new, and there is indeed no room for such invention, which would at best be a waste of time and at worst lead to a wrong result. In such cases there are enough data to yield the unique solution, and there is also the knowledge that the problem has this perfect solvability. Even the game of chess is, in some sense, only different in degree, for there is no doubt that an invincible chess-playing computer can in principle be built, though it would need a greater capacity than the ones we have at present. Chess is a game with completely stated rules, and it is this which brings it within the realm of calculation. Yet there is no danger (until microminiaturization produces a pocket computer with vaster capacity than the room-filling computers of today) that chess tournaments will be ruined, for within the rules of chess the possible situations and sequences of situations are beyond the power of the human brain to hold completely in view. The essential point is, however, that chess is a game with a complete set of rules, and therefore an ultimately limited, and knowable, range of possible courses of play. But is this true of business, or of life in general? If it is not true, then life and business give scope for *decision*, for the *imaginative creation* of the ranges of conceivable consequences assignable to this act and that, and for choice amongst the rival acts on this basis of original thought and even, we may say, of poetic power.

Decision is an act of choice amongst things partly created by the decision-maker. These things are schemes of action whose outcomes cannot be known and which, therefore, must be invented. Such invention, of course, is not exercised in a boundless freedom. The world in which we live has an *orderliness*. In nature there is a statistical regularity, so that a given broadly observed set of physical circumstances always produces an apparently similar immediate or short-term effect. There is, that is to say, what we call 'cause and effect'. In each physical situation the human being is presented with an array of 'levers', and may know that if he pulls this one rather than that, the immediate physical consequence will be *A* rather than *B*. The meaning to be given to the term 'cause and effect' has been an eternal bane of philosophers, but at least it is clear that a 'lever' only produces a given effect because of the existence of a mechanism to which it is connected. The existence of this mechanism is as necessary to the result as is the pulling of the lever, and it is difficult, therefore, to know whether the act of pulling, rather than the presence of the mechanism, should be held responsible for what happens. None the less, the mechanisms do exist, and are evidently interlocked into one great and comprehensive mechanism, the 'order of nature'. If unconscious nature were all that existed, everything that happened would have, perhaps, to be ascribed to the mere inexorable working of the machine after some initial push had set it going. There would be determinism, if nature is exactly regular, or 'random history', if she is only statistically regular. In the former case at least it would be surely impossible to speak of cause and effect. But when the conscious human being appears on the scene, there may be a difference. His 'conscious mind', whatever that may be, stands between his circumstances and the action which he chooses. Does it perhaps contribute something which is not to be found in those circumstances themselves? Is his selection of one lever rather than another undetermined? In order to suppose it so, we should have to suppose, either that he acts without logic, or that the basis for a logical choice of one 'lever' rather than another does not exist and cannot be found, and that this gap must be filled by invention, by imagination. The action which a man attempts will have a different sequel in a different environment, and that environment itself consists partly of the actions being performed at the same time by other men. If, because those other actions are not the mere necessitated consequence of what has gone before, but contain some element *uncaused* by that past, and because they are *simultaneous* in conception with his own choice of action, they are essentially and necessarily unknown to the decision-maker, then the outcome of his own choice is *uncertain within the orderliness of nature*. This orderliness determines the *kind* of thing that *can* happen, not the *precise* thing that *will* happen. Decision, if so, is choice in face of bounded uncertainty. How is such choice to be analysed? What sort of insight into it is possible?

There has been spreading and consolidating in recent years an attitude of mind according to which all problems are solvable. There is, according to this tacit assumption, no ultimate uncertainty. If we are strenuous and thorough enough in our gathering of 'information', advanced enough in our statistical techniques for drawing from this information a knowledge of the deterministic structure and principles of society and the world (especially in its business life), and careful enough in analysing some stretch of recent history so as to see on what paths the world's affairs are moving, we can calculate the future. How different this doctrine is from what one would expect to find in men of basic spiritual audacity, the 'New Elizabethans', desiring to make history and a new world! For the view of the 'all is solvable and foreseeable' school is fatalism; the reverse of hope, the opposite of freedom. It is uncertainty which gives room for hope, at the price of also being afraid.

If uncertainty means that there is not and cannot be at any moment a sufficient basis for reasoning out the infallible consequence of electing this course of action or that, what is the use of reason? Is an incomplete and fragmentary basis of reasoning about the respective outcomes of rival available courses of action a meaningful conception? Is not pragmatic knowledge like a bridge, no use at all unless every span is complete? How can choice of action in face of uncertainty be other than arbitrary and capricious? All our conduct and careful deliberation, our weighing of what suggestions the scene around us offers of its possibilities, our formal or opportunistic research, our planning, our anxious attempts at judgement, our figments of hope and despondency, belie the notion of our abandonment of our lives to the inscrutable tide and our acknowledgement of helpless ignorance. We are not hopelessly ignorant, for we can *set bounds* to what can happen. These bounds of course cannot claim to be 'objective fact'. They are judgements, but they are based on experience of that orderliness, that repetitiveness 'in the small', that recognizable validity of stereotypes of everyday, small-scale action aimed at immediately visible results, without which the world and our life in it would not make sense. If, in this world, there are indeed fountains of sudden essential novelty, sources of new streams of impulses in affairs, these impulses can only propagate themselves at a limited speed. People, however sensitive and receptive, do not transform their beliefs in a moment, except in rare crises of illumination. The material equipment which must body forth the fresh ideas if they are to be effective cannot be built overnight. The world's business and political and diplomatic organization, the 'lines of force' of its educational systems, its fashions and ingrained habits change slowly. Thus the pace of technical and business change, even though constantly accelerating, can do only so much in a given time. Thus there are two things the business man can do: he can set himself a *horizon*, beyond which he will not try to peer, beyond which he will count on nothing; and he can so choose his choice of action that *at worst* it will not ruin him. If, as may well happen, there are many courses which at worst will not ruin him, he can choose amongst these the one which seems to leave open the possibility of greater success than any other.

What has theory to do with policies or prescriptions so obvious and instinctive? Their soundness may need no argument, it is their execution which calls for all the knowledge, judgement and imagination that the firm can muster. Knowledge is produced by gathering masses of observations and showing how they can be all interpreted as manifestations of a few general principles. Today, compared with yesterday, these processes have been rendered incomparably faster and more powerful by electronic machines. The interrelations between sets of measurements, the statistical structure of society and of its physical environment, can be explored with a scope and speed undreamed of twenty years ago. Does all this mean that caution, improvisation, awareness of the edge of the pit of time that we must always be just peering over without ever seeing clearly into it, will soon be no longer necessary? Some voices are already ringing with a note of aggressive assurance: we can do this, we shall do that, we can *predict*. There are, perhaps, two basic thoughts on which a warning can be founded. One is that to improvise, to invent, is possible only in a world of unknowns and uncertainties. Can the world really be turned, by an advance of technique, into a place so different *in essence* from the one where history, in the past, has staged its untidy, unorganized, wild play? The other is the question whether the predictive techniques will free themselves, in practice, so completely from 'wishful thinking', from building into their basic assumptions the *desired* results, that the same course of things will be foreseen by rival interests? Can NATO and the Warsaw Pact really be supposed to agree on how things will go? The new techniques, the new tools of the computer revolution, are new and more powerful means of doing what we have always had to do: feel for the edges of the possible, elect those plans of action which leave, so far as we can judge, *disaster* outside that edge, while leaving a generous, a satisfying success inside it. We cannot tell, any better now than yesterday, what *will* happen. We can hope only to judge, with some presumption of skill and a fair basis of experience, what *can* happen, at best and at worst, if we do this or if we do that.

At this point the reader may feel that some explanations are due to him. In all the above, what has happened to the word *probability*? We have several times referred to statistics, and probability, in its more 'operational', objective, empirical meaning is the basis of statistical reasoning and conclusions. Statistics is a means and an expression of *knowledge*, knowledge about the orderliness of the non-human world and about many aspects of society. Without such knowledge, uncertainty of the outcome of our actions would be absolute and unbounded, the anarchy of existence would leave no meaning or role for *decision*, for the study of policy or the considered seeking of ends. It is because statistical methods, and the probability theory that underlies them, help to *bound* our uncertainty that they are important, not because they help us to cope with that irreducible uncertainty which is part of the nature of life. When the choice to be made is a routine, repetitive one, statistical study of a long series of results of this or that elected course will give knowledge of what policy is best. It is when the choice to be made is crucial, once for all, such as to put us on one road out of many and never let us retract and retreat to any other road thereafter, that there is true uncertainty, and that the only safety is in limiting the stakes, if we can. In face of true uncertainty, it is *possibility*, not probability, that is ultimately relevant, and these two things cannot (except arbitrarily) be mapped upon each other.

For the business man, the immense array of 'things that can happen' if he adopts this or that particular course can be somewhat simplified. For on the understanding that he will impose a horizon on his expectations, some given amount of profit or loss will be the equivalent of *each of several* different paths which future developments might follow. The 'things that can happen' can be gathered in groups, each group corresponding to an interval along a gain-loss axis. This is where possibility comes in. For if all these things are judged to be on an equal footing as to possibility, if all of them 'can happen' without any distinction of different degrees of ability to happen, then it is the best and the worst that matter to the decision-maker. The policy, which follows from this view of things, is to choose that course of action whose 'worst' is not intolerable, and whose best outshines that of all other such 'safe' courses. Such 'safety', of course, is still a matter of judgement. But judgement can more efficiently grip 'what can happen' than 'what will'.

Between the best and the worst, expressed as profit and loss, there will be an interval, a range. This range will be bigger or smaller, and differently located on the gain-loss axis, for different rival available actions. But there will be times when all or most of these ranges seem to close, and others when they seem all to get wider. A general narrowing of these ranges may be called a 'clarifying' of expectations. There will be times when such a clarifying can itself be expected. If society's institutions provide for an annual budget, a four-yearly Presidential election or the monthly issue of important statistics, any estimates made before these events about the course that affairs will take after them will include widely diverse hypotheses of that course, corresponding respectively to this or that character of the event itself. Such an event is like a blind corner, blocking the view ahead as we approach and suddenly revealing it when we arrive. It is widely agreed, amongst financial editors and the City generally, that the wider uncertainty, the greater spread between 'best' and 'worst' for any given scheme of action, which prevails while a crucial event is awaited inhibits decision, or to speak more strictly, since daily and hourly choice is inescapable, leads to defensive choices being maintained until the clarifying event has occurred. Once it *has* occurred, many of the rival available actions whose 'spread' of possible outcomes was widest will close up, either towards the bad end or the good. They will continue to threaten while ceasing to promise much, or will cease to threaten while continuing to promise, and the remaining range of plausible rival actions will be easier to choose from. In this way we may account for the business man's insistence on the importance of 'timing' in that class of decisions which makes the severest demands on him, namely, decision to invest large sums in buying durable, expensive, complex, specialized and invention-vulnerable equipment.

We may look on the foregoing either as a prescriptive or as a descriptive treatment of the act of decision. But these two interpretations converge. A man whom circumstances compel to make a choice, when the grounds which would be relevant to his choice are partly hidden from him, cannot be 'rational', if rationality means calculation on the basis of sufficient data. Is he, then, severely crippled in his pursuit of success? On the contrary, he is liberated. If he could know for certain what the outcome of each available act would be, the act of decision would have shrunk to mere mechanical response, and the scope for imagination, invention and hope itself would have vanished. Decision is a central strand in conscious human life, and conscious life is incompatible in meaning with complete knowledge and foreknowledge, for consciousness is continual discovery.

So far as the account we have given is accepted as self-consistent (its realism is a matter for separate judgement), is it nearly related to the policy which emerges from von Neumann and Morgenstern's *Theory of Games*? The most fundamental difference lies in the very word 'games'. A game is a set of explicit, exact and complete rules prescribing the limits of action in every situation which can arise within the context of the game. The rules define the game and, *in abstracto*, they *are* the game. Every 'play' (every instance of playing the game) is merely an illustration of the rules. Where is the counterpart of such rules to be found in life in general, or in business life? If the rules are not perfectly known, there can be no 'minimax strategy', no adopting that line of play which frustrates, to the greatest logically possible extent, the inimical endeavours of an infallible reasoning-machine which is perfectly programmed with the rules and objectives of the game: no knowable rules, no minimax strategy. But we can go further: it is only in very special and unusual circumstances that a business man's situation is even approximately represented by a game in which he is opposed by a consciously *inimical* opponent. In the famous 'duopoly' situation of a market supplied by just two firms, their rivalry, objective and subjective, may render them visible and conscious duellists. At the other extreme, a firm may look out upon a sea of impersonal competitors, whose names, even, it need not concern itself to know. There are so many of them that no one firm will be measurably affected by anything that our own business man can do; there is something near to what the economist calls 'perfect competition', a nameless and almost nature-like environment, neither hostile nor friendly but unconcernedly neutral and uncaring. To follow a policy specially designed to defend one against the hostility of a non-existent enemy would be futile and wasteful. Lastly, where do we find the infallible rival who never makes mistakes? The minimax strategy sacrifices all possibility of taking advantage of such mistakes, if any are made by a human, as distinct from a game-theory, opponent. The minimax strategist knows the worst, and has nothing better to hope for.

The business man, asking himself how his affairs may develop if he does some particular thing, will see a range of rival possible situations which widens into the future. In setting bounds to what can happen, of good and of bad, as a sequel to his embarking now on this or that course, he can avail himself of only two kinds of knowledge: his conception of how the world works and evolves, and his conception of the present situation from which any processes of change must start. Neither of these kinds of knowledge is any use without the other. But if he believes that there is, in the era of history where he finds himself, a limit to the speed at which fresh situations can grow one out of another, then the width of the band within which the path of future history seems constrained to lie will widen as he looks to a more remote future. The way to keep this band tolerably narrow is, accordingly, not to look too far ahead, to impose on his reckonings and hopes a *horizon* beyond which he will count upon nothing. There is strong testimony that such a horizon is a reality in the business world, and business men in some industries appear, in their investment decisions, to put it as near as two or three years, so that they will not take any notice of possible trading profit which a piece of equipment, installed now, might earn beyond that distance into the future. We can also infer the existence of such a horizon indirectly, from the yield of fixed-interest securities considered as depending on their remaining life to redemption. At 'normal' times (if we can give some meaning to such a phrase), bills carry only one or two, or even less, percentage points of interest; bonds with a year or two to run yield a little more, and so on, until we reach maturities five years ahead. About here the steepness of the curve, yield as a function of remaining life, becomes markedly less steep, and at ten years it flattens altogether, so that the yield of bonds with twenty or forty years to run is no greater than that of bonds redeemable in ten years. Why is this? Surely it is because ten years is long enough for 'anything to happen'. A bill, even when just issued, is so near to redemption that there is 'no room' for wide fluctuations of its price: the prospect of a sure though small gain will be sufficient to induce someone to buy from any unwilling holder. A bond with five years to run offers much more possibility of speculative loss, through the possibility of a need to sell, at some unforeseeable moment, when the market may be down. At ten years such possibilities have all the scope possible, and the forty-year maturity is felt to impose no greater uncertainty than the ten-year one. There is a horizon.

The ten-year futurity which appears to expose the bondholder, in the market's estimation, to all the hazards of capital loss (and gain) of fixed-interest securities, is not quite the same in meaning as the limitation which the business man, contemplating the purchase of plant and industrial facilities, sets upon the stretch of years over which he may consciously entertain hopes of profit from these investment goods. But in both contexts we have the idea of a distrust of estimates of the future, a distrust which becomes more acute as the date in question is more remote. This phenomenon has a very important, and theoretically interesting, bearing on the extent to which government manipulation of the interest rate can increase or decrease the flow of orders from the 'private' sector of industry for machines and equipment, with all that such power implies for the effectiveness of employment policy. The Keynesian 'multiplier' theory is well known. If 1,000 formerly unemployed men are given work in making something which cannot be sold to consumers as such, in the home country, then all of the extra income which these 1,000 now receive, except what they save or use to repay debt, will have to be spent on *other people's* output. Other people, therefore, also formerly unemployed, can be given work in satisfying this new extra demand for consumer goods. This second group of workers will be able to provide consumer goods for the first group to the extent that they themselves do not consume all they produce. Only that part of their output, which corresponds to their *saving*, will be available for the first group to consume. Thus a third group will be needed, and a fourth, and so on, in principle, ad infinitum, the groups getting smaller and smaller, so that we have a converging series. In fact, if the *saved* proportion of extra income is always $k$, the ultimate result of injecting one unit (say, £10,000 per annum) of extra income into the economy by employing the formerly unemployed in non-consumer-goods production, will be extra output equal to

$$1 + k + k^2 + \dots = 1/(1-k)$$

times £10,000. If $k$ is $\frac{3}{4}$, for example, this Keynesian multiplier will be 4, and by giving 1,000 men governmental employment, another 3,000 will get 'private' employment. But this powerful lever depends on the willingness of somebody, government or other, to buy or build *investment goods*. Such buying or building ought to be more profitable, more attractive, when funds for the purpose can be borrowed at low interest rates than when the rate is high. But is this so in practice?

The text-book argument is plain. Expected profits from the use of equipment (the sole incentive for buying it) are *deferred* profits. £1 deferred $N$ years is not the equivalent here and now of £1 available here and now, for a smaller sum than £1, if lent today at compound interest of $r$ per annum, will amount to £1 in $N$ years. If we write $V$ for this present or discounted value of £1 deferred $N$ years we have

$$V = 1/[(1+r)^N],$$

and so the larger is $r$, the smaller will be $V$ for any given $N$. When all the instalments of expected profit are similarly discounted, using the various appropriate numerical values of $N$, the sum of all the results is the spot-cash equivalent of the series of deferred instalments, provided the latter are looked on as certain to be duly earned. The spot-cash equivalent of the expected profits, on this same crucial assumption of his feeling certain he has got them right, is the most that it is worth the business man's while to pay for the equipment. Since this 'demand price' goes up when the rate of interest goes down, the profitable gap by which it exceeds the 'supply price', the manufacturer's list price or the contract price for construction, gets bigger, and more attractive, as the interest rate falls.

So much for the text-book. Business men themselves have often denied any connection between their investment decisions and the rate of interest. What, then, has the text-book overlooked? Simply the consequences, the mere *arithmetical* consequences, of the fact that *certainty* is the very last thing a business man can feel about his 'expected' profits.

In appearance the business man has a variety of schemes for coping with his dependence on an unknowable future. His inevitable temptation, as Keynes pointed out, is to assume that it will be like the present, though all experience suggests that it will not. None the less, for a little while, perhaps, the relevant divergences will be small, and the problem is to decide how long this little while is. For many purposes the business man seems to reckon it at only two or three years. But when only those profits are counted on which will accrue in two or three years, the discounting process has no leverage. We can see this plainly by asking ourselves *which*, out of a supposed long series of future annual 'instalments' of profit, will have its present value affected to the largest *absolute* extent by a given change in the (supposedly uniform) interest rate. If the reader can be patient with a trifling piece of analysis, let us speak of a *unit* instalment of profit of futurity (deferment) $x$, discounted at interest rate $r$ per annum. Its present value will be

$$V = \frac{1}{(1+r)^x} = e^{-\rho x} \quad \text{where} \quad \rho = \log_e (1+r).$$

The happy circumstance which, for ordinary levels of interest, makes $\rho$ approximate to $r$ allows us, if we wish, to speak of $\rho$ as the interest rate. We have

$$\frac{\partial}{\partial x}\left(\frac{\partial V}{\partial \rho}\right) = (\rho x - 1)\, e^{-\rho x}$$

and putting this equal to zero we have $\rho x - 1 = 0$, or $x = 1/\rho$, as the only solution short of an infinite futurity. Thus the sole extreme value of $\partial v/\partial \rho$ lies where the number of years' futurity is the reciprocal of the interest rate. At $\rho = 1/20$, for example, the greatest leverage of a small fall in $\rho$ will be exerted on the present value of the profit instalment looked for, not in two or three but in twenty years' time. But who is going to count on profits twenty years hence, to be earned by a machine which may be obsolete in five? The curve connecting $\partial v/\partial \rho$ with $x$ is of the type shown (Fig. 1).

It is plain that the main weight of an interest-rate change is exerted on instalments which lie far on the other side of the 'horizon' when the business man decides, as for many purposes he must, to ignore all but the nearest few annual instalments.

But now suppose that instead of cutting off the further future with a curtain, he discounts it at a very high annual percentage, to allow for the uncertainty of future years in a way whose effect gets more powerful with increasing futurity. If the discount which covers both deferment and uncertainty is 33 per cent per annum, that is, $\frac{1}{3}$ per annum, the greatest leverage will be exerted on the 3-year-hence instalment, and discounted values of the more remote instalments will be too small, in absolute size, for even a large *proportionate* change in them to make much difference to the total. Thus a high rate of discount for uncertainty comes in practice to the same thing as a near horizon.

One more step of reconciliation is possible. What of the possible profits which, although deliberately neglected or discounted, may accrue in the further years? To ignore them in all investment proposals is to short-list only those proposals which offer a wide margin against the business man's misjudgement. For in setting a horizon of, say, three years, in requiring an investment project to promise to repay its first cost in three years of operation, he well knows that at the end of the three years it may be working as profitably as ever, and may at that time still seem likely to be profitable for several years more. Beyond the

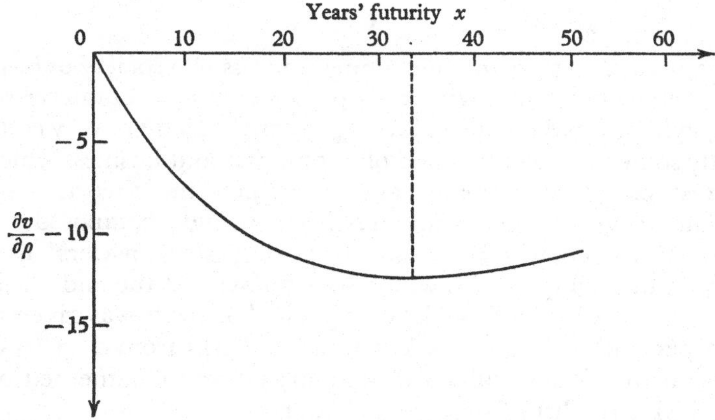


Fig. 1. The curve shows $(\delta/\delta\rho)\, e^{-\rho x} = -x\, e^{-\rho x}$, when $\rho = 0{\cdot}03$. The curve has an extreme value at $x = 1/\rho$, thence approaches zero asymptotically.

horizon which he sets when deciding what equipment to buy, the *possible* profits are pure gain, for the equipment will already have been paid for. The *possibility* of these further profitable years, the freedom which uncertainty itself confers upon the business man to imagine them without straining the bounds of realism, serves as a counterpoise to the disturbing thought which also he cannot quite exclude (for there is an intellectual, as well as a moral, conscience: truth is in the end invincible inside our minds if not outside them) that despite all care, caution and calculation, even the early years within the horizon may be a disappointment and a failure. So long as the world is what it is, there will be no escaping the basic uncertainties, there is no freedom to imagine high success without the inseparable shadow of exposure also to misfortune. Scientific prediction is *conditional* prediction, and it is only in the laboratory, or in the game completely described by its rules, that we can govern the conditions.

# 14
# BUSINESS MEN ON BUSINESS DECISIONS

## I

Being invited to give an after-dinner address to a society of business men engaged in engineering production and commerce on Merseyside, I had the idea of trying to convey to them very compactly some notion of the kind of questions about business which interest economic theorists and on which the theorists are anxious to get direct testimony. I accordingly composed the explanatory remarks and the list of 'suggested answers' to a number of such questions which here follow. At the end of my explanation a copy of the list of suggested answers was given to each person, and he was asked to allot marks from 0 to 10 to each answer. The results are summarized and commented on along with the list of suggested answers.

## II

If there is one question more than another which causes economists to stammer in confusion and tie themselves up in verbal knots, it is 'What is economics about?' Now, when I started to write this paper I had an inspiration. Economics is about business. That answer, generously interpreted, really covers everything. We must understand 'business' to include the housewife devising her household budget so as to get the most out of a given expenditure, the bread-winner seeking that particular type of job where his aptitudes will be most valuable to the community and therefore best rewarded, the business man in the more ordinary and restricted sense trying to discover or invent, and produce, as cheaply as possible, something which will please and satisfy the public and so give him a profit, and the Government, which, regrettably as some of us think, has been taking over more and more the functions both of the consumer and of the enterpriser. But here I want to use the word 'business' to mean the special activities of those who initiate and organize production and marry themselves for better or worse to the hazards of so doing. We can, I think, find a single heading under which all these special activities come, a name for the whole of the business man's business: it is *decision-making*. Business decisions ought surely to be one of the focal points of the economist's study of his field. It is in the act of making a decision that the business man gives a fresh thrust to affairs, that in greater or less degree he helps to make history. Perhaps we can break the problem down somewhat. When the business man makes a decision, he presumably has in mind some guiding purpose or objective, some general policy, and either some immediate plan or at least some pressing problem or emergency. Using a military analogy, we can say that a general's basic purpose is to win a war. His policy may be to wear the enemy down, or perhaps to bring about one decisive engagement in which the enemy's whole force can be annihilated; his immediate plan, by which he hopes to give effect to his policy and achieve his ultimate purpose, will specify in more or less detail, with more or less rigidity, the course of action of all the forces and arms under his command up to some more or less precisely stated future time or situation. Has this analogy any application to the world of business? The text-books on economics, using the central principle of theory-building, radical and ruthless simplification and abstraction, have usually assumed simply that the business man's basic purpose is to 'maximize his profit' or his 'net revenue'. This proposition, that the enterpriser has at the back of his mind all the time the dominant purpose of making his firm's income as great as possible, opens up a host of questions falling under several different headings.

First, there are the interpretive or definitional questions: What precisely is it that is sought to be maximized? Is it

A (i) Net profit before tax?

(ii) Net profit after tax payable by the firm?

(iii) Net profit for the immediate future, for example, a quarter or half year or one year?

(iv) Net profit averaged over the next five years?

(v) Net profit averaged over the next ten years?

(vi) Net profit averaged over the next thirty years?

(vii) If it is net profit averaged over a period, is the average 'unweighted', so that as much importance is given to the profitability of the firm ten years hence as next year, or is greater weight given to the more immediately future years?

Or is it not profit at all but

(viii) The general prosperity of the firm, where we include in general prosperity the maintenance of the goodwill of a body of customers or the esteem of the public at large?

(ix) The firm's net worth as estimated within the firm?

(x) The firm's liquid position or balance-sheet strength?

(xi) The firm's prestige as an enterprising, efficient, technically progressive, financially sound, humane and high-principled concern?

Or is it rather

(xii) The personal reputation or self-esteem of the moving spirits of the firm, their prestige as heads of a firm which has the attributes listed under (xi)? Does the head of the firm identify himself with his business so that its success is his success?

I would like to try to make clear the point of some of these distinctions.

In the economic text-books we find sentences like this: 'In order to maximize its net revenue, the firm must set its output at that level where marginal revenue is equal to marginal cost.' Now the actual behaviour that conforms to this rule may be quite different according to whether the net revenue considered is merely that of the ensuing week or month, or is reckoned in some way over a long future period in the life of the firm. If the firm's object is to maximize its profit from month to month, it will perhaps take advantage of any general shortage of the type of product it makes to ask a higher price so long as the shortage lasts. But what will be the effect of such action on its market and its customers' goodwill in the long run? The maximizing of profit in the short term and in the long term may be incompatible objectives, calling for different policies.

So much for questions A (iii) to (vi). What arises from question (vii) is both more subtle and more topical. It really amounts to asking: How do we reckon the *success* of an enterprise? Is a firm to be called successful if it has for a long time been making good profits, or if it has made them for a short time in the recent past, or if it 'is making' good profits (but what, precisely, do we mean by 'is making'?) or if it seems to be going to make good profits? Is success something which is reckoned at a point of time or over a period? And if over a period, is this a past or an expected period? Or shall we say that a firm is successful if its recent history gives promise of prosperity over the next few years? In calling this question topical I have in mind the bearing it seems to have on the topic of take-over bids.

I do not think there is any need for me to discuss questions A (viii) to (xi), and I shall pass on to A (xii). It is sometimes said that the classical 'enterpriser' of the text-books is dead, his mantle torn in two and his functions divided between the equity shareholder on the one hand, as provider of risk capital, and the salaried executive on the other, as decision-maker. The text-book enterpriser was a man who owned capital which he was ready to risk on ventures of highly uncertain outcome, ventures which might bring him a very large gain, or might equally well lose him his stake. He was thus the uncertainty-bearer. One decision at least was evidently taken by him, the decision which venture or what type of venture to back. But he was also the director of the enterprise, deciding the precise character of the product, the method of production and the scale, type and timing of extensions and improvements of plant. The text-book enterpriser did not merely subscribe to the share issue of a shipping company: he bought a ship of a specified type, decided what trade it should engage in, and indeed assumed the business responsibility for the venture in all important respects. Nowadays, it is said, such people only exist in a small way of business. Typical of them perhaps is the barrow-boy, who nevertheless sometimes makes a fortune. In large-scale concerns, it is contended, the decision-maker has not provided the capital and therefore will not lose his own fortune if things go wrong, and therefore (and this is the point) he will not behave as he would if the capital which he controls did in fact belong to him. Against this view, however, it has been pointed out that the unsuccessful business executive will soon have nothing to manage; his own prosperity and his prestige, which may mean more to him than money gain, are as much bound up with the firm's success as if he owned it. A third view, which to me seems cogent, is that the business executive *identifies* himself with the enterprise which he directs, and is thus strongly interested in ploughing back profits rather than paying them away to usurious shareholders, even though those shareholders are the legal owners of the firm. He wants the profits to be used to build the living tissue of the organism which provides his life with its meaning, not bled away in dividends.

So much for the nature of the ultimate objective. Let us turn now to a second set of questions, concerning the policies which business men adopt in pursuit of the objective. A policy is not a book where you can look up the answer to the question, 'What do I do in these circumstances?', whatever the situation or emergency that has arisen. The politician's habit of replying to parliamentary questions by saying, 'I cannot answer questions about a hypothetical situation', is not so unreasonable as it sounds, for it is impossible, in the nature of things, to specify in advance everything that is relevant about a hypothetical situation. It is impossible, for example, to specify fully the knowledge and experience in the light of which, at that future date, the situation will be viewed by this person and that. Thus such a question as 'What would you do if such and such happened?' is not worthy of an answer, for such and such can in the nature of things be only incompletely described. Nevertheless, a policy is a useful and necessary guide. It gives you a 'line', if not detailed directions for following it. Let us ask, then, 'What is the business man's "line" on certain matters?'

One thing that interests economists very much is how business men decide upon the prices they ask. Here I again suggest a choice of answers to be ranked in order of truth or accuracy:

B (i)–(iii) I know the total cost $T$ of any number $N$ of units of product, and for each possible output $N$ I know what difference $\Delta T$ would be made to $T$ by changing from $N$ to $N+1$. I also know the sale proceeds $S$ of any output and consequently what difference $\Delta S$ would be made to $S$ by changing from $N$ to $N+1$. I choose $N$ so that $\Delta T = \Delta S$ and then set price equal to $S/N$. (This is what the text-book says.)

(iv) I select a figure for my intended or expected output $N$, and divide the total $Q$ of my overhead costs by $N$. To this I add the unit direct cost (for labour, power, materials, etc.), say $D/N$, and an arbitrary percentage mark-up for profit, say $p$, so that my price comes out as

$$(1+p)\,[(Q+D)/N].$$

This is the answer that business men themselves sometimes appear to give. It raises the further question of how the business man decides upon his output. Here he might perhaps say:

(v) I take the largest output that I can produce without overtime.

(vi) I take an average of the experience of the corresponding month in the past three years.

(vii) I produce what I think I can sell at the price which covers direct and overhead costs and allows me my usual percentage mark-up. When trade is bad, I am willing to take a cut in my percentage of profit, to the point where I think my total profit over the whole output (as distinct from profit per unit of output) will be kept up to the highest figure possible. This total profit will be $p(Q+D)$, and I am willing to reduce $p$ if the resulting increase of $N$ and therefore of $D$ is sufficient to increase $pD$ by more than the associated decrease of $pQ$. In extremely bad trade conditions I would even reduce price below $(Q+D)/N$ to any level where it gave me any contribution at all towards overheads, the absolute lower limit being $D/N$, since below that I should be actually out of pocket on current expenses (*direct* costs not covered by sale proceeds).

The answer B (vii) calls for comment. A little reflection will show that it amounts to the same thing as answer B (i). The point and purpose of the policy described in answer (i) is to make the total profit $S-T$ as large as possible by pushing output $N$ up to that level where to push it any further would add more to its total cost $T$ than to its sale proceeds $S$. But this is also just what policy *B* (vii) aims at. Under B (vii) that price is sought which, taken together with the output that it will enable to be sold, will keep the excess of sale proceeds over direct costs as high as possible. Economists have been tremendously exercised by the apparent collision between the policy recommended by the text-book and the policy which business men themselves, in the enquiry conducted by the Oxford Economists' Research Group before the war, affirm that they adopt. Some economists have maintained that the text-books must be rewritten, others that the two policies come to the same thing in effect, and that what has come to be called the 'full cost principle' described by the business men really applies the textbook criterion of rational conduct through a process of trial and error.

I turn now to the second matter on which I should like to find out what is the business man's line, a matter which to me personally is even more interesting than the basis of price policy, namely, how does the business man decide when, on what scale, and in what precise form to enlarge or improve his productive or commercial facilities, his plant and equipment or his premises or his material business outfit in any sense? Economists call such acts 'investment'. By *investment* they do not mean the act of subscribing to a new issue of shares or of buying existing shares on the Stock Exchange, but the act of ordering new machines, installations or buildings for use in their own business. The question of how the business man's mind works and what materials it works with in approaching a decision whether or not a particular investment proposal is worth while or not is one of the most fascinating, to my mind, in the whole of economics. Here again we have a clash between the text-book and the business man's own testimony. The following are some of the answers which have been put forward:

C (i) A block of equipment will be bought if its expected net earnings in future years, when each such annual instalment is discounted to the present at the current market interest rate on loans of the appropriate term and the resulting 'spot-cash equivalents' are all added together, give it a valuation not less than its supply price.

I interpolate here a more extended statement of the suggested calculation. Actuaries constantly use the notion of the 'present value of £1—deferred $t$ years'. Let us represent this present value, which with an interest rate of $r$ per cent per annum is of course $1/(1+\frac{1}{100}r)^t$ by $x_t$. And let the number of £s which the proposed block of equipment is expected to add to the firm's profit in future year $t$ (counting the immediate future year as 1) be $G_t$. Then $v$, the 'present value' of the piece of equipment, means, in the economists' vocabulary, the total of all such terms as $x_tG_t$ for every value of $t$ from 1 up to the most distant year in which the equipment will earn anything at all. If the equipment can be bought for less than $v$, says the text-book, it will be bought. Or, more precisely, such a volume of orders will be given per month or per year for equipment of this type as will drive up its supply price to equality with the valuation set on such equipment by the least sanguine of those who actually give such orders.

This answer, C (i), is the *formal* answer to be found in Keynes's *General Theory of Employment, Interest and Money*. I will leave comment on it until later.

C (ii) To be deemed worth buying, a block of equipment must be expected to pay for itself in from three to five years, or, in other words, the expectation must be that in each of the first three to five years of its life it will add to profits, over and above what they would have been without it, an amount equal to one-fifth or one-third of its first cost. Sometimes the required expectation of annual earnings is put as high as one-half of first cost. This is the answer given by business men.

Now this answer is to me, and I think to many other economists, extraordinarily puzzling. A large firm may put several hundred thousand pounds to reserve each year; does it keep the accumulated amount on current account at the bank, earning no interest? Until the money is needed for some purpose connected with the firm's proper business or some enlargement of its interests, will not the money be put into Government stock or some other form in which it will earn from 2½ to 5 per cent per annum? Would not the directors of such a firm regard a policy of keeping their reserves on current account at the bank as wasteful, as implying the throwing away of a perfectly good annual income of several tens of thousands of pounds perhaps? But, if so, how can they possibly explain their reluctance to put such money into blocks of equipment (improvements or enlargements of plant) which would earn annually five or ten times as much? It is this question which, more than any other, I should like to discuss here. As before, I suggest an explanation, which is to be awarded marks according to its closeness to the truth:

C (iii) A business man is willing to instal a new machine even if he *does not count on its doing much more than pay for itself*, provided it promises to do this in a very short time. Why should he insist on being able to expect this swift recoupment of his outlay? May it not be because he feels that he can see fairly clearly and confidently only a year or two ahead, that while he feels he can dismiss from his thoughts the possibility of the machine being superseded by a better design or a radically new method immediately after he has installed it, he feels no such confidence about the future beyond two or three years ahead? It would be reasonable for a business man to argue thus:

I should be glad to earn 8 or 10 per cent on the money I have put to reserve, instead of the 3 or 4 per cent I am getting by keeping it in Government stock, but the only reasonably safe way of doing this in my own business is to find some scheme which will give very great benefits over a few immediately future years, since any benefits are more likely than not to disappear at the end of that short time through imitative action by my competitors, or the invention of still better methods.

If the business man said this, we could suppose him to have in mind this sort of picture:

| Year ... | 1 | 2 | 3 | 4 | 5 | 6 |
|---|---|---|---|---|---|---|
| Difference made by the machine | −£100,000 (first cost) | +£25,000 | +£50,000 | +£30,000 | +£15,000 | |
| | | Operating profits | | | | |

Such an explanation would fit at one and the same time all three of the statements:

(1) The proposed block of equipment is expected to earn in each year, for a few years, between 20 and 50 per cent of its first cost.

(2) It is expected to pay for itself in three years.

(3) If the initial outlay of £100,000 were a loan repayable by instalments according to the same schedule as that of the expected earnings, the *yield* in the actuarial sense would be about 8 per cent.

I shall conclude with one or two supplementary questions on investment decisions. Answer C (i) implies that a decision whether or not to buy a block of equipment will be influenced by the prevailing market interest rate, represented, for example, by the yield of Consols. For this is one of the important rival uses of the money which would have to be laid out on the equipment. If the business man is proposing to invest his own reserves, this market rate of interest is one possibility which he is sacrificing; or if he is proposing to borrow money on debentures, this is one of the important counter attractions which he will have to out-bid. The particular form in which answer C (i) introduces the interest rate may strike the business man as unfamiliar, but the essential point is not affected: a rise in the system of interest rates will *reduce* the spot-cash equivalents $x_t G_t$ of earnings of a given amount expected at a given future date, and thus weaken the inducement to buy the block of equipment in question. Thus I would like to ask:

C (iv) In deciding whether or not to instal a specified block of equipment, is the business man influenced by the prevailing market interest rates as represented by the yields of Government securities?

In 1938 I ventured to put forward a theory of the business cycle in which the central idea was that when a business man has just installed an important new block of equipment, he will not immediately proceed to consider further improvements or extensions but will need a period of a year or two to get the new equipment which he has just acquired assimilated into his existing outfit, to get it run in and tuned up, to find out its effect on the flow of production in his whole works, to see how far the increased capacity is matched by increased sales and so on. So my last question is:

C (v) Does a business progress by alternating phases of active enlargement or modernization of equipment and of consolidation, running-in and experiment to get the best out of the equipment as it exists?

## III

The list of suggested answers to the questions which have been introduced above and which were handed to each member of the audience is reproduced below as Appendix I. The marks assigned by the audience are tabulated in Appendix II.

There are many evident difficulties in interpreting the markings given by the business men. This enquiry, in which only a small roomful of people took part and in which, after listening for some fifty minutes to the explanatory address, each business man gave well over an hour of concentrated study to the written list of suggested answers and the process of marking it, is plainly far removed from the ordinary procedure of sending a short list of tersely expressed questions by post to a relatively large number of people. Doctors sometimes express a preference for 'clinical evidence' over 'statistical evidence', presumably on the ground that it is better to have detailed pictures of a few cases than formal cut-and-dried particulars of many cases. Perhaps a somewhat similar idea may do something to make my experiment seem worth while. What I am attempting to explore on this exceedingly modest scale is a technique of 'systematic impressionism' rather than statistics, for there can plainly be no question of applying formal statistical techniques, or indeed of doing anything except the very simplest grouping, tabulation and inspection of the marks. In the accompanying Table I the mark given by each business man to each answer is separately shown. Each row of the table belongs to one answer, each column to one business man, whose description of his firm and of himself heads the column. Some of those taking part have put a dash, or nothing at all, against some of the answers instead of awarding an explicit nought, and Table I reproduces these dashes and blanks, which in interpreting the marks I have treated as noughts. It will be seen that towards the left of Table I there are nine firms described as 'small' or 'medium' and towards the right there are four firms described as 'large' and one whose size was not indicated, while on the extreme right are the marks given, on the basis of his contacts with business men, by a Youth Employment Officer. He, and the firm of unstated size, have each given two sets of marks, one referring to small firms and one to large firms. Thus we have eleven columns of marks referring to 'small' or 'medium' firms and six columns referring to 'large' firms. For each row of the table, that is, for each answer, I have taken the total of the eleven marks for the small and medium firms, the total of the six marks for the large firms, and the grand total for all firms. The result is shown in Table II with the maxima that could have been scored if every firm had given the answer ten marks.

The business men were in effect asked to give opinions on three questions:

A. What does the business man seek to maximize?

B. How does the business man decide his price?

C. How does the business man reach his investment decisions?

I think their evidence warrants the following comments:

## A. *What does the business man seek to maximize?*

The marks suggest that it is net profit after rather than before tax; that for small firms it is, above all, profit of the immediate (up to one year) future, and secondly, profit over the next five years; for large firms 'the next five years' gets slightly more marks than 'the immediate future'. The suggestion that it is net profit over a period of years with more weight given to the more immediately future years gets about half marks. 'The general prosperity of the firm [and] maintenance of goodwill' and 'the firm's prestige' both get very high marks. These high marks, which are one of the most striking features of Table II, suggest that firms are more far-sighted and prudent, and also less materially minded, than the economist's ordinary assumptions suggest. There is no great enthusiasm for internally estimated net worth or even for balance-sheet strength, but this latter gets slightly better marks than 'the personal reputation of the head of the firm'.

B. *How does the business man decide his price?*

Equating marginal revenue to marginal cost gets distinctly poor marks. One of the most definite verdicts in the whole enquiry is that in deciding his price the business man does not ignore his competitors. This suggested prevalence of an oligopolistic market attitude may reflect the character of the sample, which consisted largely of engineering firms. The 'kinked demand curve' gets a very modest vote. 'Full-cost pricing' is better supported than the equating of MR and MC, but there is no enthusiasm. On methods of estimating output for the purpose of full-cost pricing the marks are more interesting: they show a distinctly favourable response to a suggestion—B (vii)—which would go some way to reconcile 'full-cost pricing' with the equating of MR and MC.

C. *How does the business man reach his investment decisions?*

Amongst the suggested answers on investment policy, the comparison of marginal efficiency of capital with market rate of interest gets a poor mark. There is general agreement that two years is shorter than the time in which most firms require a proposed new block of equipment to pay for itself. 'Five years' gets far the highest mark of the three suggestions. Answer C (iii), which I think may be a new interpretation of evidence obtained in past enquiries, also gets a comparatively high mark.

No more is claimed for this little experiment than that it may indicate a possible way of securing the interest and attention of very busy and pre-occupied business men in questions of economic theory for which they would otherwise have no time. It only remains for me to thank with the utmost sincerity those who entered so kindly and so keenly into the spirit of this 'game'.

## APPENDIX I

***You are requested to assign a mark from 0 to 10 to each suggested answer to each question. The marks assigned to all the suggested answers to any one question need not add up to any particular total. If, for example, a high mark is given to every answer to one question, this marking will be understood to mean that each answer would be right in one or other set of frequently arising circumstances.***

*Question* A — The business man is chiefly anxious to increase: — *Mark awarded*

(i) Net profit before tax
(ii) Net profit after tax payable by the firm
(iii) Net profit for the immediate future ($\frac{1}{4}$, $\frac{1}{2}$, or 1 year)
(iv) Net profit over the next 5 years
(v) Net profit over the next 10 years
(vi) Net profit over the next 30 years
(vii) Net profit over a period, giving greater 'weight' to the more immediately future years
(viii) The general prosperity of the firm, including the maintenance of the goodwill of a body of customers and the esteem of the public at large
(ix) The firm's net worth as estimated within the firm
(x) The firm's liquid position or balance-sheet strength
(xi) The firm's prestige as an enterprising, efficient, technically progressive, financially sound, humane and high-principled concern
(xii) His personal reputation, prestige and self-esteem as head of a firm having the attributes listed under (xi). The heads of the firm *identify* themselves with the firm

*Question* B — The business man decides the price of his product in the following way:

(i) I choose a price such that, having regard to the respective outputs which various prices would enable me to sell, a small lowering of this price would add more to the total cost of the output than to the total sale proceeds, while a small rise of price would take away more from sale proceeds than from costs
(ii) In deciding on the price of my product I ignore competitors
(iii) I have to reckon that a lowering of my price will be immediately followed by a lowering of my rivals' prices, but a raising of my price will not be imitated by them
(iv) I select a figure for output $N$, and divide the total $Q$ of my overhead costs by $N$. To this I add the unit direct costs (for labour, power, materials, etc.), say $D/N$, and a percentage mark-up for profit, so that my price comes out as $(1+p)[(Q+D)/N]$. In deciding output $N$ for this purpose I use the following principle:

| *Question B* | | *Mark awarded* |
|---|---|---|
| (v) | I take the largest output that I can produce without overtime | |
| (vi) | I take an average of the experience of the corresponding month in the past three years | |
| (vii) | I produce what I think I can sell at a price $(1+p)[(Q+D)/N]$. In times of bad trade I cut $p$ and in very bad trade I am willing to cut price almost down to $D/N$ | |

*Question* C The business man decides whether or not, at a particular time, to instal a specified block of equipment, by applying the following test:

(i) Let $G_t$ stand for the addition to profit which the proposed equipment would be expected to make in year $t$, counting the immediately future year as year 1. Let $x_t$ be the present value of £1—due in year $t$. Then if the sum of all terms $x_tG_t$ comes to more than what it would cost to instal the equipment, I order it

(ii) To be deemed worth while, a block of equipment must be expected to pay for itself in
   (*a*) 2 years or earn in each year 50 per cent of its first cost;
   (*b*) 3 years or earn in each year 33 per cent of its first cost;
   (*c*) 5 years or earn in each year 20 per cent of its first cost.

The interpretation of this requirement is:

(iii) The block of equipment would have to be expected to earn 20, 33, etc. per cent of its first cost for a just sufficient number of years to cover its first cost and yield a moderate net gain

# APPENDIX II — Table I

| Questions | Small private company (engineering). Staff approx. 50 | Small firm of machine tool merchants controlled by proprietors | Director of a small private limited company | Small firm in personal ownership, capital £40,000 with 50 employees | Company Secretary of small private limited company manufacturing mass-produced articles | Managing Director of small private limited company (hardware manufacture) | Small firm of manufacturing mechanical engineers, individually owned | Sales engineer of firm of electric motor manufacturers | Medium-sized engineering family business | Non-ferrous metal and cable manufacture on a large scale | Large public company in the electrical industry | Large public company | Chief plant engineer, large company (telecommunications) | Firm's own size not indicated. Marks refer to the practice of: Small companies | Large companies | Youth Employment Officer. Marks refer to the practice of: Small companies | Large companies |
|---|---|---|---|---|---|---|---|---|---|---|---|---|---|---|---|---|---|
| A (i) | 2 | — | 3 | — | — | — | 1 | — | 7 | 6 | 4 | — | 7 | 4 | 4 | 8 | — |
| (ii) | 3 | — | 6 | 10 | 4 | 5 | 1 | 5 | 4 | 8 | 8 | 10 | 4 | 5 | 5 | — | — |
| (iii) | — | 10 | 10 | 10 | 3 | 3 | 2 | 8 | 4 | 1 | 4 | 10 | 8 | 1 year [10][d] | 1 year [10][d] | 10 | 2 |
| (iv) | 5 | — | 6 | 5 | 9 | 10 | 2 | 5 | 5 | 10 | 3 | 10 | 6 | 7½ | — | 4 | 8 |
| (v) | 3 | — | 4 | — | 7 | 5 | 2 | — | 6 | 10 | — | 3 | 1 | — | 2½ | 2 | 9 |
| (vi) | 3 | — | 2 | — | — | 1 | 2 | — | 3 | 10 | — | — | — | — | — | — | 4 |
| (vii) | 3 | — | 8 | 7 | 5 | 7 | 2 | 4 | 4 | 5 | 10 | 6 | 5 | 8 | 8 | 6 | 3 |
| (viii) | 5 | 10 | 8 | 10 | 6 | 10 | 10 | 10 | 10 | 10 | 10 | 8 | 10 | 10 | 10 | 2 | 6 |
| (ix) | 3 | 5 | 3 | 2 | 4 | 6 | 8 | — | 4 | — | 8 | 2 | 5 | 7½ | — | 4 | 4 |
| (x) | 5 | 5 | 10 | 5 | 5 | 7 | 8 | — | 8 | 5 | — | 8 | 8 | 7½ | — | 5 | 5 |
| (xi) | 7 | 10 | 4 | 10 | 8 | 10 | 10 | 10 | 8 | 10 | 10 | 10 | 10 | 6 | 10 | — | 8 |
| (xii) | 3 | 5 | 5 | 5 | 5 | 8 | 10 | 2 | 6 | — | 2 | — | 7 | 6 | 10 | 4 | 6 |
| B (i) | 1 | 10 | 10 | — | 3 | 8 | 2 | — | 3 | 5 | — | 8 | 1 | [8][c] | [8][c] | — | — |
| (ii) | — | — | — | 10 | 2 | — | — | — | 5 | 1 | 5 | — | — | 'This is never done except in monopoly' | | — | — |
| (iii) | 4 | — | 8 | 2 | 8 | 1 | 5 | 5 | 6 | 1 | — | 6 | 7 | — | — | 2 | 6 |
| (iv) | 5 | 10 | — | 10 | 7 | — | 3 | 10 | 8 | — | 10 | 9 | 3 | — | — | — | — |
| (v) | 5 | — | 3 | 10 | 5 | 5 | — | — | 8 | — | 6 | 6 | — | — | — | 8 | 8 |
| (vi) | 3 | 10 | 5 | — | 5[a] | 6 | 5 | 6 | 7 | 5 | 6 | 8 | 8 | — | — | — | — |
| (vii) | 5 | 10 | 1 | — | — | 8 | 5 | 10 | 8 | — | 8 | 8 | 3 | — | — | 6 | 6 |
| C (i) | 8 | 10 | 3 | — | — | 5 | 6 | 10 | 5 | — | 8 | 2 | — | — | — | — | — |
| (ii) (*a*) | — | — | 6 | — | — | 3 | 1 | 0 | 6 | — | — | 6 | 3 | [10][d] | — | — | — |
| (ii) (*b*) | — | — | 10 | — | 8 | 7 | 1 | 10 | 7 | — | 8 | 6 | 8 | — | — | — | — |
| (ii) (*c*) | — | 10 | 4 | 10 | 4 | 10 | 5 | 4 | 8 | 10 | 9 | 10 | — | — | [10][d] | — | — |
| (iii) | 5 | 10 | 7 | 10 | — | 6 | — | 8 | 4 | [8][b] | — | 7 | — | — | — | 8 | 8 |

[a] Depending upon the article. [b] '20 per cent is on the high side. 10 per cent nearer' [interpreted as a mark of 8 for the answer].

[c] Written comments suggest a mark of 8. [d] Written comments suggest a mark of 10.

Table II

| Answers | Firms: Small and medium (possible mark 110) | Large (possible mark 60) | All (possible mark 170) |
|---|---|---|---|
| A (i) | 25 | 21 | 46 |
| (ii) | 43 | 35 | 78 |
| (iii) | 70 | 35 | 105 |
| (iv) | 58 | 37 | 95 |
| (v) | 29 | 25 | 54 |
| (vi) | 11 | 14 | 25 |
| (vii) | 54 | 37 | 91 |
| (viii) | 91 | 54 | 145 |
| (ix) | 46 | 19 | 65 |
| (x) | 65 | 26 | 91 |
| (xi) | 83 | 58 | 141 |
| (xii) | 59 | 25 | 84 |
| B (i) | 45 | 22 | 67 |
| (ii) | 17 | 6 | 23 |
| (iii) | 41 | 20 | 61 |
| (iv) | 53 | 22 | 75 |
| (v) | 44 | 20 | 64 |
| (vi) | 47 | 27 | 74 |
| (vii) | 53 | 25 | 78 |
| C (i) | 47 | 10 | 57 |
| (ii) *a* | 26 | 9 | 35 |
| (ii) *b* | 43 | 22 | 65 |
| (ii) *c* | 55 | 39 | 94 |
| (iii) | 58 | 23 | 81 |

# 15
# BUSINESS AND UNCERTAINTY

If an economist of former days had been asked to identify the very hub of his subject upon which all of it turns and from which or upon which all other ideas radiate or converge, he might have said that the key idea was that of price and its natural, impersonal and unconscious regulation of a freely competitive economy. He would often have rejected the idea that economics is concerned at all with the insides of men's minds, and would have declared that once their tastes and desires are known we have done with them as thinking and feeling beings. Nowadays, I believe, the emphasis is different. The central theme of economic theory is no longer simply the logic of choice amongst alternatives each fully, precisely and certainly known, but it is instead the business of choice amongst unknowns.

Does this seem an absurd and impossible task? It is, nevertheless, what all of us, and in especial business men preparing to supply as yet non-existent markets and even unborn customers with goods which are only now being dreamed of, are every day engaged in doing. A mass of our daily acts, it is true, are aimed only at immediate and routine results whose character and effect upon us, nearly enough for all practical purposes, we know for certain. But some actions look for their relevant consequences months and years into the future, and what contact have we with those non-existent times? The times themselves are non-existent until they have ceased to be future, and until, therefore, it is too late to make choices about them. All we can do is to put something in their place, to *imagine* the consequences of present acts and choose amongst these figments of imagination.

These figments will, of course, not be mere fantasies or day-dreams. To be interesting, they will have to seem *possible* consequences of present acts. No one will elect to do such and such a thing today for the sake of later consequences which he believes cannot happen. But the mere fact that different individuals are free to construct their own imagined futures independently of each other, together with the other fact that the realizations, when they come, will inevitably be interlocked and necessarily forced into consistency, sufficiently suggests the depth of uncertainty in which our choice of present acts must work. The kind of choice which nowadays we think of as bearing the weight of economic success and well-being not only for single enterprises but for the whole country is *choice in face of uncertainty*, that is, *decision*.

In advanced communities people insist on saving, that is, on leaving unspent part of the income they have earned in helping to put goods upon the market. Farmers and miners, transport workers, factory hands, shop-keepers, technicians, office staff, accountants and managers, all contribute to the production of goods, all receive pay or hope for profit, and the whole process must seek its justification, and its warrant for continuing at full pitch, in the sale of those goods for the expected prices. To buy all these goods for those prices will take *all* the money earned in producing them, wages, salaries, rent, interest and profit. But if part is saved, must not some of the goods remain unsold? Plainly, if all had to be sold to consumers as such, or not at all, some could not be sold in an economy which saves. But others besides the home consumer buy goods. The foreign consumer buys exports, though he may cancel this by selling imports. The Government buys goods and services. But even if there were no foreigner and no Government, there would still be the business man himself wishing to extend and improve his plant or equip a brand-new enterprise. Economists, giving a familiar word a quite special meaning, call this business of ordering and paying for equipment, *investment*. Full employment, or any given level of employment, depends upon the saving gap corresponding to that level of employment being filled by investment. Thus the *decision to invest* has its special strategic importance for the economy.

What makes a business man decide to invest? What kinds of circumstances induce or inhibit him, when it is a question whether and in what particular shape to get new equipment in exchange for a large sum of money which he already has at his command, or in exchange for money which he would have to borrow? A preliminary formula on which business men and economists can agree seems easy to find: a business man will invest whenever a profit opportunity and the necessary funds can be brought together. Thus we have boiled the matter down to the question: What is a profit opportunity?

There is a danger at this point that differences in form of expression will seem to be differences in the substance of their thinking between the business men and the economists, so I propose to try to answer the question: 'What is a profit opportunity?' in the two languages as I believe business men, on the one hand, and economists, on the other, would answer it. Both parties, I believe, would start from the idea of the market value of what will be produced by the new plant and the total operating costs of the new plant including materials, power and human services of every type and for every purpose connected with it. The difference between these two amounts in a year let us call the earnings of the plant in that year. It is at this point that the ways divide, and it is here also that the real difficulty has to be faced. For who knows 'what will' be earned by the new plant? No one knows or can know; the most expert and diligent reckoning can result only in a plausible figure. It is on the question of how this uncertainty is to be expressed and incorporated into the arguments for and against embarking on the venture that the great differences of thought, expression or attitude appear. For his part, the business man places a hurdle to be jumped over, a hurdle whose enormous height used greatly to puzzle the economist. In form, the figure the business man concerns himself with is simply annual earnings divided by first cost. To be acceptable, the proposed investment has to be able to offer, with some credibility, a figure of thirty or even fifty per cent.

Why should this ever have puzzled the economist? Because he is trained to think of the business man as one who constantly seeks out all the profit there is to be had, and surely a business man who takes up only those investment opportunities which offer thirty or more per cent per annum is neglecting all the gains to be had from those which offer only fifteen or even ten or anything *above the percentage per annum at which funds can be borrowed*. The explanation is of course overwhelmingly obvious and can be expressed in several alternative ways. Its essence is suggested by another form of words that the business man sometimes uses. 'We do not invest', he says, 'unless the proposed investment promises to amortize itself in three years' (or sometimes 'in two years'). To amortize itself in three years an investment will of course have to earn thirty-five or forty per cent *in each of those first three years of operation*, and this apparently enormous percentage means no more than that only those first three (or two) years are to be taken into account at all.

When, on this basis, the economist does his own sum, he gets an answer which no longer surprises him at all, since it leaves no gap of unexploited gain. The economist asks himself: If the first cost of the plant is *E* and the earnings in each of the first three years are respectively *A*, *B*, *C*, what rate of discount will make the total of discounted *A*, discounted *B* and discounted *C* equal to *E*? That rate of discount may come out at 5, 7 or 10 per cent, something that is not in the least surprising to the economist and leaves no gap between itself and the borrowing rate. Thus for example, if *E* is 100 and *A*, *B* and *C* are each 40, a compound interest rate of 10 per cent per annum used for discounting *A*, *B* and *C* will bring their total discounted value to equality with *E* at 100. That discount rate which makes the total discounted expected earnings equal to the first cost is called in academic circles the marginal efficiency of capital, and the economist's logic tells him that there ought, in some sense, to be a tendency for it to be pushed (by a sufficiently large investment programme) down to equality with the borrowing rate. Well, why not?

But the matter is not, after all, so tidy as all that. For the economist, when he has pulled himself together, may still ask: What about the earnings of all the years *beyond* the first three? And he may answer his own question: They are a risk premium, or an allowance for uncertainty. I have no doubt this is part of the truth, but there is a more important aspect, what we might call the *uncertainty horizon*. Our only means of making guesses or imaginative pictures of the future is to use the memories or the records we have of the past to provide us with principles, with knowledge of the way things can happen, and to apply this knowledge of the forms which historical development can take to the situation which we see existing in the present. Within a given time, say two years or three years, relevant things, we argue, can go this way or that way or that other way, but *only so much*. The present does throw light on the future, for a limited distance. Up to that limit it may be sensible in certain ways to count on the future; beyond that limit, wherever we reckon it to lie, it would be silly to count on the future.

This, as it seems to me, is how the business man argues. He has two defences against the essential uncertainty that must attend any investment venture. First, he reduces it by confining his assumptions to matters that are in some degree illuminated by his knowledge of the present. Secondly, he gives himself a presumption that things will turn out better than this restricted reckoning suggests. For any profit earned in more distant years will be a pure bonus.

So much for the business man's method. The economist also resorts, usually, to a risk premium, but he incorporates it into his theory in a very neat and explicit way. The borrowing rate, the 5 or 6 per cent per annum that the business man will have to pay for money borrowed or that he can get on money lent, is one of the costs that hoped-for profit from an investment has to cover. The risk premium is another. Why should not the risk premium be given exactly the same arithmetical form as the borrowing rate of interest? There is, indeed, a strong reason why it should be. The uncertainty, the lack of solidity and cogency of any guess about the size of the new plant's earnings in a particular year will surely increase the more remote the year selected. The shape of things next year may be dimly discernible, or we think so; even the possibilities of the year beyond that may be subject to some constraint. There is a limit, perhaps, to the speed at which science, politics and personal ascendancies can change and develop. But ten years hence is for all practical purposes as unknown as the end of time.

Thus an uncertainty allowance ought to get more powerful when it is applied to more remote years. But this is precisely what will happen if we give it the form of a discounting rate. The present value of £1 deferred $n$ years at $100r$ per cent per annum, is, of course, £$[1/(1+r)^n]$. Now if $100r$ per cent per annum is the borrowing rate of interest, let us increase it by an extra 25 per cent to allow for the uncertainty of the expected earnings which are being discounted, making, say, 33 per cent in all. What is the present value of £1,000 deferred 5 years at 33 per cent per annum? About £237. Deferred 10 years the value is about £57. In fact, the effect of applying an uncertainty allowance, in the form of an additional discounting rate of such a percentage per annum as to make the total discounting rate equal to the ratio that the business man says he requires, in each of the first few years, between the promised earnings and the first cost of his proposed new investment, is that the present value of all 'expected' earnings beyond those few years into the future will be rendered negligible. Discounting expected earnings at 30 or 40 per cent per annum is equivalent to saying: We shall not bother about anything that may be earned after four or five years.

It is gratifying, at any rate to an economist, that the two roads, seemingly so different, converge upon the same destination. And yet I would like to probe a little deeper.

It cannot be true that investment never results in a loss, that the first cost is always covered by the earnings even when those earnings, and the first cost itself, are discounted back to the date when the decision to build the new plant is taken, or when the first cost and the earnings are all accumulated at compound interest at the borrowing rate up to the date when the plant is obsolete or worn out. Sometimes the whole calculation of expected earnings, when put to the test of practice, comes tumbling down like a house of cards. Someone else gets in first with a better idea, fashion goes off at a wild tangent, the government of the country where the plant is sited changes colour, the rock strata give out against all reason, the product fails to stand up under consumer treatment, and so on and so on. Business men know that such things happen. How do they find a place in their calculations for these possibilities?

For purposes of persuasion, even of self-persuasion, I can easily understand the advantage of a single figure for 'estimated rate of earnings', a single assumption about the profitability of a proposed investment. I do not in the least suggest that such a figure need be in any sense dishonest. No one, it might be argued, would embark on an investment project unless he felt there was some presumption that it would make a profit rather than a loss, and so a formula which is by its nature incapable of saying 'The result may be a profit *or it may be a loss*' cannot be simply condemned as inherently one-sided and misleading. But can it be true that a business man never says to himself in his detached, unemotional and private thoughts: 'If this comes off it will be immense, but if it doesn't come off we shall lose a million pounds'? If the total of the discounted expected earnings comes to less than the first cost, the difference is a loss. Is the business world so united in defence, so telepathically cohesive, that each business man says to himself: 'I can see a possibility of profit in such and such a venture (and of loss, too, of course), but I realize that the reason why A.B.C. Ltd., D.E.F. Ltd. and all the rest have not plunged in already is that they think that if we all plunged in, it would be too risky; so it would not be quite the thing for me to seize a chance which their combined (but not concerted) restraint has made pretty well a sure-fire success'? Is there such partly unconscious solidarity? I do not believe it. There is competition for profit and, in the manner which has been a classic piece of text-book theory for eighty years or so, the realizable profit is thus pushed down. It is not within the bounds of credibility that all ventures make a modest profit, none ever make a loss, none ever make a large profit. I could believe that, by a sufficient degree of explicit or tacit 'investment restraint' or 'investment solidarity', the business world could ensure that at best the result of an investment was immense success and at worst was merely a break-even. If there is not this solidarity (which would be much against the canons of social responsibility to which business men seem anxious to subscribe) I can only believe that there are big profits, break-evens, and *big losses*. Can it be true that the business man's private formula does not recognize this?

For, if the argument of my earlier paragraphs is accepted, the business men's formula makes them out to be extremely conservative. First, they require the project to hold some promise of amortizing itself within a period short enough for today's situation to seem to throw some light on it. Thus the uncertainty is reduced as far as is at all practicable. But secondly, this period is so short, and the rate of earnings sufficient to amortize the plant within it so high, that if the best hopes are realized and this rate of earnings continues for something approaching the *physical* life of the plant, the total discounted earnings will enormously exceed the first cost. What stops business men from pursuing these large gains, if the worst they have to fear is that they may break even? Surely the answer is that the worst they have to fear, in many cases, is not a break-even but a large loss.

I would like to suggest an alternative formula which the business man might use, and to ask whether in fact he does not sometimes use it, in his inmost and private thoughts: 'At best, we might make a profit of such and such, a very attractive thing; at worst we would make a loss of such and such; can we stand that? And if we can stand it, is the hope of that first-rate success worth the knowledge that we stand to lose this other amount?'

# 16

# SCALE, RISK AND PROFIT

Let us take it that we wish to understand the thoughts by which a business man, possessing a stated sum of money which he is free to distribute between the two purposes of retaining money and of buying the equipment needed to make a certain product, chooses the type and the size of this equipment. We shall refer to the stated sum as his *fortune*, and to any complete outfit of equipment suitable to the making of the product as a *plant*.

If he felt certain that a plant of some given type and size would give him a profit, as distinct from a loss, and that this profit would be larger than he could obtain from a plant of any other type and size within his power to buy, there would be nothing to analyse or discuss. The analysable quality of an investment decision arises from his not being sure what type or size of plant, including a zero plant, will, when he commits himself to buy it, most greatly increase the present value of his fortune. We wish to discover a general scheme of analysis in which the relevant considerations can be brought together.

The elements of his thought about any one of the rival investments which he has in mind, any one type and size of plant, will be vectors or number pairs, in each of which one member will name a hypothetical profit or loss from the investment over its life as a whole, and the other member will qualify the force that this idea of profit or loss from the investment exerts on his mind. By our definition of investment decision, no such hypothesis is accepted by him as certain to prove true, and no hypothesis which he regards as certain to prove false can be of concern to him. Thus the second member of each number pair expresses, in some way, his uncertainty. What this second number has to express is a personal judgement arising in the investor's own mind, no matter what is the material or evidence on which this judgement is based. If we, as outside observers or students of his thought, assume that we have before us the precise evidence on which he will base his judgement, and that we can ourselves exactly reproduce the thought process by which he will interpret this evidence, then we may carry our analysis of his decision straight from evidence to act without explicitly recognizing that there is involved an individual judgement or set of such judgements which are not our own. Such a short cut in analysis cannot in general be justified. The investor's judgement is his own, it is personal and subjective and cannot be ignored in favour of some standard method of interpreting a body of evidence which itself is arbitrarily assumed to be relevant.

Recognition that each such judgement is subjective still leaves us with, at least, two options as to how we shall suppose the investor to express it. Referring to the second member of each pair of numbers as an uncertainty variable, we can state the two options by saying that one type of uncertainty variable is *distributive*, the other *non-distributive*. A distributive uncertainty variable requires the investor to assume that he has in mind all relevant hypotheses as to the outcome of investing in the plant in question. He must suppose that he can make a list of such hypotheses, which will be complete in the sense that if any hypothesis not included in it were mentioned to him, he would dismiss such hypothesis as certainly false. By definition of this list, he feels certain that the outcome will prove to be one or other of the hypotheses in it, and this certainty he represents by unity. The values of the uncertainty variable to be respectively attached to each hypothesis of the list must be such, therefore, that they sum to unity. Certainty is *distributed* over the hypotheses, and each is assigned a 'portion of certainty', a mark indicating a degree of 'partial confidence' that it will prove the true answer. This type of uncertainty variable is familiar under the name of 'subjective probability', and it is always, so far as we know, taken to be subject to all those manipulations which are appropriate to probability of an entirely different kind, namely that which arises, objectively and impersonally, from the counting of cases.

In those statistical contexts where, within a reasonable interpretation, the same answers would be obtained by each counting process no matter who performed it, the combinatory laws are a matter of arithmetical logic and impose themselves ineluctably. But have these laws the same status in subjective probability? The latter is *distributive*, therefore *additive*, but it is not proven, in our view, that all the theorems which can be obtained for frequency-ratio probability are necessarily valid in subjective probability. We leave this question aside in the present paper.

The second option is to use as an uncertainty variable, a measure not of positive, if partial, confidence but of *anti-confidence*, of doubt or disbelief. This offers two prime advantages. First, we can escape from the need for the values of the uncertainty variable, assigned to the various hypotheses of the outcome of an investment, to sum to unity, or to any other particular total. Thus we escape from the need to suppose that the list of hypotheses is in any sense *complete*. For what should 'completeness' mean in this context? How, on what grounds, and in what circumstances, can a decision-maker justifiably feel sure that his list of hypotheses is *exactly complete*, that it contains neither fewer nor more items than those which he would not, if he examined them, reject as certainly false? Plainly, unless his list is looked upon by him as exactly complete in this sense, he cannot use a distributive uncertainty variable.

Secondly, when we invert our problem and use as our uncertainty variable some indicator of *disbelief* rather than one of positive confidence, we can interpret our procedure as a concern with *possibility* rather than with *probability* in any of its senses. And this brings us to the heart of the matter of risk. For those things constitute danger which are both damaging, if they occur, and also *able to occur*. To run risks means to put oneself within the reach of injury, and the essential question is not 'How often does a man, who takes the sort of action I propose, come to grief?' but 'What is the worst misfortune which my proposed action *can* lead to?', for it is only a satisfactory answer to this question which will allow the investor to embark on his venture with composure of mind.

Our proposal, then, is to use an uncertainty variable whose zero value will stand for *perfect possibility* and which will range up to some absolute maximum standing for perfect impossibility. 'Possible' and 'impossible' here mean possible or impossible *in the judgement of the particular investor*. The idea of possibility is always the idea of a human judgement, for it refers to the outcome of some experiment yet to be made, and only in the human mind can an action be *anticipated*. The experiments made by unconscious nature are either non-existent or already performed.

Those *elements* that we spoke of as composing the investor's thought are thus vectors of two entries, the first being a hypothesis of profit or loss, the second a measure or indicator of the degree of possibility which he adjudges to this hypothesis. Which of such elements will occupy the forefront of his mind? Those, surely, whose profit or loss hypothesis is numerically *the largest* amongst those elements which seem fairly possible. A large profit is, in itself, more interesting than a small one, and so is a large loss, which, in contrast to a small one, could be crippling or finally disastrous. But large hypothetical profit or loss is only interesting if it is possible. The nearer a *given* hypothesis of profit or loss approaches to adjudged impossibility the less interesting it will be. Thus arises the notion of focus elements, a pair of hypotheses, one of profit and the other of loss, which because of their peculiar combination of numerical size and fairly high adjudged possibility, capture the decision-maker's thoughts and represent for him the potential of the investment in question.

Loss is not merely the cancellation of an equal amount of gain. The significance to the business man of a given possible loss is by no means, in general, merely the mirror image, as it were, of a numerically equal gain. Suppose a bettor has wagered a considerable sum at evens on some outcome, so that he stands to win a known sum or to lose the same sum. Is his situation the same as if had made no bet? To find the total effect upon the business man of a given combination of possible gain and possible loss, it will not do simply to add these quantities. The combination of a possible gain of $M$ and a possible loss of $N$ need by no means affect the investor in the same way as the combination of a possible gain of $2M$ and a possible loss of $2N$. To resolve this problem, we can represent the investor's reaction to different pairs of focus outcomes, which reaction will of course be a matter of his own temperament, personal experience and current circumstances, and in particular, of the size of his 'fortune', by means of an indifference map. Since in this map distance on the horizontal axis will stand for something disliked, namely focus losses, while the vertical axis will show something desired, viz. focus gains, the indifference curves will slope upwards from left to right. Something can be inferred as to their shape from the consideration that no meaning can be assigned to any part of such curves which, if drawn, would correspond to losses larger than the investor's fortune. There will on this account be a barrier, erected perpendicular to the loss axis at a point representing a focus loss equal to the investor's fortune. If any indifference curve attains this barrier, the meaning is that the investor is willing to contemplate the possible loss of his whole fortune, provided this exposure allows him to contemplate a large enough (finite) possible gain. Should he be unwilling,

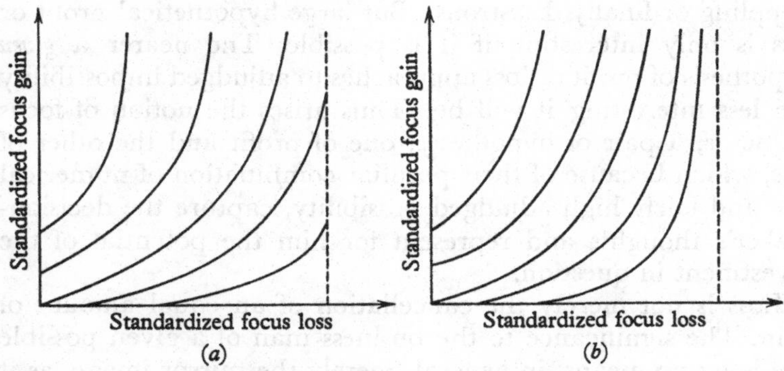


Fig. 1. The broken vertical line at the right-hand side of each diagram represents, by the abscissa at which it is erected, the investor's whole uncommitted fortune. In (*a*) the investor is of reckless, and in (*b*) of cautious, temperament.

for no matter how great an imaginable reward, to expose himself to the loss of his whole fortune, the indifference curves, in their broad shape, must approach the barrier asymptotically, sloping upwards ever more steeply as they are traced from left to right. Now if we see reason to assume that one class of investors will have indifference curves of increasing slope, may we not infer that even those of the other class, who are willing to face total disaster in hope of a big enough prize, will also require larger and larger increments of focus gain to compensate given increments of focus loss? By this argument, we draw all indifference curves concave to the vertical axis. These ideas are illustrated in Fig. 1 (*a*) and (*b*).

An investment indifference map thus defined is concerned with the disposal of the investor's whole uncommitted fortune, that is, the whole of his fortune except such part as he does not mean, on the present occasion, to withdraw from those assets in which it already is. In so far as the map deals with only part of the whole fortune, the shapes of its indifference curves depend on how the rest of the fortune is invested. A man who was holding three-quarters of his fortune in a form which he regarded as subject to only small losses might be willing to contemplate the loss of the whole of the remaining quarter and so the indifference curves of a map referring to this quarter would attain the barrier, standing for the possible loss of the whole of this part of the fortune, at some finite focus gain. If the three-quarters were dangerously disposed, however, the possible loss of the remaining quarter might be unacceptable and the relative indifference curves would approach the barrier asymptotically; and so on. We thus suppose the investor's fortune to be divided into two parts: on one hand, a committed part whose disposal is not in question, which will remain invested in its existing assets and offer, in his judgement, an unchanging spectrum of possibilities of gain or loss; and on the other hand, a disposable part, the whole of which must be accounted for by each scheme which is to be represented on his investment indifference map. *Each* such scheme can then be represented on the map by one or by several points. One problem which confronts us is how, if a scheme falls into several technically distinct structures, such as different plants for the production of different commodities, the several points respectively corresponding to these different structures can be combined into one point; or alternatively, how several schemes, each accounting for the whole of the investor's disposable fortune, can be compared if each is represented by a constellation of points on the investment indifference map. When the comprehensive scheme for the disposal of the whole uncommitted fortune consists of several parts of such a kind that it is natural for the investor to assign to each such part its own pair of focus outcomes, it will not do in general simply to add together the various focus gains to obtain a focus gain for the scheme as a whole, and the focus losses to obtain its focus loss, since, as Mr R. A. D. Egerton has pointed out in a remarkable book,* the circumstances which favour one venture or type of plant may be the opposite of those which favour another. The success of one investment may imply the failure of another. The

* R. A. D. Egerton, *Investment Decisions under Uncertainty* (Liverpool University Press, 1960). See pp. 80 et seqq.

combination of the investor's expectations concerning a set of subschemes must be performed at an earlier stage in his process of thought, at that stage where we suppose him to assign to each hypothesis of gain, from some one subscheme or particular plant, a degree of doubt concerning its possibility. Doubt or potential surprise is at that stage treated as a function of hypothetical gain or loss, and we have elsewhere proposed a rule* by which a set of such curves, one for each plant or subscheme, might be combined into a curve relating to the comprehensive investment scheme for the whole uncommitted fortune. This latter curve would then supply a single pair of focus outcomes for the comprehensive scheme. We need not, however, complicate our main argument with these considerations, for if we suppose, in a quite realistic way, that such part of the investor's uncommitted fortune as is not to be invested in a unified plant to which, as a whole, it will be natural for him to assign a single pair of focus outcomes, will be retained by him as money; and if we further suppose, without any loss of generality for our central purpose, that the investor is concerned only with gain and loss in today's money, and does not concern himself with its possible decline in purchasing power during the life of any proposed plant; then the focus outcomes for the comprehensive scheme, embracing investment in a single plant and the retention of the rest of the uncommitted fortune in money, will be simply those of the plant itself; for the part retained in money can yield, in terms of money, neither gain nor loss.

Let us take stock of our preparations. On the investment indifference map, abscissae stand for focus losses, ordinates for focus gains. Any scheme for disposal of the investor's uncommitted fortune, for which he has determined a pair of focus outcomes which belong to the scheme as a whole, can be represented by a point on the map. The preferred scheme is the one whose representative point lies on an indifference curve above and to the left of all those containing other points. A scheme whose focus loss and focus gain are both zero will be represented by a point at the origin, and any scheme whose focus loss is exactly compensated by its focus gain, so that this scheme is neither preferred to, nor rejected in favour of, a scheme promising zero

* See, for example, G. L. S. Shackle, *Decision, Order and Time in Human Affairs* (Cambridge University Press, 1961), pp. 199 et seqq.

gain and loss, will lie on an indifference curve passing through the origin. Since by assumption the investor concerns himself only with gains and losses of money, he need accept no scheme whose representative point lies below this *origin indifference curve.*

To avoid complications which are not to our purpose, we have elected to consider only those schemes according to which any part of the investor's uncommitted fortune, which is not absorbed in the construction of some single, self-coherent 'plant' whose profitability it is natural to treat as a problem on its own, will be kept in the form of money. The focus outcomes of any such scheme will be those of the plant concerned, and thus we can compare with each other the relative attractiveness to the investor of plants of different technical type and different scale, since all can be meaningfully plotted on a single investment indifference map. Let us finally remind ourselves that by the 'outcome' of constructing such a plant we mean the difference, positive or negative, between the total of time-discounted assumed future operating profits and the total construction cost of the plant. The formula for any one hypothesis concerning such an outcome, $G$, is the familiar one

$$G = \sum_{n=1}^{L} \{v(n) - u(n)\}(1+r)^{-n} - \sum_{n=1}^{K} s(n)(1+r)^{-n},$$

where $v(n)$ stands for assumed sale proceeds of product of the plant in year $n$; $u(n)$ stands for assumed outlays in year $n$ on operation of the plant (outlays for materials, power and labour to make the product); $s(n)$ stands for assumed outlays in year $n$ on construction of the plant; $r$ is the market interest rate, prevailing at the investor's temporal viewpoint, on loans of money, this interest rate being treated here, for simplicity, as one and the same for loans of any length of term; $L$ stands for the plant's assumed economic life in years from the investor's temporal viewpoint; and $K$ stands for the number of years required for construction. We may simply write $G = Z - S$.

By *output* we mean the number of physical units, of some product of constant composition, produced per unit of time. By a *factor of production* we mean a worker of given skill, an acre of land of given soil, climate and type of location, a machine of given design and size, and so on. By a *technique* we mean the use of factors of production combined in given proportions. Within each technique, factor proportions ('technical coefficients of production') are constant. We assume that a plant is designed to produce a single product by a single technique. By the *scale of the plant* we mean its maximum output, which, because of the singleness of its technique, may be taken to be sharply defined.

How will focus outcomes respond to changes of scale: (i) with a given technique; (ii) when advantage is taken of larger outputs to adopt a cheaper technique; and as a cross-classification: (*a*) when construction cost of the plant per unit of scale is constant irrespective of scale; (*b*) when, beyond some scale, construction cost per unit of scale increases with scale; and again: ($\alpha$) with a perfectly competitive product market; ($\beta$) with variously imperfect product markets? These are the questions into which we wish to gain insight.

A *scale-opportunity curve* is the locus of all standardized* focus outcome pairs (gain–loss points) belonging to plants of given technique and differing scale. Laws of nature will impose upon some techniques a lower bound to the outputs they can produce, and there will correspondingly be some smallest size, and smallest construction cost, for which a plant employing this technique can be constructed. Such a bound will often take the form of a smallest practicable size for the plant itself or some part of it. A plant of zero scale will promise no gain and threaten no loss, and therefore if the design of a plant is such as to permit production on an exceedingly small scale, the scale-opportunity curve for this design will pass through the origin. If the product market and the factor markets for this technique (including the market in which the plant itself is bought) are perfectly competitive, and if, as seems formally assured by our assumption of constant technical coefficients, there are within this technique no economies or diseconomies of large scale, it follows that scale makes no difference to the price, or to the cost per unit, of the product, and there seems in consequence to be no reason why the ratio of standardized focus gain to standardized focus loss for such plants should not be uniform for all scales over that range of outputs where the technique in question is the cheap-

* See G. L. S. Shackle, *Expectation in Economics* (Cambridge University Press, 1949 and 1952), pp. 18, 25 et seqq. Also *Uncertainty in Economics and Other Reflections* (Cambridge University Press, 1955), p. 47; *Time in Economics* (North-Holland Publishing Co., 1958), p. 53; and *Decision, Order and Time in Human Affairs* (Cambridge University Press, 1961), pp. 154 et seqq.

est. Over this range, therefore, the scale-opportunity curve would be a straight segment bounded at one end by the origin. This gives us the answer to the combined questions (i), (*a*) and ($\alpha$). If, while still assuming the product market to be perfectly competitive, we suppose that the construction cost of the plant per unit of its output capacity begins somewhere to increase with increase of this scale, then the total discounted construction cost, say

$$S = \sum_{n=1}^{K} s(n)(1+r)^{-n},$$

which must be deducted from total discounted operating profit, say

$$Z = \sum_{n=1}^{L} z(n)(1+r)^{-n},$$

will at each larger scale be bigger than before while the operating profit itself will be the same as under the assumption of constant unit construction cost. Whatever the investor's particular hypotheses about possible operating profit and construction cost, therefore, consistency will compel him to adopt a numerically larger focus loss and a smaller focus gain, for all sizes of the plant beyond the size where unit construction cost begins to increase with size, than he would have done had there been no such increase. Thus beyond this size the slope of the scale-opportunity curve will steadily decrease and eventually turn downwards as in Fig. 2. This is our answer to the set of combined questions (i), (*b*) and ($\alpha$).

There may, of course, be several techniques which allow the scale of production to approach zero. All of these will be represented by scale-opportunity curves which pass through the origin, and amongst them, the one with the steepest curve will evidently be preferred. At some scale, however, the smallest practicable size will be reached of a cheaper technique which we may refer to as the larger-scale technique in contrast with the smallest-scale technique with which we are for the moment concerned. At any scale where it is open to the investor to choose either technique (that is to say, at any scale large enough to make available the larger-scale technique), the smallest-scale technique will surely be assigned a larger focus loss and a smaller focus gain than the larger-scale technique which can produce the product at a lower unit cost. For amongst the investor's uncertainties may be the market price which will prevail, at this and that future date, for the product, and the lower the unit cost at which he can produce it, the less doubtful will seem any supposed operating profit, and the more doubtful any supposed operating loss or the necessity not to operate at all. Thus the smallest practicable scale of the larger-scale technique will be represented by a point *above and to the left*

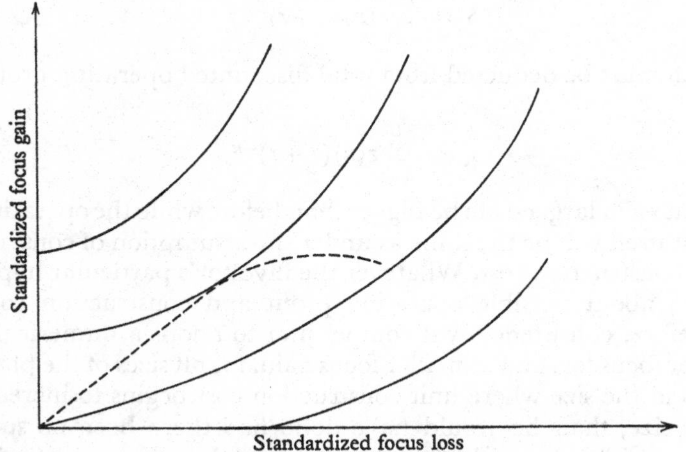


Fig. 2. The scale-opportunity segment is concave downwards because, beyond some scale, construction cost increases with scale.

of the point representing the same scale of the smallest-scale technique. The scale-opportunity curve of the smallest-scale technique could be produced in the same straight line, radiating from the origin, as before, but it would evidently be irrelevant over the range where the larger-scale technique was available.

The notion of a 'larger-scale' technique arises from the supposition that there is some item of equipment which has a smallest practicable size. We shall not here complicate the argument by supposing that such an item can be made only in *one* size, so that the scale-opportunity curve for the larger-scale technique would have to consist of discrete points corresponding to the discontinuous jumps in scale imposed by the need to use one, two, ... items of this fixed size along with similarly multiplied quantities of co-operating factors. The investor, planning his plant *ab initio*, is free to choose any size of each item of equipment, above the sizes appropriate to some smallest practicable scale. So long, then, as we assume perfectly competitive product and factor markets, the scale-opportunity curve of the larger-scale technique will again be a segment of a straight line radiating from the origin, but this segment will start some

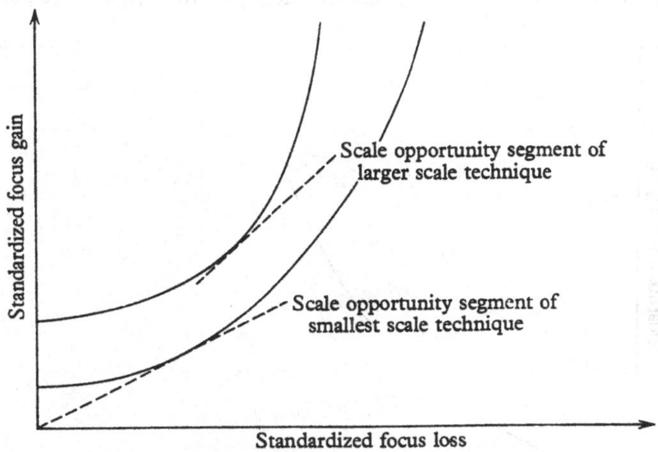


Fig. 3. A fan of scale-opportunity segments contained in straight lines radiating from the origin, these segments having their left-hand extremities successively farther from the origin.

distance away from the origin. It will extend, perhaps, to a point dictated by the existence of a still cheaper technique which becomes available only at a still larger scale; and so on. Thus the picture which answers our combined questions (ii), (*a*) and ($\alpha$) is that of a fan of scale-opportunity segments lying along straight lines radiating from the origin, these segments having successively steeper slopes, and having their left-hand extremities successively farther from the origin, according as they correspond to cheaper and cheaper techniques with larger and larger smallest practicable scales. When we substitute question (*b*) for question (*a*), each segment is concave downwards beyond that point where construction cost per unit of capacity becomes an increasing function of capacity. These conclusions, shown in Figs. 3 and 4, complete our argument under the heading of a perfectly competitive product market.

Concerning this heading, it remains only to remark that the question whether an investor, proposing to set up a plant for manufacturing a particular product, will find himself operating in a perfectly competitive market or not, is one which can be ultimately answered, like all other questions that bear on his investment decision, by his own judgement in the light of a dossier of information of which he alone is fully possessed, since

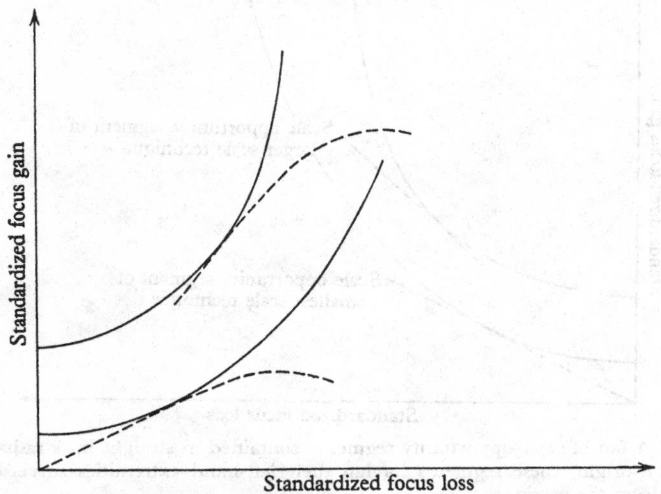


**Fig. 4. Beyond some scale, scale-opportunity segments become concave downwards, because of construction cost increasing with scale.**

this information, as well as his means and standards for interpreting it, is personal to his own mind.

We are bound to recognize that perfect competition is not a highly fruitful assumption for the study of decision-making. In perfectly competitive product and factor markets a business man has, paradoxically, no rivals, but only an impersonal environment which he can treat as a part of nature. He has no need to wonder how other firms will react to his own economic conduct, for they will be unaware of that conduct. Thus his task in selecting focus outcomes for a proposed plant is not complicated by the thought that realized trading profit will be determined largely by his own week-to-week price and output strategy, and by his use of his power to change his customer's image of his own product, either by changing that product technically or by advertising it with this or that special slant. The perfectly competitive trader cannot win and hold a market, nor can he lose one, except by technical inefficiency in production which would make his costs too high.

Competition in general, according to the literature, falls under four or perhaps five chief headings. These form, in the first place, a cross-classification into many-firm and few-firm industries, and into homogeneous-product and differentiated-product industries. Under few-firm or oligopolistic competition we have also the subdivision into cases where firms are of roughly equal size and cases of price-leadership where one firm is dominant. Perfect competition guarantees a market for whatever output a firm can produce at a low enough cost. The business man, projecting a plant to sell its product in such a market, still has to guess what price, in this year and that, the market will set and whether he can produce at a unit cost less than that price. But an intending monopolistic competitor has no assurance of any market at all. It seems inevitable that he will regard given sizable losses as more possible for him than if he were projecting a perfectly competitive plant of the same construction cost, and also that given sizable profits will seem more possible. Physical output comparisons are of course impossible between different types of commodity, and since our monopolistic competitor is, by definition, selling a product which is in some respects unique, we cannot attach any meaning to the notion of plants of equal scale selling in perfect and in monopolistic competition. However, we can connect plants of equal construction cost by a *trace* linking their respective points on the investment indifference map, and this trace, if our argument above is accepted, will move rightward and upward as in Fig. 5 as it passes between plants of equal construction cost, one perfectly and the other monopolistically competitive. Our declared purpose, however, is to consider how focus outcomes will respond to changes of scale. Will the monopolistic competitor judge, as we have supposed the perfect competitor to do, that a doubling of scale should double both focus gain and focus loss? Will he not have in mind some scale, beyond which it will be increasingly difficult and costly, either in terms of price reductions or selling campaigns, to extend his market by each unit amount? If so, will not his scale opportunity curve tend to flatten and even, eventually, to slope downwards?

Product differentiation gives a man a market of his own, without, in itself, appearing to rob other men of their markets. To seek to compete with established oligopolists must surely seem more dangerous still. They may act in concert to ruin the intruder, and, if so, he may be able to hope, at best, only for expensive survival. Not much can be discovered *a priori*,

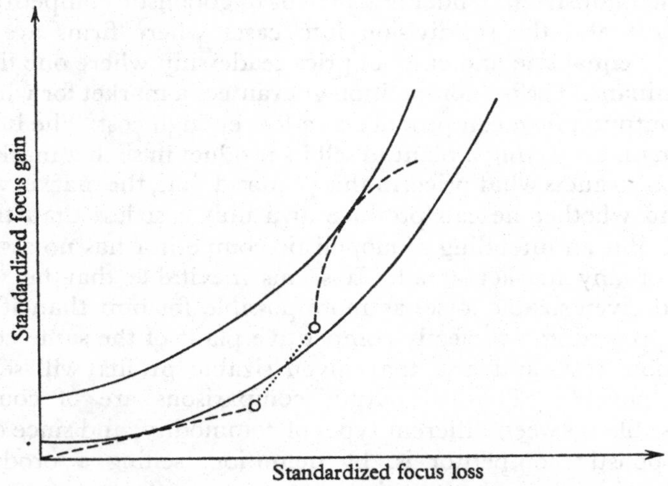


Fig. 5. The 'trace' shown by small dots ... links the respective gain–loss points of two plants of equal construction cost, one intended to sell a perfectly competitive and the other a monopolistically competitive product. The scale-opportunity segment for perfectly competitive plants does not necessarily attain, at best, a lower indifference curve than the segment for monopolistic plants.

however, about the shapes of scale-opportunity curves in complex market situations. If the notion of this curve is found to correspond to business men's ways of thinking, or if they can be induced to translate their thoughts into its terms, the study of its shape can be pursued empirically. We wish to conclude this paper by considering how the scale-opportunity curve will be affected when we suppose the investor to be able to borrow funds at fixed interest so as to construct a bigger plant than he can afford from his own uncommitted fortune.

There are two types of case. If we suppose that the investor's uncommitted fortune is his whole fortune, or if we suppose that for some reason his creditors, if he were to borrow at fixed interest, would have no claim on his committed fortune in the event of his defaulting on his debt to them, then it remains true that he can lose, in the contemplated investment, at most the whole of his uncommitted fortune. In this type of case, therefore, we shall continue to erect a barrier at the abscissa representing this uncommitted fortune, and to say that to the right of it indifference curves are meaningless. But if we suppose that the investor has a committed fortune, the whole of which can be pledged as security, then the barrier must be shifted to the right through a distance representing the amount he can borrow at fixed interest, provided this amount does not exceed the amount of his committed fortune. The barrier can in this case stand anywhere between the two abscissae, representing respectively his uncommitted and his total fortune, its position depending on the total of loans for which he can find lenders.

The first of our two types of case quite transforms the investor's situation, and shows, in a perhaps rather too dramatic way, how a firm can increase both its profit hopes and its exposure to loss or disaster, by increasing the 'gearing' of its capital: scale, risk and profit (understood as *hoped-for*, *ex ante* profit) can all be increased by borrowing at fixed interest. For suppose that the scale-opportunity segment is contained in a straight line which passes through the origin. Amongst the indifference curves which this line encounters, there will be a most preferred indifference curve, and if the point in which it meets this curve belongs to the scale-opportunity segment, this point will show the focus outcomes of the preferred plant, so that the preferred scale of plant can be inferred as the one which has that pair of focus outcomes. If, near the origin, the slope of this line, which we may call the scale-opportunity *line* in distinction from that segment of it which contains the attainable gain–loss points, is greater than that of the neighbouring indifference curves, the meeting of the line with the preferred indifference curve may be a point of tangency, for we have shown reason to assume that the indifference curves will be concave to the vertical axis. We may thus regard as a rather central type of situation that in which the scale of the plant is determined by a tangency between the scale-opportunity *segment* and an investment indifference curve. It is easy, but rather needless, to enumerate those practically relevant types of case which surround this central type. Amongst them will be those in which the indifference curves meet the barrier, representing the investor's losable fortune, without their slope having increased to equal that of the scale-opportunity line. In this case the preferred point will lie on the barrier where the segment meets it, if the *segment* extends so far. There will be the case also where, although the *line* has a tangency with an indifference curve, the *segment* lies wholly to the left or right of this point. Then the preferred point will be at that extreme of the segment, right or left, which lies nearest to the tangency. If, more generally, we take account of non-linear scale-opportunity segments, the curvature of the segment in conjunction with a possibly less tight curvature of the indifference curves opens many other possibilities. What we have now to consider, however, is that when the investor can obtain a loan secured only on the plant he is about to build (a *mortgage* on this plant) it will be possible, so far as finance is concerned, for his scale-opportunity segment to run up the vertical barrier whose abscissa defines his uncommitted fortune, and so carry him perhaps to a higher indifference curve than that with which his scale-opportunity *line* has a point of tangency, provided his indifference curves attain the barrier.

In the circumstances we have just supposed, where the investor cannot mortgage his committed fortune even if he has one, he cannot, by building a plant with his uncommitted fortune and with borrowed money, expose himself to lose more than his uncommitted fortune. Hence he cannot reach any point to the right of the barrier defining that fortune. But as he passes in review larger and larger plants, whose construction would be made possible if he were able to borrow larger and larger sums, approaching and even exceeding equality with his uncommitted fortune, he will steadily increase his focus gain and thus will attain points lying on the barrier at a larger and larger ordinate. Whether this movement up the barrier can or cannot eventually carry him to a point which he will prefer to the point of tangency, will depend on the shape of the indifference curves. If these approach the barrier asymptotically, the one which contains the point of tangency with the scale-opportunity line plainly cannot contain any point on the barrier, and so the point of tangency will be the preferred point. But if the indifference curves attain the barrier, then a higher indifference curve than the one containing the tangency may be attainable. These contrasting situations are illustrated in Figs. 6 and 7.

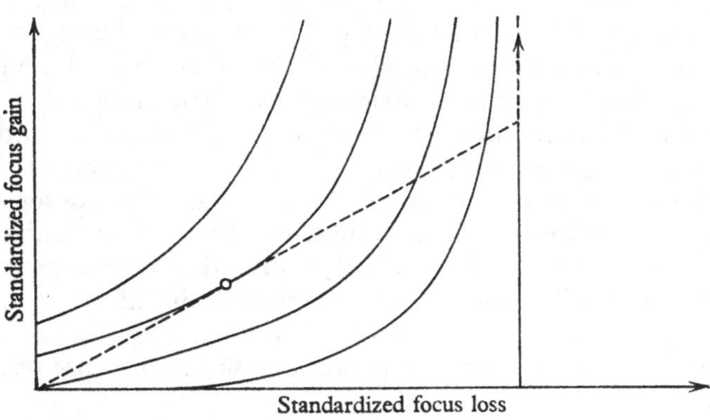


Fig. 6. Because no indifference curve has a point in common with the barrier, borrowing at fixed interest cannot place the investor on an indifference curve preferred to that with which the scale-opportunity segment has a tangency.

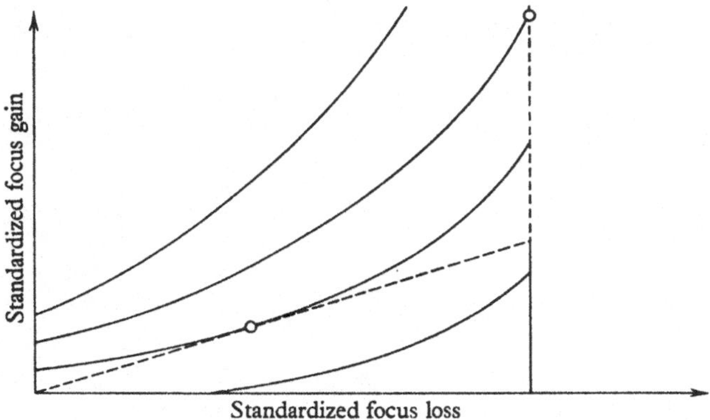


Fig. 7. Borrowing at fixed interest can increase the focus gain but not the focus loss. Thus if indifference curves attain the barrier at finite ordinates, a curve preferred to the 'tangency' curve may be attained.

What is contributed to economic theory in general by the use we have made of the investment indifference map and the scale opportunity curve? Our constructions provide the answer to a paradox or dilemma that is implicit in the notion of long-period perfect competition. For if a firm can sell its product, and obtain *all* of its factors of production, in perfectly competitive markets, so that the demand for the product and the supply of every factor is infinitely elastic; and if (as is the case in the Marshallian long period, or with an investor freely planning an investment on paper), the amount employed of every factor, or the size of every instrument, can, above some lower bound, be precisely chosen in a quite unrestricted way; then there is nothing to prevent the individual firm from being set up on an indefinitely large scale quite incompatible with perfect competition, which thus becomes a self-contradictory idea. To make sense of perfect competition, we need to show what it is which limits the scale to which the individual plant, operated as an independent undertaking, is planned. The investment indifference map shows that the limitation arises from the investor's, and, if he borrows, also his creditor's, reaction to risk in our sense of that term.

# IV

# RESOURCES AND DEMANDS

# 17
# RESOURCES AND DEMANDS

Resources are limited by Nature and the Scheme of Things, but demands are not, and that is why we have a science of economics. Resources are not only limited, but versatile. In a year, the people of a nation, or the world, can produce this set of quantities of a variety of goods, or that set, but if they are using their resources fully and to best advantage, they cannot have more of one thing without having less of another. Amongst these possible sets of outputs, they must *choose.* It is with the principles of this choice, and the institutional means of giving it effect, that economics is concerned.

Amongst these latter institutions there has, up to now, been one of such pervasive and commanding importance that we may well suppose it indispensable to the modern organization of life, or to any organization of our lives which could remotely approach today's civilization in its wealth, convenience and technical power. This institution is money. The basic principle, which has given the modern Western world its previously unapproached command over the physical conditions of life, has been in organizational matters that of specialization and interdependence. These two words name two aspects of a single phenomenon. What we have done is to multiply enormously the number of technically distinct sorts of operation that go on, and the number of distinct tools or parts of tools used in these operations, and to accommodate this complexity to human limitations by giving each man only a minute, simple and constant role in the business as a whole. Finally we have so designed this total business machine that it interlocks almost completely, and every part is in some degree supporting, and in some degree supported by, every other part.

What is the meaning of the activities we gather under the name production? All of these activities are designed to help make our environment more usable and enjoyable, to make our circumstances easier or more agreeable to live in. This environment can be thought of as a collection of things, such as fields and forests, mines, rivers, oceans, stores of seed corn, truck-loads of iron or copper ore, petroleum in tanks, steel billets and sheets, paper and ink, flour, sugar, leather, cotton yarn and an unlistable diversity of other things, and the activities of production can be seen as making these things *more useful*. What we create, by production, is not essentially material objects but the capacities of these objects to serve and satisfy us. For this purpose we turn one thing into another. Fields and seed corn are arranged so that they turn into wheat, which is milled into flour and passed on in that form to the baker to be mixed with sugar from another works, and ultimately from another farm, and so made into cake. The cake is a *consumer's good*, something directly useful to human beings. All these activities are not, in Western countries, centrally organized like a school time-table, which decrees who shall be doing what at each hour of the day. And yet all these activities make up an orderly *system* which can be made sense of as a whole in a way in which it would not be possible to make sense of the individual activities if they were unrelated to each other and were considered in isolation from each other. One man, one factory, one firm, passes on his or its product to another man, factory or firm to be further worked upon and combined with other things until there finally emerges a consumer's good. The total business of production results each day and year in an immense variety of consumers' goods, and some share of these outputs is passed back to each of the people in the factories and firms who have contributed, somewhere along the line or, more truly, somewhere in the web of interlocking processes, to the ultimate emergence of these streams of consumers' goods. All this amounts to the *exchange* of one thing for another. Even in a centrally organized system there would be exchange in a literal sense, for the farm-worker cannot live, and so cannot produce, without clothes and tools made by factory-workers, who in turn cannot live without food produced by the farm-worker. But in the sort of society we live in, the word *exchange* has a special and extra meaning: it means exchange in the *market*, exchange not merely qualitative, of some arbitrary number of ounces of butter for some arbitrary number of yards of cloth, but quantitative and such that the market process settles the quantities exchanged.

The things which are exchanged can be set under three headings. There is, first, human work of all kinds; secondly, the things which are being worked on or with, but which do not directly serve human needs; and, thirdly, the consumers' goods themselves, which are for the direct satisfaction and support of human beings. The business of exchanging these things does not consist in simple bilateral transactions in each of which a Mr A faces a Mr B and each hands to the other just one thing, whereupon the account between them, for that occasion, is held to balance and be closed. Each participant parts with something, his week's labour or his year's crop, to one or many other participants and receives in return, as his real reward, a great collection of things from a quite different group of participants from those to whom he gave his own contribution. If we look upon this seething pattern of activity as barter, as the exchange for each other of things useful in themselves, it is not simple two-sided barter multiplied daily in a thousand million instances, but exceedingly complex barter which requires very peculiar institutional arrangements to make it possible, arrangements which have until now consisted in a *market* whose transactions are *indirect* exchanges each involving *money*. Direct, two-sided barter would of course be utterly unable to meet the case. The farmer cannot get from the miller all the various things he wants for his household and his farm; the steelworkers cannot get from the engineering firms the food, clothes and football matches they need to keep them going, the motor-car firms need components from a hundred other kinds of firms who cannot be paid for these things in motor-cars. The social convention, the universal tacit agreement which makes specialization possible, is that each thing exchanged, whether it be a productive service or a result of production, shall be exchanged in the first instance for *money*.

Here let us ask why we should call the use of money a convention. Is it not just as natural to exchange things for money as for each other direct? It is not, for modern money is not a thing useful in itself and wanted for its own sake. Ultimately and fundamentally, money is usable and valuable only because we are confident that it will be accepted in exchange for things that *are* wanted for their own sake. For what does money consist of, in its overt physical manifestation? Marks in a bank ledger, or small pieces of paper, or small pieces of very cheap metal. Then, what purpose does money serve? Formerly it was often spoken of as a 'medium of exchange'. We might express its primary function better as that of a means of multilateral exchange. But, more briefly, we can call it, in this primary capacity, a means or medium of *account*. The business of production is like a vast river into which streams of goods and services of all sorts are poured, to mingle with each other in a way which utterly blots out the individual source and ownership of the services which produced each item. We have but to ask ourselves *who, by name*, make possible our bus journey? Who mined the coal which smelted the iron which formed the steel, who shaped the steel, who tended the trees which yielded the latex which made the rubber which forms the tyres, who built the ship which carried the rubber, who drilled the well which yielded the oil which drives the engine, who lent the money which built the works which stamped out the body, who? Who, by *name*? For you cannot give something to someone anonymous and unlocated, you cannot pass it from your hand to his. We all know what happens in reality. The great river of goods, drawing in its substance from a hundred million tributary streams, is redistributed like the river which flows out through a spreading and complex delta. For this, what has to be done is to keep account, in some way, of how much, in some sense, each person put in so that he may draw out an equivalent amount, and no more. For if the total of the amounts which people seek to draw out is too great, the system breaks down. Somebody will get less than his due. This is what happens when there is inflation.

'Less than his due': but what is his due? He *contributes* to the river of production one specialized kind of service, he wishes to *draw out* from it a great variety of things. How is the question answered: How many units of his own service will buy him one unit of any one of the things he desires? Or if he is himself a business man, say a farmer, selling things he has produced rather than the means of producing them, how is the *price* of one product in terms of another settled? Or finally, to reduce all these questions to one, how does the market work?

The market is a computer. Its function is to pool information and draw inferences from the combined stock of data. People tell it what things they like and what they can do in exchange for such things, and it tells them how much of these things they can accordingly have. To gather, collate, and interpret information is the whole business of the market. Like other computers, it needs a language, and this language is *price*. Price is expressed in money, and so we come back to my earlier statement, that money, like verbal language, is an indispensable and dominant institution of the modern world. What I have to say further is, first, to elaborate a little my account of the organizing business that the market performs in its language of price, and, secondly, to modify and add essentially to my statement that money is the means of expressing price. It is, for good or ill, much more than that, and hence all the trouble that we experience under the headings of unemployment, or inflation, or both. I do not mean that money is the ultimate *source* of this trouble: that lies in the scheme of human things and particularly in the nature of human beings and the unalterable, bedrock conditions which are 'existence'. But money is the vehicle and seat of the trouble. From it we can trace back the threads to their source, and see what it is in human nature and society that we have to cope with.

Let us, then, make a wild supposition and imagine that instead of going to the shops and refusing, let us say, to pay half a crown for a cauliflower, thus causing the greengrocer to mark it down to two shillings when another customer appears, each householder each week fills in a very large and detailed shopping list, stating not what she *will* buy, come hell and high water, but what she *would* buy at such and such a price, what different amount she would buy at such and such a different price, and so on through the whole list of household requirements. All these forms are then, we are to imagine, sent in to a computer which also receives from farmers and market gardeners and manufacturers similar tables showing how much of this and that they *would* put on the market, that is, make available to the shoppers, at each of a range of different prices. At the very same time, also, the husbands of the shoppers, or more probably their trade union representatives, are sending in forms showing how many hours, in total, the potential workers are willing to work at this rate of pay and that. Having all this information, the computer can get to work. It must allocate to the shoppers in total no more milk, bread, eggs, pairs of shoes, units of electricity and so on than the quantities which it is going to require the potential producers to produce by offering them this or that rate of pay or rate of profit. The prices it puts on things will, of course, affect the value of given rates of pay, and so in principle the potential producers will have to state their offers of work in terms not of a 'money' rate of pay but of a 'real' rate of pay, in which a pound or a shilling means so much actual purchasing power. Here we come, in practice, face to face with the index-number problem, the fact that a pound's purchasing power may change by a larger amount for a man who wants petrol than for one who wants books. In principle, if all the forms could conceivably be filled in in sufficient detail, the computer could dispense altogether even with that de-natured money which we might call a 'unit of account' or a *numéraire*. In theory, it could deal purely in physical quantities of real things (including, of course, real work of hand or mind) and never mention money. But in practice the *conditional shopping lists* and the *conditional work offers* would have to be made in terms of prices expressed, if not in money, then at least in some universal unit of value or unit of account. Subject to this slight limitation, or blurring of the sharpest edge of precision, we can say that the computer would not give anybody 'something for nothing'. It could, indeed, be programmed to pay taxes in kind to the government out of people's pay or profits, but overtly, so that they would know what was happening. The computer, doubtless, would be *programmed by consent* in this respect. In a respectable social system, it would not be open to any Cabinet Minister or official to tamper with this programming, to make the computer give the Government control over resources by a channel which evades, or makes nonsense of, the Budget. The computer would not allow inflation.

Back, then, to reality. What we have in fact is not a computer but a market. The greater the number of units of any one thing, which come to market in a day or a month, the smaller the quantities of other things which the market will give in exchange for each of these first units. For the importance we attach to one extra weekly unit of anything, an extra ounce of tea or gallon of petrol, depends on how many units we are already counting on getting. This importance or urgency of getting a little more translates itself naturally into pragmatic terms, into the quantity of something else that we will *give up* to get that little more. This is the famous 'law of diminishing marginal utility'. Now when money comes to market, it, like everything else, finds its purchasing power to be less, the more of it that arrives in any one day or hour. But there is one great difference. In order to bring more bushels of wheat or bales of wool or bottles of beer or bicycles or books to market, I have to work hard, sacrificing my leisure and my opportunity to make something different. Nature and the scheme of things limit my efforts and the market is seldom flooded with excessive quantities of any of these useful and desirable things. With money, however, it is different. Even as a private citizen, it is quite possible that I can persuade somebody to *make some money* for me, and hand it to me to spend, without my having had to sweat and toil to provide something *useful in itself* in exchange for the things I want to buy, and without the *money-provider* having had to, either. For money can be created by a stroke of the pen, by a nod of the head, if it is the right head, the *banker's* head, and, in particular, the Central Banker's head, nodding with the consent of the Chancellor of the Exchequer and of Parliament itself. If, instead of being a private citizen, I am the Chancellor of the Exchequer representing Government and Parliament, there is no question but that I can obtain all the money I want, by having the banking system create it for me. Let us consider the method of this creation of money, and its consequences.

You and I, and all private persons and ordinary firms who do not act as banks, if we wish to lend money, can only lend money which already exists. We can lend some of the money which has been paid to us as wages or which we have gained as profits, to the Government by buying Savings Certificates or to a company by subscribing to a new issue of its shares. But banks can lend money which has not, up to that moment, existed. The Bank of England can do this for the Government, and the ordinary commercial banks can do it for ordinary people and firms. It is true that the commercial banks, before they will lend to you or me, require some assurance that they will be repaid. We have to pledge our growing crops, if we are farmers, or our stock in trade or our houses or our insurance policies or what not. But these things would exist anyhow. The money the bank lends on this 'security' would not exist anyhow, unless it so happens that the fresh loans the banks make on any day are exactly cancelled by the repayments to them on that day. When the bank gives me permission to overdraw, it allows me to write cheques assigning to other people money which I have not paid in to the bank. If I assign that money to someone whose bank account is already in credit, someone, that is to say, to whom the bank already owes money, then quite plainly he now has, say, an extra £100 over and above what he had before, and this is an addition to the nation's stock of money. But the size of that stock of money, if we are to be consistent, ought to be reckoned by asking: 'What total amount of payments could be made *simultaneously at any one instant* by all the people and firms and institutions, other than banks, in the nation? By saying 'simultaneously' we mean that we shall not allow Mr A to wait until he has paid in a cheque from Mr B before he writes a cheque for Mr C. Now in answering this question, we shall have to include not only all the money *owed* by the banks to the public, but also all the money which the banks have given their customers permission to sign away in excess of what the banks owe them. We shall have to include unused permission to overdraw. So even if the money which Mr A borrows from his bank and pays to Mr B merely serves to reduce Mr B's overdraft, still it makes an addition to the nation's stock of money. But why bother with Mr B at all? The very moment when the bank gives Mr A permission to overdraw is the moment when the extra money comes into existence.

If, then, we ask 'Where do the banks get their deposits from?' the answer is 'From themselves, as a body'. The nation's stock of money is, for the most part, money which the banks have lent to the non-bank public and borrowed back from it. The existence of a stock of money is, as I have reminded you, essential for the working of a modern economic system of high specialization, and the banking system not only provides this stock but offers us a means of making payments to each other, and of storing the money we wish to keep on hand, which is marvellously convenient and safe. We must not blame the bankers for the dangers and drawbacks inherent in the system they operate. Some of these drawbacks are inherent in any money system, even one which uses gold coins and has no banks whatever. Yet it remains true that bank lending, to public or to the Government, when it increases in particular circumstances, can redistribute purchasing power while the flow of goods coming into the market remains unchanged. When this happens, some people have to forgo goods which they would otherwise have been able to buy, which they have reasonably counted on being able to buy with the wages or salaries in exchange for which they gave the labour of their hands or brains, or with the pensions to which a lifetime of hard work has entitled them. Extra creation of money may in some circumstances thus work injustice or provide the vehicle of injustice. But in other circumstances it may be the great irrigating flood of a depressed and infertile economy. We have to consider what these contrasted sets of circumstances are.

We saw that *production* means activities which add usefulness and therefore value to an initial outfit of tools and materials. The *value added* in a week by productive activities can be measured by pricing the things we start with and those we end with, *before* the latter are depleted by consumption, and deducting the total initial value from the total final value. The prices used must be the same for both the initial and final possessions of the society, so far as the things composing each set are of the same kinds. Other prices must be consistent with each other, and will in fact be kept so by competition; for if the market value of some commodity gets its price out of line with the prices of the materials and activities needed to produce it, many firms will step in to try to reap the potential profit. They will produce this commodity at a lower price than it has been fetching, take away custom from the high-cost producers and eliminate the 'supernormal' profits. Thus we see that aggregate *value added* by productive activities throughout the society or the economy (call it what we will) is a measure of the amount of production being done. It is a measure, in units of market value, of the *general output* of the economy. This river of newly produced value belongs to those who have produced it. It is the *income* of its producers. The firms who have organized and fired the spark of this activity have promised *contractual* incomes to their employees, and because no one can know in advance how the goods will sell, these firms and their owners stand a chance of profit or loss when they have paid the wages and salaries, settled their bills for materials and power, and sold the products on the market. Profit and loss are not characteristics of a capitalist economy, they are the inevitable accompaniments of an *uncertain* world.

Who will be willing to risk his energy and nervous strength, his time, peace of mind and money in making things to sell at no one knows what price? Only the man who is willing to gamble, to make a bet. It is *hope of profit* that impels him, *uncertainty* that leaves room for such hopes. But this is by the way.

What becomes of the income gained from production, or rather, what is done with the money which represents this income? Or, in still another form of words, what purpose is served by paying out wages, salaries, rents, interest and dividends? The purpose served is to *distribute* the goods whose production is represented by these incomes. The money incomes are part of the economy's accounting system, giving people claims on shares of what they have themselves helped to bring into being. But now we have to ask: What happens if they do not exercise these claims? Or if they do not fully exercise them?

Let us remember that the aggregate of all the incomes is the aggregate value of all the production. These are two ways of looking at one and the same thing. So if less than all the income is spent, *less than all the production can be bought.* Now income is something which flows like a stream from day to day, from hour to hour, from minute to minute. For production itself goes on like this. If, then, the products are to be sold at the prices that were counted on when it was decided to make them, the relevant income or its equivalent must be spent contemporaneously with the production. If you say to yourself, 'I shall not spend that £1 this week, I shall spend it next month', you are not spending it, you are saving it, so far as *this week* is concerned. And this act of saving, as we shall see, may be a blessing to your fellow men, but only on a certain condition.

If goods are not bought in the quantities in which they are flowing out from the great productive machine, soon it will seem not worth while to produce so much. General output will be reduced. That means that employment will be reduced. When fewer people are employed at given wages and salaries, aggregate income is reduced, and so we get the vicious spiral of deflation. And we can have a vicious spiral of inflation, by precisely the opposite counterpart of the mechanism I have just described. But first let us look more closely at deflation.

Am I saying that if some people save some part of their incomes, it is *impossible* for all the goods, whose production those incomes represent, to be sold? Not at all. For the money saved can be borrowed, and spent instead by someone else. What for? To buy *equipment*, tools, machines, buildings, docks, and all the other things which are not wanted *directly*, by consumers, and are not even wanted by business men themselves to keep their existing facilities in good shape, but are wanted by the business men in order to *improve* their facilities and productive power.

When business men give orders for equipment and spend money on buying it and having it installed, we call these actions *investment* and measure their total amount in value per unit of time. Investment, like production, consumption and saving, is a flow. If all the goods produced in a month or a year are to be successfully sold in that month or year at the prices expected when the production decisions were taken, the gap between income and consumption spending, the *saving gap*, must be filled by *investment*. Now there are two quite distinct interpretations of this proposition. When we look back on a month or a year that has just elapsed, and is now over and done with, we see that certain quantities of goods were produced and the incomes representing them paid out by the firms and received by the individual producers. Any part of this total production which was not bought by consumers must, of logical necessity, still be in the hands of business men, either because these business men invested *intentionally* in goods produced by other business men (other firms) or because they invested *unintentionally* in goods produced by themselves, by producing goods which they meant to, but in the event could not, sell. Thus in any *past* period, investment, intentional or unintentional without distinction, cannot help having been equal to saving. For the goods not sold to consumers are investment, and the portions of income representing the production of these goods, which have, by assumption, been withheld from being spent on these goods, are saving. But this *identical*, unbreakable and logically necessary equality is quite beside the mark when we are asking whether general output, and employment, can continue on their present levels. It is voluntary, *intentional* investment which counts for this question. If the saving gap was filled partly by unintentional investment, by the piling up of unsalable goods, there will be no willingness to go on producing as large a general output in future. What we must look at is the other interpretation of our statement, the forward-looking interpretation referring to what people *intend* to do in a time-interval which has not yet elapsed. If the *intended* investment of this coming period equals the intended saving out of the expected income of this coming period, all the goods intended to be produced in this coming period can be successfully sold and employment in the further future beyond this immediately impending period can continue at the same level as now.

What have we now discovered? That when intended investment (*net* investment, the purchase of equipment *over and above* what is needed for replacement of tools worn out) is equal to intended saving, the total demand, or weekly (etc.) quantity of money offered, for all the goods produced will be just equal to the total value assigned to those goods in advance, by their intending producers, when the decisions to produce them were taken. The outcome will give rise to neither a decrease nor an increase of general output and employment. But suppose that intended investment is *greater* than intended saving? Then the total effective demand (the total of money offers) for goods will be greater than the expected value of production. Prices will tend to rise at first. In the further future period, there will thus be an incentive to increase output. Can this be done? Only if there are unemployed people and surplus machine capacity. If there are, output will go up and prices will not. But if there is no unemployed labour or equipment, output *cannot* go up, and prices will. So long as production cannot keep up with demand for *goods in general*; so long, that is to say, as intended saving is less than intended investment, the prices of things in general will tend to rise. And a rising general price level is what we mean by 'inflation'.

Now there are a number of details to be added to this picture. In the first place, we have to make explicit our tacit inclusion of the Government as a firm. For matters of production and physical consumption (that is, destruction) of goods, it is quite appropriate to consider the Government as a firm. If we regard all that the Government, including its various limbs such as the nationalized industries, produces as part of general output, and all that it buys as part of investment, the formal condition that we stated as the condition of *employment equilibrium* still holds good. That is to say, if we start with a state of full employment, the equality of intended investment and intended saving, *including taxation*, will ensure its continuance. If we start with a condition of underemployment of people and equipment, an excess of intended investment over intended saving will increase general output and employment. But if we start with a state of full employment when intended investment, by business and Government together, exceeds intended saving including the compulsory saving represented by taxation, we shall have a rising general price level.

One further question brings us full-circle to our departure point, the essential nature and operation of money. For how can business men spend more on investment than their current incomes? They can borrow from the public money which has been lying idle in people's bank accounts, money held by these people over and above what they need for day-to-day transactions, money held in reserve, as a precaution against emergency or unforeseeable opportunity or a fall of prices of other assets. The business men will have to pay interest to these people as compensation for giving up the advantages of having money in reserve. (Or if the business men use money which they themselves have been keeping in reserve, they will themselves have to sacrifice the safety and power of manoeuvre which such 'liquid' assets give them.) Will it be worth the business men's while to overcome other people's, or their own, desire for *liquidity*, for money instantly available? This depends, of course, partly on the strength of that desire, on how uncertain, confused and dangerous they think the general business and political situation is; and partly on how profitable they deem the investment opportunities open to them, how large and how *possible* are the gains which these investment ideas suggest. Suppose they decide in favour of investment, what will be the effect? The active money stream, pouring into the market to buy goods, will be augmented by there being discharged into it these still pools of money in reserve. The stream of investment *demand* can thus become bigger than the *supply* of investment goods which saving leaves available.

There is something else that the business men can do. Instead of increasing the *velocity of circulation* of the money stock by borrowing money formerly idle, they can increase its *size* by borrowing from the banker money formerly non-existent. And when we ask what the Government can do, if they want to spend more money per month or year than they are taking by taxation from income-disposers, they indeed have unlimited power to command the creation of extra money by the Bank of England for their use.

Let me try to sum up in one sentence. Price miraculously matches supplies with demands in a world-wide commerce. Price is expressed in money. But money has qualities beyond those by which it serves as the language of the market computer. It is not a rigid system of rods and beams but an elastic rope, which can be stretched and twisted to serve individual desires, and especially those of the Government, not always to the general benefit of society.

# 18
# THE NATURE OF INFLATION

## I. DEFINITION

Suppose I make a list of all the different kinds of goods and services that I bought, for the subsistence and enjoyment of my family and myself, in June 1947, stating exactly the quality and the quantity of each kind, and that I then work out how many pound notes I paid in June 1947 for this 'basket of goods'. And suppose I also work out how many pound notes I should have had to pay in June 1955 for a precisely similar basket of goods. If I now find that the figure for 1955 is 48 per cent greater than the figure for 1947, I shall perhaps put this result into words by saying that between June 1947 and June 1955 'the cost of living rose to about half as much again', or that between those dates 'the value of money fell by a third'; or perhaps I shall merely say, in the autumn of 1955, 'Since 1947 there has been a lot of inflation.'

Another man, working out the corresponding calculation for his own case, might get a ratio of 40 per cent, or 56 per cent, and he too could say, with as much justification as myself, 'Since 1947 there has been a lot of inflation.' The precise ratio might differ in every pair of families. But, moreover, each family could perform a second calculation which would in all likelihood yield a different ratio. Instead of starting with the basket of goods I bought in June 1947, I might start with the different one I actually bought in June 1955 and work out what that would have cost in June 1947. Suppose this showed a 45 per cent or a 60 per cent increase. Which of the two calculations ought I to regard as the true measure of the 'rise of the cost of living', 'the rise of the general price level', 'the fall in the value of money' or 'the amount of inflation'?

The conclusions I would like you to draw from what I have said so far are the following:

First, before we can seek the causes or the consequences of 'inflation' or the means of controlling it, we must be clear what we are going to mean by this word. I am proposing to use it simply as an equivalent for 'a rise in the general price level' or 'a fall in the value, or purchasing power, of money'.

Secondly, there is no uniquely valid way of measuring the degree in which 'the general price level' has risen or 'the value of money' has fallen. There is no end to the number of different kinds of sum we could do to get a figure for the percentage rise or fall between any two dates or short time-intervals. You may feel that it would be inexcusably vague for an economist to say, 'There has been a lot of inflation since 1947.' Ought he not to say how much inflation there has been? He can, indeed, select a kind of calculation, he can use a particular 'index number of prices', which commends itself as being fairly representative, fairly relevant to the circumstances of most of us. But there is no sense in calling some precise percentage '*the* rise in *the* general price level' between two dates. The phrases 'the general level of prices' and 'the value of money' are perfectly sensible ones that we are all quite justified in using. They mean something which is qualitatively clear in essence and which is important and worth studying, but which is also logically incapable of having a unique, universally agreed, exact figure set upon it.

## 2. THEORIES

How did we come to adopt the portentous word 'inflation' to mean no more than a general rise of prices? I think this usage must have had its origin in a particular theory of the mechanism or cause of such a rise. When a given weight of gas is released from a steel cylinder into a large silk envelope, there may appear to be more gas, but in important senses the amount of gas is unchanged. In a somewhat analogous way, we can make our total stock of currency spread over a larger number of paper notes, but this action in itself will not increase the size of the basket of goods (where various goods are present in fixed proportions) that this total stock of currency would exchange for on the market. Bank-notes, of course, are not the main part of our present-day stock of money and I refer to them here only by way of vivid illustration. Some such image as this may perhaps have been in the mind of the man, whoever he was, who first spoke of inflating the currency. This idea, that the general price level is closely related to the ostensible, apparent size of the money stock, the actual total number of money units which at the given instant are standing to the credit of bank customers (leaving aside those who are overdrawn) or are lying in the shop tills or the pocket-books of individuals, has become formally enshrined in what is called the Quantity Theory of Money, which until twenty-five or thirty years ago was the explanation which almost all academic economists would have given of the movements of the general price level.

To state the Quantity Theory we must again begin by seeking a definition. What do we mean by the 'quantity of money' existing in our country at some instant? It seems to me most reasonable to mean the total number of pounds which could, at that instant, be handed over, by everybody in the nation all taken together, including not only private persons but firms and local governments and charitable institutions and so on, in a single simultaneous act to somebody else. I say 'simultaneous act' because, of course, we must not count as two pounds a pound handed by A to B and then by B to C. Now this total of simultaneously expendable pounds will consist, in our modern economic system, of all the bank-notes and coins which are *outside* the banks, plus all the money that the banks owe to their customers, plus, finally, all the *as yet unused* portions of the 'lines of credit', or permission to overdraw, which the banks have given to their borrowing customers. The total of all these three kinds of item is, I think, what we ought in strictness to mean by the Quantity of Money or the total stock of money. And for theoretical purposes we can accept this definition, although if we want to be able to trace actual movements in the size of the money stock we shall have to omit the third item, the unused permission to overdraw, since no statistics of it are available.

## 3. THE VELOCITY OF CIRCULATION

Now just as the size of a gang of navvies does not by itself tell us how much earth will be shifted, since we need also to know how hard each man will work, the size of the money stock needs also to be supplemented by knowledge of the velocity of circulation. Imagine a country where the whole stock of money consisted exclusively of one-pound bank-notes, and suppose a law was passed by which, during a whole year, everyone who received a note from someone else had to sign his name on the back of it. If the number of notes in circulation remained constant throughout the year, the total number of signatures on the backs of all the notes at the end of the year, divided by the number of notes, would tell us the number of times the average note had changed hands during the year: it would give us the velocity of circulation. The total number of signatures would also itself directly tell us the total value of money payments made during the year, and we could consider ourselves, in working out the velocity of circulation, to be simply dividing this total value of all payments by the size of the money stock. Looked at in this way, the calculation of velocity can be performed regardless of whether the stock of money consists of tangible pieces of paper which actually change hands, or whether this 'changing hands' consists merely of the mutually corresponding ups and downs of book-entries in bank ledgers.

The 'total of money payments made in a year' needs further definition. We might make it all-inclusive, comprehending in it not only those payments, such as wage, salary, rent, interest and dividend payments and the spending of money in shops, buses, theatres, the payment of taxes, and so on, which belong to one or other side of the circular income–expenditure process, but also the payments by the baker to the miller, by the miller to the farmer, and so on, and also the payments for 'second-hand' rather than newly produced goods, in particular, the payments for 'old' securities bought on the Stock Exchange. For our purpose it is perhaps more relevant to include only the income-circuit transactions, the total of which would give us twice the national income. Let us, then, use the letter $M$ for the number of pounds constituting the nation's stock of money, which we may suppose to remain approximately constant during, say, a year; the letter $V$ for the velocity of circulation obtained by dividing the total value of income-earning and spending transactions during the year by the stock of money; the letter $T$ for the total number of such transactions, and the letter $P$ for the number of pounds changing hands in each such transaction, on the average of all the transactions. By these definitions, the total annual value of income-earning and spending transactions will be $P \times T$, and $V$ will be equal to $(P \times T)/M$. So, *by definition*, we have $M \times V = P \times T$, the famous 'Quantity Equation' on which, until thirty years ago, most explanations of the movements of the general price level were based. In what sense can this truism, as it undoubtedly is, 'explain' anything?

## 4. THE QUANTITY THEORY

A modern defender of the Quantity Theory might, I think, argue somewhat on these lines: The velocity of circulation depends largely on such business habits as paying wages weekly and salaries monthly, with the corresponding tendency for people to have, at each particular stage of the week or the month, some fairly regular proportion of a month's earnings in their pockets or their bank accounts. Thus (it might be claimed) the velocity of circulation will not change in a wild and arbitrary way over periods of a few years, and as a first approximation we can treat it as a constant. Next, so long as we have full employment, the size (in some broad, vague but perhaps still meaningful sense) of the stream of newly produced goods and services, and that of the stream of services being yielded by factors of production in the making of these goods, will vary only with the building up of equipment and with the advance of technique, and its growth within a period of a few years will only be by a few per cent. Thus $T$ also, in our formula, can be taken as a constant. This leaves us with the result: average price level multiplied by some constant equals quantity of money multiplied by another constant. If we accept this, it follows that any given percentage increase in the size of the money stock must be accompanied by an equal percentage increase in the general price level. And it would further follow, of course, that if you want to prevent prices from rising, you have only to prevent the money stock from increasing.

Few economists nowadays would advance the crude argument that I have outlined. But there are still some whose policy recommendations are plainly and avowedly founded on the Quantity Theory, and who say in effect: 'Even if changes in the general price level are not rigidly linked with changes in the quantity of money, at least it must surely be admitted that if only you keep the quantity of money strictly within some limit, there will be a definite 'ceiling' above which the general price level cannot go. It is perfectly easy to prevent an indefinite rise of prices simply by keeping the quantity of money fixed.' Let me make my own position clear. I agree with the statement. But I think it ought also to be admitted, first, that if policy consists in no more than rigid limitation of the quantity of money, there is every possibility that we shall bring back a violent manifestation of the trade cycle, the ghost of which still disturbs the slumbers of some economists; secondly, that the political courage needed to enforce such a limitation at the present juncture is very great, and if a sharp fall in employment from its present 'flood' level (which fall, as I shall try to show, is a necessary condition for the stabilization of the general price level) begins to appear, the government may lose its nerve; and thirdly, that as a theoretical basis for monetary policy the Quantity Theory is exceedingly crude and can be replaced by something far better.

## 5. HISTORY

Historical facts, and our feelings about what constitutes an 'explanation' in economics, alike condemn the Quantity Theory. It becomes informative only if we can assume, for one thing, that the velocity of circulation, defined in a way which is relevant to the price level of newly produced goods and services, is virtually constant over periods of years. But history affords little support for this assumption. It has been estimated that the velocity of circulation of the money held in current accounts in the banks of Great Britain and Ireland, in making payments arising directly from industry and commerce (excluding, that is to say, those involved in Stock Exchange and other purely 'financial' transactions) was equivalent to over $14\frac{1}{2}$ annual changes of owner in March 1920 and less than 9 annual changes in July 1921. In the late 'twenties it was often around $11\frac{1}{2}$, and in 1933 it twice dropped to below 9. The amplitude of these latter fluctuations is of the order of 25 per cent of the mean level of about 10. But, after all, is there any strength in the argument that unchanging business habits ensure a steady velocity? Individuals and firms do not at all times keep only so much money in their current accounts as will just suffice to enable them to make their regular and foreseeable out-payments. At ordinary times they may keep enough to give themselves convenient elbow-room, and perhaps to provide some reserve against contingencies, being able at a pinch, on the other hand, to manage their affairs on very much smaller balances. There is an even larger loophole. All the money on deposit account can, if necessary, be drawn into the 'active' stream, and this consideration means that the velocity of circulation of the nation's stock of money as a whole, the stock over whose size the Chancellor of the Exchequer, via the Banking System, has control, can, in principle, fluctuate far more widely than that of total current accounts alone. Let us, then, abandon the Quantity Theory and consider an alternative, which I shall call the Keynesian theory, although its origin can be traced back to the great Swedish economist Knut Wicksell and the closing years of last century.

## 6. KEYNES'S THEORY OF THE GENERAL PRICE LEVEL

If we divide the means of production into broad classes or 'factors of production', such as land, labour and equipment, it is plain that these differ widely in the ease with which the productive machine as a whole can avail itself of a larger quantity of one or other of them. Labour can work overtime and people who do not normally work outside their homes can be induced to do so. But the farmer's fields are working 24 hours a day, and cannot do overtime. The same applies to blast-furnaces and ships, and although double or treble shift working can enable some kinds of machines to serve a much larger labour force than they normally do, this often entails extra expense per unit of output. Let us use an analogy. The nation's outfit of land and of machines is like a basin of fixed size and shape, into which a smaller or larger quantity of labour can be poured. The output of goods and services can be represented by the area of the liquid in the bowl. This area will get larger as we pour in more water, but while at first the water will spread rapidly over the saucer-like bottom of the bowl, it will spread more and more slowly as it rises up the steadily steepening sides. You may object that the nation's outfit of machines and buildings, its 'equipment' in a very broad sense, is *not* fixed in quantity and is, indeed, being augmented every day. But in comparison with the rapidity with which the number of man-hours per week in a particular industry can be changed, this building up of equipment is a relatively slow process. In the economist's language, equipment can be taken as given 'in the short period', a period which is still long enough for the quantity of labour engaged in production to be treated as highly variable. Thus when we want to increase output, successive equal increments of man-hours a week yield successively smaller increments of output. Yet each of these extra man-hours costs just as much in money wages as each of those that were already being worked, indeed the extra hours probably cost more, because they often represent overtime, or double shifts. So as we increase output by putting more and more labour to work within a more or less fixed frame of fields and factories, the money cost per unit of goods produced goes up.

## 7. THE SIZE OF OUTPUT AS A WHOLE

This is only the first stage of the theory. For although it may be easy to grant that money cost per unit of output will rise as the size of the total stream of output increases, we still have to ask: What governs the size of this stream, what influences make it get larger or smaller? It was in answering this latter question that Keynes's special contribution was made. Keynes wrote in a situation the exact opposite of today's, a time of the heaviest unemployment ever known, and it will be easiest to understand his theory if we look at it first with that sort of background in mind.

If output as a whole is to remain at any given level, all of the goods produced have got to find buyers at the prices in expectation of which they were produced. If the buyers are not forthcoming, goods will pile up unsold and prices will be reduced to clear these unwanted stocks at the smallest loss, and output will, of course, be reduced. Reduction of output reduces incomes, and reduction of incomes keeps away buyers, so that the decline of effective demand, of employment, incomes, output and prices goes on, as it did in the early 'thirties, until they reach levels where people even with their reduced incomes are buying the whole of the very greatly shrunken stream of output. How is it that a new 'equilibrium' can thus be attained? Why does not everything go on falling until there is no output and correspondingly no income? To answer this we have to break the total demand for output down into its main components; or, taking a slightly different point of view, we have to ask what various main channels can be distinguished which, between them, must necessarily carry away the whole of output. For the whole of output, the totality of all the goods and services produced in each month or year, has somehow to be accounted for, something must happen to it, and it is accounted for in four main ways. Either it is consumed, that is, simultaneously enjoyed and destroyed, in our own home country; or it is exported; or it is added, whether by original design or because nobody has bought it from the producer, to our accumulated store of useful goods; or it is bought for some purpose other than consumption in households and other than investment, by the Government. We may call these four channels consumption, export, investment, and Government demand respectively, and it will be perceived that amongst them there is a 'balancing item' which ensures that, when we look back on any period, say a year, from the end of it, the total of the goods which have gone down these four channels is exactly equal to the total of goods that have been produced. The balancing item is unintended investment, the piling up of goods which have not succeeded in getting sold, and this item may, of course, in opposite circumstances become the selling of goods out of store, goods which have not been currently produced. Thus it may be best to make our four channels into five and say that they are consumption, export, designed net investment, unintended accumulation or depletion of inventories, and Government demand. How is the size of each of these channels governed? And in what various sets of circumstances can it come about that the balancing item is nil, so that we have an 'equilibrium' situation?

## 8. CONSUMPTION AND INVESTMENT

Many of us are painfully aware of the difference between income before tax and income after tax, between gross income and disposable income. It is the size of a person's disposable income which, given his tastes and family circumstances, mainly determines, according to Keynes's theory, that person's yearly expenditure on consumption. Out of a small disposable income he will have little or nothing left over, after he has paid for current necessaries. If he is a person enjoying a modest affluence his expenditure will naturally be larger, yet he will leave some of his income unspent on consumption, will save it; and in past days when some disposable incomes ran into tens of thousands of pounds a year, there were no doubt men who lived lavishly, yet saved much the greater part of their incomes. Thus the rule goes: pick two men at random out of different income brackets, and much more often than not the one with the larger disposable income will both spend more *and save more* each year than the other. All this may sound almost too obvious to need saying, but it leads to a very important conclusion: As a person or a family is pressed down into relative poverty in one way or another, by unemployment or by high taxation, the absolute amount saved by him in a month or a year gets smaller and ultimately vanishes. Thus when unemployment is heavy and many people are very much worse off than they are used to being, they spend nearly all the income that is left, and the self-reinforcing process of falling employment, falling incomes, and falling effective demand is at last arrested because effective demand refuses to fall any further. This is how we get a 'depression equilibrium'.

It is, of course, by no means only the poorest of the poor who save nothing. Incomes in low brackets can be greatly increased without any great increase in the amount their recipients save. Thus it is possible to increase a nation's total annual expenditure on consumption by taxing income away from those with relatively large incomes and giving it, in the form of subsidized housing, free health services, free education, free school meals, and so on, to those with small incomes, who thus have more of their incomes left for other forms of consumption and do actually so use it. The rich pay their taxes partly out of what they would otherwise save, the poor spend the proceeds of this taxation on consumption; and in the result the nation spends more and saves less out of any given aggregate income. All this is unavoidable if we are to have a Welfare State; and it goes a long way to explain why the employment situation has been, since the war, so unrecognizably different from what it was before the war.

Now let us look at the scene from the other direction. When aggregate disposable income is high, and especially when its distribution is such that a large proportion of it is in large and very large disposable incomes, the stream of saving, the annual number of millions of pounds of disposable income that are not spent on consumption, will be large. Now this stream of saving is, from one point of view, a gap that has to be filled. For it is a part of *income* and has therefore been earned in the production of goods which, if equal quantities are to go on being produced, have got to be sold. By assumption, they cannot be sold to consumers, and so they have got to be sold to one or other of the three remaining possible buyers: the foreigner, the investing business man, or the Government.

## 9. INVESTMENT

By investment, let me emphasize, economists mean the actual business of installing machines, of building factories, power stations and pipelines, of sinking wells and mines, and so on. What induces men to do this? The prospect that the use of these things will produce goods salable for more than the things themselves cost to operate; the prospect that, in each of a series of future years, the operation of each such piece of equipment will yield a profit. How big must these hoped-for future profits promise to be in order to make it seem worth while to lay out a given sum on installing the piece of equipment?

There is in relation to this question an argument as familiar to professional economists as it seems strange and esoteric to business men, which I must bring in here for the sake of the light it throws on some extremely topical issues. We are all familiar with those massive books used by actuaries and others, in which one can look up the 'present value of £1 deferred so and so many years at such and such an interest rate'. The longer the deferment and the higher the interest rate, the less is the present value of £1. Now the prospective profits from using a piece of equipment are, evidently, deferred, and by the same token we are not justified in taking them at their face value in judging how much they must amount to in order to make the investment in this equipment worth while. We have to take their 'present value' as shown by the actuaries' tables for the appropriate rate of interest. This is one way of looking at the mechanism by which a high rate of interest is said to discourage investment.

But *does* it discourage investment? If we consult the officers of local authorities concerned with housing, who have suffered three or four times in the past few months a raising of the interest rate they must pay to the Local Loans Board, we shall hear harrowing tales of the consequent need to raise rents to prohibitive levels. Certainly a high rate of interest discourages the building of houses. But if we ask business men whether rates of interest make any difference to their decisions whether or not to instal new or additional machines, we shall be told no. What we ask ourselves, they say, is whether a proposed installation will 'pay for itself in three (or four, or five) years'. How can this paradox be resolved?

In the reckoning whether a highly complex plant or machine is worth installing, there is a far more potent factor than any ordinary change in interest rates; there is the impossibility of knowing for sure whether it will in fact enable large quantities of goods to be sold at a paying price or whether a change of fashion will cause demand to veer away, or whether, again, the machine will be superseded in a year or two by something much more efficient still. The business man may feel that he can look ahead for two or three years; he will not feel that he can guess much about what may have happened in ten years. Thus prospective yield from a machine means the profits it may yield in the next two to five years; beyond that they are a will-o'-the-wisp. Now it is easy to see that the present value of sums of money deferred only a year or two is not much affected by a change of interest rate from, say, $3\frac{1}{2}$ to 4 per cent, and correspondingly the 'present value' or 'demand price' of a machine, whose claim to be profitable will only be taken seriously by the business man in so far as it rests on promised profits, at the rate of 30 or even 50 per cent of first cost, to be earned during the first three or four years of its life, will also respond in only an unimpressive degree to such changes.

How different it is with houses! The need for house-room can hardly go out of fashion, nor are revolutionary designs of house thought of as likely. The bulk of houses built this year can reasonably be counted on to go on earning a rent for 30 or perhaps 60 years, and the present value of such streams of earnings, stretching far into the future, is very greatly affected by changes of interest by, say, one percentage point.

## 10. EXPORTS AND GOVERNMENT SPENDING

In its immediate effects on income and employment, the making of goods for export is very much like the making of goods for augmenting our capital equipment. In both cases incomes are earned in making goods, but the goods which result are not available to be bought for consumption with the incomes their making represents. Thus exporting, like investing, is a way of filling the gap between production on the one hand and consumption demand on the other, though we have to remember that that gap is made bigger than it would otherwise be by the fact that consumption demand is partly satisfied by imports. If the value of goods exported and that of goods imported were exactly equal, exporting would in a sense make no net contribution to filling the gap.

And lastly, and of a like order of size as investment and exports, there is Government expenditure on goods and services, much of which expenditure, like that on defence, is a 100 per cent effective creator of employment, since the goods and services produced do nothing whatever to satisfy any kind of economic demand.

## 11. THE PICTURE UPSIDE DOWN

Hitherto I have spoken as though the great problem was how to find channels of demand to carry off the excess of full-employment output over the private consumption corresponding (with given tax rates) to this state of employment. This is the picture which Keynes saw in the 'thirties, and the one I have deliberately used to explain his system of thought. But now we have to turn the whole thing upside down. Instead of thinking of the gap between output and consumption as something difficult to fill, we have to think of it as a quite inadequate hole into which an unwieldy total of exports, investment, and Government expenditure has somehow got to be crammed. The basic explanation of our present inflationary troubles consists in showing how it is that the hole has become too small or the bundle of things to go in it too big.

First, there is the great rise in the standard of living of a large part of our people, who now enjoy clothes, domestic gadgets, entertainment, and holidays strikingly different in quantity and quality from what some of them used to have. Taken by itself, this increase in consumption tends, of course, to make the gap smaller than it would otherwise have been. And there is another thing which has the same effect. Our imports of goods, which in themselves (apart from the question of how we pay for them) serve largely, of course, to meet our needs as consumers, have decreased in annual quantity by about one-eighth since 1938, and this has left more of our consumption to be met directly by home production than would otherwise have been the case. But even more important than these hindrances to the widening of the gap is the fact that the bundle of things which have to go in it has become so much vaster.

The annual quantity of our merchandise exports, compared as well as may be by value adjusted for price changes, is more than one and a half times what it was in 1938, yet this quantity must not be allowed to fall if we can help it, for it barely suffices, taken with our 'invisible' services to foreigners and what is left of our income from overseas investments, to buy what we need from abroad and meet our obligations to other countries. The annual value of our merchandise exports is nowadays equal to about one-sixth of the annual value of our output as a whole.

Next there is the acceleration of the pace of growth of our stock of capital goods, our buildings, plant and machines, vehicles, roads, forests, flocks and herds, and so on. Taken over all these sorts of things, the stream of newly produced capital goods needed to make good the wear and tear and the obsolescence of the existing stock and provide, on top of that, for this pace of growth was, in real terms, that is, measured by value adjusted for price changes, one-sixth greater in 1954 than in 1938. This stream of newly produced capital goods, the stream of gross investment, is also equal, like exports, to about one-sixth of the value of our output as a whole.

Lastly there is the expenditure of central and local government on goods and services, which is nowadays equal to one-fifth of our national output,* compared with one seventh in 1938.

* Gross national product.

## 12. THE EFFECTS OF INFLATION

A general price level which has for a decade or more been rising at, say, 8 per cent per annum, and, because of this prolonged past climb, is widely expected to go on rising at a similar pace, has some advantages. In such circumstances it is unprofitable to hold large bank balances, and these tend to be spent quickly on goods or on equity shares in firms which own concrete equipment. Such action, of course, reinforces the inflationary pressure, but it also promotes production and employment. Full employment, if only it is full enough (that is, as at present, 'brimming over') is for this reason in some degree self-maintaining. If prices are going to go on rising everyone wants to get 'out of money into goods' and there is a strong demand for more goods to be produced. But inflation, even of the 'walking' as opposed to the 'galloping' kind seen, for example, in Germany in 1923, has also some extremely undesirable consequences.

Unless there is a capital gains tax, or unless profits taxes are so heavy as to make business impossible, inflation is in one sense tax-defeating. For the owners of ordinary shares are tempted to treat as income the tax-free capital gains which they enjoy, and to spend them on consumption. This leads evidently to an injustice, for poorer people who are not shareholders are thus in effect taxed more heavily on their disposable spending power than those who can live by gradually killing the geese which are laying the golden eggs. But this is a minor matter, in view of the small numbers rich enough to live on capital, compared with the injustice, still miraculously tolerated, which inflation inflicts on holders of fixed-interest securities. What is the use of receiving 3 or 4 or 5 per cent gross on one's savings, paying nearly half of this back to the Chancellor of the Exchequer in tax, and being left with, say, 2¼ per cent net to compensate for an annual fall of 7 or 8 per cent in the value of the principal? Why, after sixteen years of a persistently falling value of money, do people still buy ordinary Government securities, or even tax-free Savings Certificates and Savings Bonds with their rather better net yield to payers of standard-rate income tax?

I believe the reason is, at bottom, a basic ingrained human desire for some safe means of storing wealth. One method, which limited liability and Stock Exchange organization make possible, is to 'spread the risks' over a number of ordinary shares, but when the quantity of wealth is only a few hundreds or thousands of pounds effective spreading is very expensive. People are no doubt aware of the inflation that has occurred, but they are still much under the spell of the so-called 'money illusion', and think that, at worst, the pace of fall of the value of money will get no worse, will not be allowed to become disastrous, and so it is better to hold Government securities whose money value (if we ignore the unhappy post-war experience with irredeemables) is known, rather than put all one's eggs in an industrial basket which may smash.

The negative reward effectively paid to those who trust the Government with their savings is, however, only part of a larger matter. Great numbers of people besides those, often quite poor, who depend mainly for their livelihood on trustee securities, have salaries fixed by law, custom or accident at some level which stays the same, regardless of all changes in price levels, until someone takes deliberate action about them. The action is usually overdue, slow when at last it comes, and insufficient even then to catch up with the inflation. The case of the High Court Judges' salaries is only the most spectacular instance of something which affects the entire professional and administrative classes of the nation, and not them only, but skilled manual workers also, who are continually being made relatively worse off when all workers, skilled and unskilled alike, get the same *absolute* rise of wages.

The injustice that arises from inflation, in the mulcting of creditors and the penalizing of those whose incomes are more 'sticky' than the prices of goods, leads on to further troubles resulting from the attempted remedies. Those who borrow on mortgage may be required to repay the principal at a rate which bears very heavily, because otherwise their creditors think they will prove to be financing them at a negative rate of interest. This seems very well, but it presupposes a continuance of the inflation and a further rise of the borrowers' incomes, and who can tell? I have chosen a trifling illustration of what may, after all, be a pervasive effect of uncertainty about the future value of money affecting very many people.

The hindrance that inflation imposes, unless compensated by repeated exchange depreciations, on our efforts to export, and the serious drawbacks which attend depreciation, if we resort to that remedy, are even more serious; for, literally, we live by exporting, and anything which makes it harder to sell goods abroad is desperately dangerous.

And, lastly, there is the constant nuisance and frustrating disorganization and inefficiency, affecting every single person in some measure, that springs from the strikes by which people seek to prevent themselves from getting left behind by the inflation.

## 13. INFLATION A BLESSING OR A CURSE?

On balance, then, is the kind of 'walking' inflation we have now been experiencing for sixteen years a good thing or a bad? This really means, of course, is it better or worse than the alternative? We do not really know what the alternative is. We do not know whether 'full employment', in some sense which would satisfy all reasonable standards of 'welfare' without being at all like the present absurd excess of jobs over workers, is compatible with a constant value of money. A constant value of money would not, let us remember, mean a constant level of money wages. Productivity per man-hour goes up by several percentage points every year, and to that extent money wages can go up too without causing the prices of goods to rise. But our experience of the last sixteen years has been that when unemployment vanishes, money wages are pushed up several times as fast as the rise of productivity.

This is the form, then, in which I think the question about inflation should be put, this is the really vital aspect of the matter: how much unemployment should we need in order to have a stable price level of goods? In this form it becomes plain that inflation is a sociological and psychological matter and not a narrowly economic one only. For plainly, if all of us guided our conduct with a sufficiently enlightened self-interest and enough self-restraint, we could have a stable price level along with no matter what degree of full employment. Whether there is any hope, in our scheme of things as it is, with universal suffrage and the consequent temptation to politicians to buy votes by spending money, and with trades unions which, naturally and inevitably in fulfilling their nature and *raison d'être*, act as monopolists of the supplies of the various kinds of labour; whether in such a set-up there is any hope of combining tolerable freedom from unemployment with freedom from all the frictions, frustrations and injustices of a constantly rising price level, I doubt if anyone can yet say. Let me turn briefly, then, to the purely economic mechanisms by which we could seek to bring inflation to a halt, and consider which of them offer the best hope of doing this without also destroying prosperity.

## 14. HOW INFLATION CAN BE HALTED

A large part of this chapter has been taken up with the attempt to show that essentially it is the size of the flow of outlay, the total stream of effective demand from consumers, foreigners, investing enterprisers and the Government together which, taken in relation to the size and shape of the channel of productive resources that must carry this stream away, determines the level of prices and whether or not this level is going to rise. If demand is only, so to speak, a small stream, in a wide estuary where there is ample reserve capacity, the flow can be greatly enlarged without causing the depth of water to rise markedly. But if the channel is already occupied from side to side, any increase of the flow must carry the level rapidly and far up the steep sides. The flatness or the steepness of these sides represents the flatness or steepness of the 'supply curve of output as a whole' or of 'goods in general'. Now although we can steadily dig the channel out, and this is in fact being done all the time so long as our stock of machines and other equipment is being augmented by saving and net investment, and so long as improvement in technique is increasing the productivity of each man and each machine, yet the stream of effective monetary demand can rise far more swiftly than the productive channel for carrying it can be enlarged. To prevent inflation the only way sometimes is to reduce the stream of demand. For this there are, broadly, three kinds of policy: monetary, fiscal, and what I will call 'regimentary'. By this last I mean the statutory imposition of rationing and dictated prices.

Regimentary policy offends against what, I hope, is still a national passion for freedom and for the dignity of the individual. But in addition to this, if more is needed, it frustrates the free expression of consumers' desires, not only reducing their effective demand but preventing them from getting as much satisfaction as they might even from their reduced consumption. It distorts the relative profitability of different products and attracts resources away from those very kinds of production which, because the demand for them is so insistent and their output so insufficient, are the first to be rationed and price-controlled. Regimentary control is fit for war but not for peace. Let us turn to the other two.

Monetary policy has three types of action. By a ukase from the Chancellor of the Exchequer bank advances can be rationed; and this could be done without any raising of interest rates. Or again, by his edict, interest rates charged by the banks could be raised without any rationing of advances. Or, as is happening in the autumn of 1955, both rationing and higher interest charges can be applied. The direct squeeze upon overdrafts is inevitably more arbitrary and more liable to cause hardship than the simple raising of interest rates. It is even doubtful whether this measure should not come under the heading of regimentary policy. The mere raising of interest rates on overdrafts without any other kind of monetary action might have small effect in a strongly running tide of prosperity. Real monetary policy consists in causing interest rates of all kinds to rise as a market response to a reduction, through open-market selling of securities by the Bank of England and the consequent reduction in the credit base, of the size of the money stock. Higher interest rates make it more worth while to postpone consumption but less worth while to construct durable equipment. Thus, in theory and principle, the effect of the raising of interest rates is to lessen the pressure of immediate demand for consumable goods and to release resources from capital goods production to increase the current output of consumable goods. From both the demand side and the supply side we thus restrain the tendency of their prices to rise. And the effect is more subtle than appears in that statement. For, in the way I tried earlier to explain, it is the construction of those kinds of instrumental goods whose usefulness is stretched out furthest into the future, and which do least to help satisfy consumer demand in the near future, which is most strongly discouraged by high interest rates. Like a lens which focuses all the rays of a torch upon the spot where they are needed, high interest rates tend to concentrate productive effort and power upon satisfying the demand which is near in time at the expense of the demand which is remote. In doing this they act in the respectable, traditional, impersonal way of market forces.

Lastly we have the latest invention for opening and shutting the economic throttle. In the old days taxes were levied because the Government, like any private person, needed money to spend. Nowadays it is realized that by merely spending more on its own account, for goods and services, than it concurrently takes out of the incomes of the citizens, the Government can increase the stream of effective demand; and by spending less itself, in any year or month, than the amount which, by taxation, it prevents the private citizens and firms from spending in that year or month, it can *pro tanto* decrease the total stream of effective demand. By merely putting heavy taxes on what would otherwise be a stream of saving by individuals or firms, and spending just the resulting revenue without deficit or surplus, the Government can increase demand. It is impossible in a paragraph to even touch upon the immensely subtle and complex questions of the effects of different schemes and levels of taxation. It is enough to ask whether, with a tax system under which the most able, audacious and imaginative members of society, the most skilled, highly trained, responsible and self-disciplined citizens, when they make a special effort on top of an arduous and strenuously lived existence, to improve and augment the nation's stream of production, receive as their own reward sometimes less than three-fifths, perhaps even less than half, of the market value of the fruits of this extra effort, we are likely to cure inflation by a still heavier imposition of tax penalties upon productive effort. It is for this reason that I applaud Mr Butler's present efforts to restrain demand by monetary means; and why, still more, I applaud his efforts to abate the folly of unnecessary spending by Government departments and local authorities.

# V

# INTEREST AND INVESTMENT

# 19

# RECENT THEORIES CONCERNING THE NATURE AND ROLE OF INTEREST*

## PREFACE

The place of interest rates in the economic process has since 1945 been mainly discussed, within the literature in English, along three lines: first, criticism and defence of Keynes's position; secondly, advocacy of a stock or of a flow analysis, or of the need to combine them; thirdly, examination of the claim of interest to be a suitable and effective regulator of the pace of growth of the nation's wealth. The following survey tries to explain and criticize this debate and to interject some suggestions into it, without aiming at more than an illustrative coverage of the literature. It is earnestly hoped that the absence of any name from this article will not be taken to imply any judgement on the value and importance of any person's work.

## PART I. THE NATURE OF INTEREST

### 1. *Types of economic theory*

When we have no theory about economic affairs, no state of those affairs and no temporal succession of states seems inconceivable. A theory restricts the conceivable states and successions of states to those in which the relations between quantifiable things in the economy conform to some specified rules. Theories differ from each other in the list of quantifiable (not necessarily measurable) things to be considered, and in the precise character of the rules about their interrelations. This meaning of 'economic theory' leaves unlimited the number of different theory-classifying schemes we can set up. But in historical fact the cleavages between groups of theories have run along a few clear lines, which can for practical purposes be

* This is the third of the series of special articles, referred to in the *Economic Journal* of June 1960, designed to give a summary of recent developments in economic theory and supported by the Rockefeller Foundation.

easily defined. These lines, of course, intersect each other and yield cross-classifications.

One dichotomy is between *equilibrium* and *development* theories. Equilibrium is a test that selects for the economist one particular situation out of an infinity of situations and justifies his calling attention to it as something special. Judged by the smallness of the ratio of what it accepts to what it rejects, no other test seems able to rival its selective power. No other test, it may also be claimed, can state so sharply in what the accepted differs from the rejected situations. By contrast, no test of comparable power and conviction can be found for selecting among paths of development. On the most general grounds, equilibrium has great claims as an economizer of thought. To dispense with it has meant, in practice, to be reduced to mere factual enumeration. For ninety years few economists, save the German historical school, have based their theories upon any other principle. Even those most anxious to disparage it as a *description of what is* and, still more, of what ought to be, have none the less needed it as a means of understanding and of accounting for what is. Even Keynes's *General Theory of Employment, Interest and Money*,* so strongly repudiating some of the conclusions of equilibrium theories, was itself an equilibrium theory in its method.

Theories may secondly be distinguished according to the mode of choice which faces their acting subjects. When a theory supposes the available alternatives to be perfectly known to these subjects in every respect which concerns them, I shall speak of a theory of *pure* choice. Under any other assumption the acting subject has, with greater or less freedom, to create his own list of alternatives before he can choose among them. If the alternatives are not *given* to him, or in so far as they are not given, he must necessarily produce them by his own thought, judgement and imagination. Choice of this two-stage kind I shall call *impure* choice.

A subject facing pure choice has no motive for not dealing at once with every question that arises concerning the details of the action he shall adopt. For he knows everything about the consequences of every available act. But a subject facing impure choice may elect a 'simple' immediate act designed to secure

* London: Macmillan, 1936.

freedom of deferred choice among more specialized alternatives. In fact, rather than decide what to buy, he may elect to retain money. In theories of pure choice there is thus room for money only as a unit of account and none for money as a store of value, an *asset*. But all the interesting properties of money arise from its use as an asset. Thus theories of pure choice are 'non-monetary' theories.

Finally, we must make a subdivision within the equilibrium method. For this method can, paradoxically, be concerned either with *events* or with *states*. *Long-period* equilibrium is, of course, a state, and its meaning may even excuse us from asking whether it would, given stability of all the 'non-economic governing conditions', eventually be attained or not. There are degrees of strictness with which long-period equilibrium may be interpreted. We may mean by it the perfect and complete adjustment of everything in the economy to everything else, a general equilibrium attained after no matter how long a time. Or we may have in mind a period sufficient for some particular impulse (such as an increase in the money stock) to have worked itself out through the system as it exists, even though that system itself may not be in complete long-period internal adjustment. Let us call this a 'middle-period' equilibrium. Middle-period equilibrium is also, then, essentially a means of studying states.

When we seek to determine a state of affairs in which, if the economy ever arrived at that state, it could remain at rest, because this state is one of long-period general equilibrium, we are not concerned with the path from the existing to that ultimate state, we are not interested in the *event* or chain of events carrying the economy from one situation to the other. But in the short period the temporary and partial equilibrium, which defines, as it were, a gravitational force acting on the economy, serves rather to describe an event than a state. It answers the question 'What will happen next to the economy?' The two meanings of equilibrium are thus rather sharply contrasted in regard to the part they play in analysis. In its short-period connotation, equilibrium can enable a dynamic tale to be told in static language.

## 2. *Keynes and the classics*

If we have spent some time preparing the foregoing classificatory scheme, our reason is that theories can appear to be widely divergent and contradictory, while in fact, because they are answering different questions, they are perfectly harmonious. An example is provided by the first source we shall consider. Professor Patinkin* finds Keynes's interest theory wrong on almost all counts. In this criticism, however, Patinkin is setting a long-period equilibrium analysis of almost pure choice, which therefore is in vital respects non-monetary, against Keynes's short-period equilibrium analysis of impure choice treating money in its full-blooded sense. No reader of Keynes's article 'The General Theory of Employment',† published in February 1937 in answer to critics, will be in doubt that Keynes looking back saw as the main theme of his book the commanding importance of uncertainty and of the conventions by which the insoluble problems it poses, and the nonsense it makes of pure 'rational calculation', can be shelved in order to make life possible at all. Professor Patinkin, by contrast, says: 'The limited objective of this [Patinkin's] book...is to understand the functioning of a money economy under perfect interest and price certainty.' And a little earlier: 'Once the Pandora box of expectations and interest and price uncertainty is opened upon the world of economic analysis, anything can happen.' Patinkin's analysis, worked out with watch-like precision, is concerned with money as a means, merely, of meeting random demands for payment, and not as a means of speculation or of deferring specialized decisions.

Patinkin, then, quite excludes those Bulls and Bears who would otherwise smash up the china shop of rational economics. They are, to a degree which Patinkin, despite an incomparable scrupulousness towards his reader, does not perhaps sufficiently make clear, the heart of Keynes's liquidity preference theory. Once the transactions motive is satisfied, all the rest of the existing money must be held by Bears (or at least, non-Bulls), of whom there have got to be enough for this purpose. The busi-

* Don Patinkin, *Money, Interest and Prices* (Evanston, Ill., U.S.A.: Row, Peterson, 1956).

† In *Quarterly Journal of Economics*, vol. LI (February 1937).

ness of the interest rate, *qua* equilibrator of liquidity preference, is to move to such a level as will create these necessary Bears, or eliminate some of them if there are too many. Nor are we, in this dynamic world of speculation, free to think of the speculative demand for money as depending solely on the *level* of the interest rate. At any moment this demand may be powerfully influenced by the most recent *movement* of the interest rate, its extent and speed. We may go further. People who are holding money because they think the interest rate will rise may decide to hold it no longer if they observe the interest rate to remain where it is. For at a constant interest rate (that is, constant prices of bonds) they are missing an income (namely receipt of interest) which they could have with no offsetting capital loss. Thus if the constancy of the interest rate has been due to a force of non-Bulls just brought to sufficiency by the presence in it of some Bears who count on a rising rate, this constancy will soon destroy itself by disillusioning these Bears, who will buy bonds, and cause the rate to fall. Interest may be *inherently restless*. All this is outside the limits of Professor Patinkin's concerns. It is, indeed, beyond the range of the equilibrium method.

His main contention is a simple and compelling one. Money's usefulness, no matter in what context, derives ultimately from its exchangeability for goods (including factors of production) of those kinds which are wanted for their own sake or for their *technical* transformability into goods wanted for their own sake. Money by definition cannot be enjoyed, consumed or made a physical tool of; it can, ultimately, only be exchanged. It can be stored, but even then only with a view to its being in the end, at some time or other, exchanged. It can be lent, but only with the result of promising more money later on, which money will then be serviceable only by being exchanged. If you are holding money with a view to paying for things, the quantity of money you need depends on the prices of the things you have contracted to pay for. The marginal utility of a given stock of money thus depends on the price level. This is true whatever the *proximate* motive for holding the money, whether it be to bridge the unforeseeable time-gap between receipts and spendings or to make the time-shape of spending different from the time-shape of income by the issue or purchase of bonds, or even (so

Patinkin says, and here we are not quite so readily convinced) to make a capital gain in the bond market.

If, by Government decree, the British unit of currency were altered overnight from the pound to the florin, everyone whose bank had owed him £100 would now be owed 1,000 florins. Everyone who had owed his tailor £20 would now owe him 200 florins. Everyone who had yesterday purchased a bond for £1,000 due to be redeemed in one year's time for £1,050 would now own a bond due to be redeemed in one year's time for 10,500 florins. If, in the familiar way, tastes, techniques and real resources were the same today as yesterday, nothing that mattered to anyone would have changed. In France the transition to the 'new franc' is almost an example, in reverse, of the very thing we have supposed. Why, in either of these cases, should the interest rate change? There is no reason.

Change of the currency unit and re-expression of all prices, debts and money stocks in terms of the new unit is, in comparative statics terms, the same thing as a change in the quantity of *each person's* money and of all prices, all incomes and all debts in one and the same proportion. Can it be claimed that this is what an increase in the total money stock will in the long period achieve? If all prices and wages were flexible; if the extra money were introduced in such a manner that everybody's holdings (positive or negative) of bonds and holdings of money were increased in one and the same proportion; if expectations were inelastic; if there were nowhere any money illusion (no tendency to regard a ten-shilling note as something in itself and not merely as ten shillings' worth of purchasing power at the prices happening at any moment to prevail); then an increase in the economy's total stock of money would leave the rate of interest unchanged for the same reason that a change in the currency unit would do so. Professor Patinkin is scrupulous to point out how far from practical reality some of these necessary conditions are. But he does believe that those which are least easily accepted are also the least harmful to the long-period neutrality of money. Equi-proportionate changes in every item of a list in which every individual's money holding is an item, his bond holding is an item and his debt on bonds he has issued is an item are wildly unlikely; but if tastes are not too dissimilar this may not make much difference. Elastic expectations he dismisses as incompatible with meaningful economic analysis. And as to absence of money illusion, he seems to be in two minds whether to make it an assumption or to claim it as a consequence of rationality.

Many who have spoken of money as a veil have failed to make explicit the conditions on which this neutrality will be achieved, and have not, in particular, insisted that money balances as well as money incomes must be supposed to be multiplied by the same factor as prices. Turning this necessary condition round, Patinkin shows that money balances cannot be increased without bringing into play forces, of that utterly familiar kind consisting in the observance of the equi-marginal utility principle, which will in the long run, and unless obstructed by law or human perversity, push prices up in the same proportion as the balances have been increased. These forces will at the same time, given this price flexibility, cause the quantities of bonds issued and held by firms and individuals to be increased in yet again this same proportion. All these consequences together constitute what he calls the 'real balance effect'. Time will, indeed, be needed for all these changes to work themselves out through the system, and while they are doing so the rate of interest will be lower than before. But when they have done so, an increase in the stock of money will, as Ricardo* and Wicksell† said, leave the interest rate unchanged.

Keynes must be supposed, according to Patinkin, to have thought that an increase in the stock of money would permanently over-satisfy liquidity preference at the former interest rate, and would therefore lower the rate to that level where the increased transaction balances required by the increased general output or the higher prices (or both) due to the increased investment flow at the lower interest rate would soak up such of the extra money as was not wanted by the lower rate's newly created Bears. How could he believe this? By believing that asset-holders as well as wage-earners were money-illusioned. We may well think it natural for those who had experienced the gentle deflation of 1920–35 to be very differently conditioned towards money from those who, in 1956, had suffered fifteen

* R. S. Sayers, 'Ricardo's Views on Monetary Questions', *Quarterly Journal of Economics*, vol. LXVII (February 1953).

† Knut Wicksell.

years of continuous quite rapid *in*flation. Circumstances alter cases. But there is more than this. Keynes saw economic life as made up of events and not of states. His method only was an equilibrium one, the picture he sought to explain was of booms and depressions, inflations and crises, continual challenge and change. 'Equilibrium is blither', he (orally) said.

Patinkin draws from his model the following conclusions on interest:

(i) In a world where each individual feels certain that he knows, for each future date within his horizon, what interest rate, what price of each good and what level of his own income will prevail (that is, a world of 'interest, price and income certainty'), a greater than zero interest rate could exist, and would be accounted for by the desire of people to consume according to a different time-shape from their incomes, and by the desire of entrepreneurs to make profits by investing in equipment. [We may note that a world of 'interest, price and income certainty' is by no means the same as a world of perfect foresight. In Patinkin's model expectations are held with certainty, but are in general not correct.] Not only does interest belong to a world of certainty as well as to one of uncertainty, but 'a proper approach to interest differentials begins in the classical manner with the determination of the rate on long-term bonds by the basic forces of thrift and productivity, and goes down from this rate to the shorter-term ones'. [The latter part of this sentence is disturbing to a reader who is basically willing to see in Patinkin's work, not a competitor to the liquidity preference or Bulls and Bears theory, but a solution of a quite different problem. That problem is indeed the 'long-period' one. But what has this to do with 'long-term bonds'? They are the objects of day-to-day and hour-to-hour speculation like any Stock Exchange security.]

(ii) The threefold role of the interest rate is to equalize for every individual (in his private or his entrepreneurial capacity) the utility of consuming a marginal amount now with the utility of having the prospect of consuming the compound-interest-increased equivalent of this amount in the future; to equalize for him the utility which his marginal unit of money holdings affords by its liquidity with the utility which a bond, purchased with it, would afford by promising interest; and to equalize for him the interest he could obtain (or avoid paying) on the marginal bond with the rate of profit promised by the equipment purchasable with the price of this bond. This 'three-fold margin' was so named by Sir Dennis Robertson.*

(iii) An increase in the economy's total money stock does not inevitably or essentially entail a change in the long-period equilibrium rate of interest. Any such change will arise from the special *distribution* of the extra money, and not from its coming into existence. To believe otherwise it is necessary to believe in money illusion on the part of asset-owners.

(iv) 'The amount of money demanded depends upon the rate of interest, the rate of interest does not depend upon the amount of money.' This merely means that the rate of interest does not depend only on the amount of money but also, among other things, on prices, which when time has been given following an increase in the economy's stock of money, will increase in the same proportion as the stock, thus leaving the 'real' situation and the equilibrium rate of interest unchanged. When we add that the amount of money demanded also depends on prices as well as interest, the paradox vanishes.

The facts support Professor Patinkin in his chosen context. Huge increases in the British quantity of money have been accompanied over the past twenty years, not by a fall but a rise in the long-term and, far more dramatically, in the short-term interest rates. But this long-period context is nothing that Keynes ever had in mind.

In his review article in the *Economic Journal*,† Professor Hicks applies his incisive diagrammatic tests to reach much the same understanding of Professor Patinkin's book as our broader approach above has led us to. That book is concerned, Professor Hicks says, with 'full equilibrium' (this appears to us identical with 'long-period' equilibrium). Full or long-period equilibrium assumes that money wages, along with all other prices, are perfectly flexible downwards as well as upwards. (The question whether this flexibility requires time or not is, let us interject, inapplicable to long-period equilibrium, for whose

* 'Mr Keynes and the Rate of Interest', in *Essays in Monetary Theory* (London: Staples, 1940).

† J. R. Hicks, 'A Rehabilitation of "Classical" Economics?', *Economic Journal*, vol. LXVII (June 1957).

purposes time is not scarce.) It is in assuming this downward flexibility that the full-equilibrium theory, which is the 'classical' theory as Keynes meant that term, differs from Keynes's theory, whose primary assumption (realistic for the 1930's but not for the early nineteenth century) is that the money wage is given and, for institutional reasons, will not fall and, for reasons of abundant unemployed resources, will not rise as employment changes. With perfect upward and downward wage flexibility, Professor Hicks shows that real income (measured in wage units) can stand at one level, and one only, given the community's income-and-consumption schedule, the marginal efficiency of capital, the quantity of money and the absence of any speculative motive for holding money. For only at one level of real income will the amount that people wish to save out of that income be equal to the investment which, given the interest rate corresponding to the given quantity of money *and that level of real income*, the entrepreneurs are willing to do. If the entrepreneurs, all taken together, tried to have a larger investment flow than this the result would be a rise of prices and money wages without any increase of employment or output, for the unique real-income point is a point both of full employment and 'full unemployment'. This rise in prices, in face of the fixed quantity of money, would shift the income–interest-rate schedule towards the interest-rate axis, and thus, by raising the interest rate corresponding to a given real income, drive investment down to its former level. Similarly, a too small investment flow would lower wages and prices and reduce the interest rate corresponding to any given real income, and so push investment and income back to their former levels. In this model it is the 'real' factors of productivity and thrift which determine the interest rate. If thrift were weaker the 'saving gap' between production (that is, income) and consumption would be smaller, a smaller investment flow would suffice to fill it, this small investment flow (given the schedule of the marginal efficiency of capital) could be induced by a higher interest rate; and prices, given the quantity of money, would adjust themselves upwards so that this quantity of money only just sufficed for the transactions and precautions needs at this higher interest rate. Or if the marginal efficiency schedule (productivity of capital) were to shift, again a different interest rate would arise just sufficient to induce the investment necessary to fill but not over-fill the saving gap. In this model it is the level of money prices, and so, given real income, the level of money income, which is altered if the quantity of money is altered. In terms of Dr Hahn's* analysis, which we shall discuss below, the classical full-equilibrium economy was effectively 'decomposed' into two independent subsystems, the 'real' system, which determined *everything* 'real', including the rate of exchange between present and future goods, and the 'money' system, which determined only the arbitrary monetary name (measure) of the real income, etc., determined elsewhere, which it was powerless to influence in any other respect.

In pointing to the absence of downward flexibility of wages as the essential difference between the full-equilibrium model and Keynes's model, Hicks neglects in the early part of his discussion, as Patinkin does throughout, a feature which is even more characteristically Keynesian, namely, the speculative motive for liquidity. For in this neglect there is involved, given the denatured marginal efficiency schedule which in the full-equilibrium model is no more than a physical productivity schedule, the neglect of the whole matter of uncertainty of expectation. Hicks does insist, however, on the third vital difference between Keynes and all the classics, including Patinkin: the classics were concerned with the full long period, which is the same as to say, with full flexibility. Keynes was concerned with the short period, in which some things are stickier than others.

Quite at the end of his article (superb in its clarity and penetration) Hicks brings up reluctantly the speculative motive like a shameful atom bomb to settle the matter. He has shown that the question whether unemployment can be cured by monetary expansion turns on whether we assume full flexibility of the interest rate so that it can fall to whatever level may be needed for the stimulation of a full-employment-giving level of investment, below which it cannot be forced by any ordinary expansion of the money stock:

> In order to show that we get a better understanding of these problems by considering effects [of shifts of the marginal efficiency schedule or the income-consumption schedule] on employment and income first, and then correcting by possible repercussions through

* F. H. Hahn, 'The Rate of Interest and General Equilibrium Analysis', *Economic Journal*, vol. LXV (March 1955).

interest, all that is necessary is to maintain that there are ranges over which the repercussions through interest will be rather insignificant. To do that no more is necessary than to emphasize the ability of speculative funds to stabilize the rate of interest against considerable disturbances. Which is effectively what Keynes did.

To treat the transaction motive as central and the speculative motive as incidental or peripheral is as though an oceanographer should study the inflow from rivers but neglect the tide. Professor Hicks has, however, preferred to defend Keynes with classical and not with Keynesian weapons, for even he, it seems, is not willing to give Keynes full applause for his great *tour de force*: the writing of *earthquake economics* within a framework of comparative statics. One more remark seems here permissible. The theory against which Keynes has to be defended is the classical theory, which shows interest to be determined by the 'real forces', productivity and thrift. That theory also shows that there can be no such thing as unemployment. It was this sort of approach which, seen from the standpoint, say, of 1933, aroused his formidable contempt.

Professor Patinkin's 'Rejoinder'* to Professor Hicks was concerned only with insisting again on the 'real balance' or 'Pigou' effect, whereby, it is claimed, a fall of prices, by increasing the purchasing power of people's stocks of money, will induce them to spend more [when? over how long a period? in how thin a lifelong trickle? or (abandoning Patinkin's unswerving assumption of 'rationality') in how disturbing a burst of extravagance?] on commodities. The question in this regard is whether people who are saving out of income take *income* or *assets* as the proper measure of the basis of their spending power. But this whole question and Patinkin's Rejoinder bear on the theory of employment rather than on that of interest.

The classical case is the long-period case. In terms of comparative statics we ideally compare, not the states of one economy at two different dates, however remote from each other in time, since then one state must precede and 'lead to' the other, and we are always tempted to ask about 'flexibility' and other things strictly irrelevant; but we compare two structurally identical and atemporal economies (with tastes, techniques and

* 'Keynesian Economics Rehabilitated: A Rejoinder to Professor Hicks', *Economic Journal*, vol. LXIX (September 1959).

nearly all resources identical between the two) in one of which the quantity of money, say, is larger than in the other; and we observe what other things must then also be different.

The same 'classical' conclusions for the long-period (or as we should say, atemporal) case, at which Professor Hicks arrives diagrammatically, had been put forward in 1944 by Dr Franco Modigliani* in an argument which, however, Dr F. H. Hahn in 1955† found self-contradictory. Dr Hahn reports as follows Modigliani's conclusions:

> If the supply function of labour is homogeneous of degree zero in all prices including money wages [that is, if equi-proportionate changes in all prices leave unchanged the quantity of labour supplied], then
> (i) the rate of interest is determined by investment and savings [saving?] and
> (ii) liquidity preference determines the level of prices and *not* the rate of interest.

If, says Dr Hahn in effect, the 'real' variables (that is, relative prices, the rate of interest and the size of the general output of all goods together) form a self-contained system sufficient to determine all its own variables and impervious to any and all other influences, while the quantity of money and the level of absolute (i.e. money) prices form a separate and independently self-determining system, then, if we reject Say's Law, we might have a situation where the 'real' system was in disequilibrium, with total demand for commodities exceeding total supply, and yet where the 'money' system was in equilibrium, with the demand for and supply of money equal to each other. But this, says Dr Hahn, would contradict Walras's Law, according to which the total demand for all goods, *including money*, cannot fail to be (is identically) equal to the total supply, since 'all goods' includes everything in terms of which demand can be exercised and likewise everything comprised in 'supply'. However, if we assume Say's Law, that is, *identical* (unconditional and logically inevitable) equality between total demand and total supply of all goods *other than* money, then by Walras's Law there must also be identical equality between the quantity demanded and the quantity supplied of money, so that, since this equality holds

* 'Liquidity Preference and the Theory of Interest and Money', *Econometrica*, vol. XII (1944).

† 'The Rate of Interest and General Equilibrium Analysis'.

regardless of any change in the size of the money stock (the supply of money), no such change can serve to determine the absolute price level; there is no need for any particular price level to equalize the demand for and the supply of money. By this dilemma, between a contradiction if we reject Say's Law and the indeterminacy of absolute (that is, money) prices if we accept Say's Law, Dr Hahn holds Modigliani's argument condemned.

We think that in this part of a highly ingenious article Dr Hahn is over-subtle. No doubt it is true that unless *both* systems, real and monetary, are in equilibrium, both must be in disequilibrium: there must be excess demand in both (numerically equal and of opposite sign) or in neither; but when the 'real' system is in equilibrium, this equilibrium includes a determinate interest rate, to which the given *nominal* money stock must accommodate itself by appropriate change of the absolute price level and so of the real purchasing power represented by the given nominal money stock. There is, we are assuming, equilibrium in the 'real' system and so, by Walras's Law, there must be equilibrium in the money system; and this latter equilibrium can be attained because by assumption changes of the price *level* do not disturb the equilibrium of the real system.

This is the escape from Dr Hahn's two-pronged fork, if we are prepared to reject Say's Law; and surely Say's Law, true in a *non-monetary* economy, can find no logical basis in an economy which uses money. If goods are in fact bought and sold for money, and a money stock exists in the economy, it seems plain that money can be withdrawn from the stock and used on the commodity market, thus upsetting Say's Law. But suppose, against all reason, we insist on believing in Say's Law in the 'real' part of a money economy? Then surely we must ask for a *complete* money economy. What is wrong with Dr Modigliani's model is that it makes no mention of bonds. How can money be lent except in exchange for bonds? If, then, the money system in Dr Modigliani's model comprises money *and bonds* it can obey a 'Say's Law' of its own in the sense that the total demand and supply of monetary assets (money *and* bonds) must be identically equal, and still determine the interest rate by an equilibrium money price of bonds.

Dismissing theories which make interest to depend only on

productivity and thrift, or on the *ex ante* equality of saving and investment, because such theories take no account of people's decisions what to do with their accumulations of *past* saving, which exist at all moments in various forms exchangeable for each other at prices which express the interest rate, Dr Hahn turns to theories which do concern themselves with the prices of *old*, as well as those of *new*, bonds. These other theories are, first, the loanable funds theory, which says that the interest rate will change unless the excess demand for bonds is zero, and, secondly, the liquidity preference theory, which some have interpreted as saying that the interest rate will change unless the excess demand for money is zero. Dr Hahn, however, rejects this latter interpretation. For people can add to their money balances by supplying, in any interval, productive services in excess of the value of goods they demand for consumption in that interval. But Keynes explained that liquidity preference enters only at the second of two decision stages involved in the satisfaction of people's time preferences. At the first of these stages the individual must decide how much of his income to consume or how much to save, and here there is no question of liquidity preference. At the second stage, however, he must decide in what kind of assets he shall hold the results of saving, and here alone liquidity preference is involved. A theory which says that the interest rate is what equilibrates the demand and supply of money can, therefore, in particular circumstances imply that the interest rate equilibrates *reluctance to save* with desire for liquidity. The next step of Dr Hahn's reasoning from this consideration is not quite easy to follow. For he is not satisfied simply to accept the consideration as a necessary consequence of discussing the interest rate in terms of a model of general interdependence. On these latter lines we might be inclined to dismiss this objection against regarding the interest rate as the price which eliminates an excess demand for money. For on what *general* ground can we elect the rate of exchange between one pair of mutually exchangeable things as worthy of attention and ignore that between another pair? Sir Dennis Robertson's threefold frontier between consumption, the purchase of earning assets and the accumulation of liquid ones, and indeed the general interdependence conception as a whole, require us to look upon the desire to consume, and the desire to accumulate liquid assets, as possible direct rivals of each other. In particular circumstances the motive to save may be the desire not for wealth in general but for the security or manoeuvring power conferred by *liquid* wealth. I may be willing to forgo wine for a year in order to have one hundred pounds in the bank, but not in order to pay off one-tenth of my mortgage debt. Apparently accepting such a view, Dr Hahn nevertheless argues that 'liquidity preference must be taken as determining the *ratio* ('form') in which assets are demanded, and *not* the total quantity of assets demanded or supplied'.* The argument which he builds on this leads us, by an interesting fresh route, to that question and difficulty which in my own view are the supreme enigma of interest theory and the real source of all its troubles.

Let us suppose, then (Dr Hahn says), that at some date *ex ante* saving is less than *ex ante* investment, and that accordingly there is an excess supply† of bonds. Suppose also that the *ratio* in which money and bonds are demanded is the same as that in which they are supplied. In this case the loanable funds theory predicts a rise in the interest rate, but Dr Hahn's interpretation of the liquidity preference theory predicts no change in the interest rate. Dr Hahn none the less reconciles the two theories. Excess-demand equations, he says, are to be understood as holding *ex ante*; that is to say, the equality of the two sides is looked to be attained at the end of some still future 'planning period' (which we may distinguish as the investment planning period). His model assumes that investment plans are (objectively; presumably within the knowledge of some super-human observer) certain to be fulfilled. This in turn implies that investors will during the (investment) planning period obtain the necessary finance. Thus within that period two transactions must take place: first, bonds must be sold for money, and then this money must be used to buy investment goods (machines, etc.). Extending from the investor's 'present' to some interior date of the investment planning period, therefore, there is a second and shorter period which we might call the finance planning period. There are in fact two planning periods, a shorter one concerned with obtaining finance and a longer one concerned with using it. Corresponding to *each* of these there is a pair of ratios, the ratio

* 'The Rate of Interest and General Equilibrium Analysis'.

† By a slip Dr Hahn's article refers to an excess *demand* for bonds.

in which money and bonds are demanded and the ratio in which they are supplied. Between the members of one of these pairs (in particular, the one referring to the end of the investment planning period) there can be equality notwithstanding that between the members of the other pair there is inequality, an inequality caused by the intending investor's temporary need to accumulate funds ready to spend on investment goods. As soon as this spending actually takes place the equilibrium of the investment planning period will re-assert itself over the disequilibrium of the finance planning period. Both theories are right: the loanable funds theory, which says that there will be disequilibrium in the finance planning period, and the liquidity preference theory, which says that there will be equilibrium in the investment planning period (in the circumstances assumed, viz. a ratio between the supply of money and that of bonds which is correct provided demand is not distorted by the need for 'finance' for investment schemes).

If, in thus reconstructing Dr Hahn's argument, I have preserved its essence, we have, I think, to recognize two very important questions which it raises. The first is whether it is useful or appropriate to think of finance and investment not merely as distinct stages in each separate equipment-augmenting operation by each individual business man but also as *observable* stages in the economy's aggregate flow of equipment augmentation. For surely the release of finance which occurs when one firm spends its hoard can supply the need of another firm to build up its hoard? To say this is not in the least to deny that when a *given* aggregate national income contains a large investment component there may be required a different ratio of money to bonds from what is required when the income consists wholly of consumption. For when all transactions are small no marshalling of great sums may be needed. It will also be true that when the investment flow is planned to increase, the interest rate will tend to rise because the necessary extra finance will have first to be marshalled and then later released. But, secondly, a much more interesting and radical difficulty confronts us. The length, in calendar terms, of the planning periods is not a matter of indifference, for the relative quantities of new and old bonds offered for sale during such a period will depend on it. More fundamentally, what is the meaning, in the theory, of the length of the planning period and what determines it? These questions raise a basic theoretical and methodological issue, that of the co-existence in some markets, and pre-eminently in the bond market, of two separate possible equilibria, an equilibrium of stocks and an equilibrium of flows, and that of the relation between these two and the question whether one or other is dominant or by what process they influence each other and can both be satisfied at once.

### 3. *Stock analysis or flow analysis?*

An essential step towards answering these questions resulted from a debate in 1950 among Professors Klein,* Fellner and Somers,† and Brunner.‡ Klein sought to show that Fellner and Somers in an earlier article§ had been wrong to treat stock analysis and flow analysis in monetary interest theory as equivalent. He asked whether they deemed the interest rate to depend, in effect, on the whole history of the demand-and-supply relation for securities since time was, or only on that relation in some current period. They replied that if the whole history up to the beginning of the current period had resulted, at that beginning, in an equilibrium, then any divergence from equilibrium in the current period must result from the events of that period. This answer was rejected by Klein as question-begging. Karl Brunner, however, carried the whole matter forward by showing that if we opt for a stock rather than a flow theory, we have then to choose between a liquidity preference and a securities theory, and that different behaviour in the securities market is implied by these two theories.

Brunner considers first whether a stock or a flow theory is appropriate to the securities market. The contrast, we may interpolate, is between a market such as that for electricity or fresh milk, where what is demanded from moment to moment or

* L. R. Klein, 'Stock and Flow Analysis in Economics', *Econometrica*, vol. XVIII (July 1950); and 'Stock and Flow Analysis: Further Comment', *Econometrica*, vol. XVIII (July 1950).

† William Fellner and Harold M. Somers, 'Stock and Flow Analysis: Comment', *Econometrica*, vol. XVIII (July 1950); and 'Stock and Flow Analysis: Note on the Discussion', *Econometrica*, vol. XVIII (July 1950).

‡ Karl Brunner, 'Stock and Flow Analysis: Discussion', *Econometrica*, vol. XVIII (July 1950).

§ William Fellner and Harold M. Somers, 'Note on "Stocks" and "Flows" in Monetary Interest Theory', *Review of Economics and Statistics*, vol. XXXI (May 1949).

from day to day must, in so far as demand is met, be produced from moment to moment or from day to day, and a market such as that for antique furniture, where supply is an existing and non-augmentable quantity existing at all times. The market for securities is evidently nearer to the antique furniture than the electricity end of the scale. Moreover, it is one where 'the decision to hold the stock is continuously appraised in the light of current market situations'. On the implied ground that the market is dominated by the effect of price changes in releasing a large volume of orders to sell *from stock* or to buy from stock, a volume which is large, that is to say, in relation to the orders which can arise from new issues, Professor Brunner simply declares that except in a stationary state where new issues are zero and where, accordingly, both stock equilibrium and flow equilibrium are achieved together, we shall find the 'momentary' price to be determined by the stock relation. In the stationary state both stock and flow relations must be simultaneously satisfied, since the stationary state is one where the stock relation is satisfied subject to a special condition, viz. that flows be zero. The non-stationary heading covers the case of stock equilibrium combined with flow disequilibrium and the case of stock disequilibrium combined with flow equilibrium.

It is not easy to tell from what Professor Brunner writes whether he regards the stationary state, with zero new issues of bonds per unit of time, as the only possible double equilibrium, that is, simultaneous equilibrium of both stock desired to be held with stock existing, and flow desired to be issued with flow desired to be absorbed. When I am in a moving vehicle I am at each instant at some particular place (my 'stock' situation) and moving at a certain speed (my 'flow' situation). The combination of these two circumstances may be exactly what I desire for that instant. Were I not moving, I might wish to be in a different place; or were I at that instant in a different place I might desire to be moving at a different speed. Thus, it does not seem inconceivable that a particular stock of bonds and a particular pace of new issue of bonds may both be compatible with one and the same interest rate and that the combination of all three of these values of variables may satisfy everybody. In terms of our analogy, I may be moving, not because I would have preferred to be in a different place *at the given instant*, but because I aim to be in a different place at a later instant. In economic terms, wealth-owners all taken together may be willing, at some particular interest rate, to increase their holding of bonds at just the pace at which borrowers wish, at that interest rate, to issue new bonds. I think that Professor Brunner does envisage this as a possible situation, since he seems in one passage to insist that, *even* in such a situation, the stock position is dominant. We must here interpolate a further passage of our own to ask whether in such a situation the stock position is indeed dominant.

The case for saying that wealth-owners' and income-earners' attitude to existing stocks of 'old' bonds is dominant, as compared with would-be lenders' and borrowers' attitude to new issues, rests in our judgement on the idea that *the quantity released on to the market* (by any considerable change in the interest rate) of old bonds *could* be much larger than that of new issues. A trespasser hesitates to walk through the farm-yard at night, not because he is menaced by one dog awake, but because that dog may wake the whole hostile household. But whether this will be so or not depends on how sound the household sleeps; or, in our own terms, on how sensitive bond-holders, actual or potential, are to changes of price. This sensitiveness in its turn depends, we now assert, on the *uncertainty* of their price expectations. For let us consider an economy where there are no new issues or fresh borrowing nor redemption of debt, but merely a constant stock of bonds. Let us suppose that each wealth-owner has in mind some specific future date (not necessarily the same for everyone) which is the nearest he cares to look to for capital gain or loss, and that each has in mind a particular price of bonds, which price he treats as *certain* to be attained on that date. Then, with due allowance for impending payments of coupon interest, any bond-holder whose expected price is higher than the current market price will be willing to hold bonds, anyone whose expected price is below the current market price will be unwilling to hold them. Using the horizontal axis of a Cartesian diagram for numbers of bonds, and the vertical axis for bond prices, we could draw a curve connecting with each present market bond price the number of bonds which, with a given set of bond price expectations (one price for each person), wealth-owners would be willing to hold at that price. It would, of course, be downward sloping towards the right, since in order to find additional willing holders of bonds we should have to lower the present market price so that it sank below the expected prices of a further section of wealth-owners, or, in market terminology, so that it turned some more Bears into Bulls.

Now unless this curve had some actually horizontal segments, any change in the existing quantity of bonds would, so long as expectations of bond prices remained unchanged, require some change of the interest rate (that is, of the current market price of bonds). If expectations of all actual or potential bond-holders, or of all those within some range of expected bond prices, changed, the 'shape and position' of the curve would change bodily, and again there would have to be some change of the current market price of bonds; that is, of the interest rate. But now let us suppose that instead of each wealth-owner entertaining with certainty a unique expected bond price, he had in mind a range of prices, all of which he regarded as possible. It might then be a reasonable first-approximation hypothesis that a bond-holder would not wish to be rid of his bonds in exchange for money unless the current market price rose above the upper limit of his range of (subjectively) possible future prices, and would not wish to acquire more bonds in exchange for money unless the current market price fell below the lower limit of the range. This supposition would require us to draw two curves, one showing, for each hypothetical existing number of bonds, the price above which the current market price must not rise if that number of bonds is to find willing holders, the other showing, for each hypothetical size of the stock of bonds existing, the price below which the current market price must not fall if that number of bonds is not to fall short of the desired number. In this case the number of bonds existing could be changed within some range without necessitating a change in the interest rate (see Fig. 1 *a*) or expectations could change to some extent without necessitating such a change (see Fig. 1 *b*).

Let us turn to a more formal aspect of the determination of price in a market which can be supplied from an existing stock as well as from new production. Suppose that output of the good in question, measured as so and so many units of the good per unit of time, can be at all times differentiated with respect to time so that, in ordinary language, changes in its size are 'smooth' and do not include jump-discontinuities. Then the quantity of the good coming on to the market from new production will, *in zero time at any instant*, be zero. Since in a market supplied *only* from new production we can suppose demand also to vanish to the same order as supply, when shorter and shorter intervals tending to zero were considered, a balance between demand and supply in every interval can be conceived, and we can perhaps further, with some artificiality, suppose such an equality *at all moments* between the demand flow and the

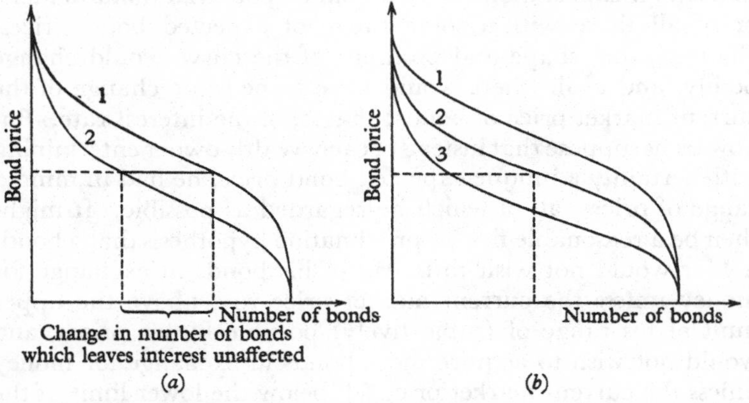


Fig. 1. (*a*) Curve 1: Each ordinate shows highest bond price at which desired stock of bonds is at least that represented by the abscissa. Curve 2: Each ordinate shows lowest bond price which will make desired stock of bonds not more than that represented by the abscissa. (*b*) Curves 1 and 2: Higher range of bond prices compatible with given bond stock. Curves 2 and 3: Lower range of bond prices compatible with given bond stock.

supply flow to be brought about by price changes. But supply *from pre-existing stock* can be of finite amount in a zero interval of time. It is this circumstance which, in the less extreme form which it would take in reality, where flows are not 'smooth' in the sense we have assumed, compels us to say that at any instant the price in such a market is dominated to some extent by the stock position. How great is this extent?

We know that except for some so-called 'tap' issues of British Government securities, and any similar arrangements elsewhere, new bond issues do not conform to the smooth-stream model, but are made in large blocks by means of subscription lists which remain open for a few days, hours or minutes. There is thus much more in common between the mechanism and market impact of a new issue and that of a sale of a block of existing ('old') securities than the extreme analogy of electricity versus antique furniture would suggest. It thus appears that the most convenient way of combining the two sources of supply in one analysis is simply to regard the interest rate, in the way we were doing a few pages earlier, as the price which must stand at or move to that level at which all existing bonds, no matter whether they have existed for a century or have only this moment been put upon the market, can find willing holders. A new issue is thus incorporated into the analysis, not as something separate which influences matters *qua* 'flow', but simply as what brings about a change in stocks and requires additional willing bond-holders to be found.

This leads to one final aspect of our interpolation. An equilibrium in the bond market may be looked on as having, possibly, two stages. There may at some instant, and some interest rate, be equality between the number of bonds requiring to be held and the number for which there exist willing holders. But the bonds existing may not be all in the hands of those willing to hold them. Thus sales must, or can, take place *at the current interest rate* (i.e. bond price inverted) in order to bring about a complete matching of desired with actual individual holdings, this state of affairs being the second state to which we referred above. It thus follows that the occurrence of bond sales and purchases is not an infallible sign of stock disequilibrium in the aggregative sense.

In the second part of his article Professor Brunner shows that even when we have accepted the appropriateness of a 'stock' approach to the bond market, we have still to choose between a 'liquidity' theory and a 'securities' theory. The former declares that the rate of interest will change unless the existing stock of *money* is equal to the desired stock of money; the latter declares that the rate of interest will change unless the existing stock of *bonds* is equal to the desired stock of bonds. Further, the liquidity theory makes the speed of change of the interest rate to depend on the size of the difference between the existing and the desired stock of money, while the securities theory makes the speed of change of interest to depend on the size of the difference between the existing and the desired stock of bonds. The securities theory embodies Professors Fellner and Somers's belief that 'in a multi-dimensional system there are a great many factors which affect the interest rate. However, in *any* system, these factors can affect the market rate of interest only through their effect on the demand and supply of interest-bearing securities.' One thing, it appears, Professors Fellner and Somers have overlooked, although it fits without difficulty into their formula just quoted. Anything which affects *equally and simultaneously* the stock of bonds desired and the stock existing, and which *also* at the same time has its own independent effect on the thoughts, feelings or mental attitudes which underly the desire for a given stock of bonds, so as to make this desire compatible with a different interest rate, can cause the rate to change *without* upsetting the equality of the desired and the existing stock of bonds. Indeed, what economist would not be willing to draw a diagram in which the demand and the supply curve of some commodity had each shifted in just such a way as to intersect at a different price but an unchanged quantity?

What thoughts, feelings or attitudes could change in such a way as to lead to such a shift? Professor Brunner's equations of the liquidity theory include among the independent variables, on which the speed of change of the interest rate might be supposed to depend, the speed of change of other prices in the system. We should ourselves prefer to say that the most relevant such influences are plainly *expectations* of price changes rather than observed, that is, *ex post* changes. Professor Brunner, however, does not refer, in his article, to expectations. In the specific mathematical form which Professor Brunner gives to it the securities theory gives no explicit place to the influence of any thoughts except those which can be resolved into functions of public *ex post* quantities.

The dilemma we found in Professor Brunner's article, which he himself seems to sweep aside, the dilemma that if there are two distinct mechanisms or sets of influences bearing on the interest rate, each by itself capable of attaining an equilibrium of its own, these two must in some way be mutually reconciled if they both bear on one and the same rate, may find a solution along lines which, for a different purpose, Mr A. Llewellyn Wright* has most ingeniously suggested. The essence of Mr Wright's proposal is that in an economy with *changing*

* 'Sequence Analysis and the Theory of the Rate of Interest', *Economic Journal*, vol. LXV (December 1955).

income, and so with changing amounts per unit of time by which equipment and aggregate idle balances ('reserve', 'speculative' or 'pure liquidity' balances, as they might alternatively be called) are being augmented, the requirement of equality between the number of dependent variables and the number of mutually independent equations (which equality Mr Wright, reasonably as we think, seems still prepared to accept as the equivalent of determinateness in many circumstances) allows *two* interest rates to operate simultaneously and separately on the market, the essential explanation being that their respective levels control the speeds of growth, respectively, of the saving-investment flow and of the hoarding or dishoarding flow. This, if in presenting it I have properly interpreted Mr Wright, seems a most fertile suggestion. It means that a person's or a firm's affairs can be in equilibrium even when, for example, he is paying one rate of interest to borrow money and receiving a different one for lending it, not essentially because of any differences in risk or other such circumstances, but because he thus achieves the desired changes in the respective speeds of growth of his accumulated stocks of assets of different kinds. He ought, according to static analysis, to borrow just so much at any time that the rate of interest he pays on his marginal borrowing equals the rate he receives on his marginal lending. In a dynamic system the loss he appears to suffer by this failure to observe an equi-marginal rule may be the price he pays for, or the loss which is compensated by, the desired changes between one period and the next of the amounts added per period to his stocks, respectively, of equipment and of money.

The foregoing is my own statement of what Mr Wright's article suggests to me. He, at least, proposes that there are two interest rates differing in their role and in the influences determining them; differing, that is to say, more essentially than in merely being 'short-term' and 'long-term' rates, although they may fall under these respective headings. One of these rates, called the 'money rate of interest', is determined on a market which is almost literally the money market: 'It can be regarded as the average rate of interest charged on bank overdrafts in any period; or, better still, it can be regarded as the Bank Rate.' The other, called the 'investment rate of interest', is 'the rate which rules in the investment market proper, the market where the demand for investible funds is brought into equality with the supply of investible funds'. His purpose in distinguishing, even in fundamental theory, two interest rates is to find for his lagged Keynesian model an extra variable unencumbered by an extra equation, since he believes the model otherwise to be over-determinate. As to the fitness of his device for its purpose, we are bound to ask whether this is not an example of that very dis-aggregation which Mr Wright in his article recognizes as in-effective, and Professor Brian Tew* has put forward the objection which must occur to every reader: can we conceptually split the loan market into halves so independent of each other that we need not have any equation connecting the prices which reign in them? We think, none the less, that Mr Wright's work may yet be found to bear usefully upon our own problem, which, if the rate of interest has really to equilibrate both stock held with stock existing, and the *time-constricted* acts of offering bonds and money for mutual exchange, is also one of over-determinateness.

The problem of how 'stock' influences and 'flow' influences upon bond prices are related to each other can perhaps be put as follows. At any instant a stock of bonds exists. The change in the size of this stock in a short enough time-interval is negligible, and thus, it appears, the bond price at any instant must be determined by those influences which make people willing or unwilling to hold a stock of bonds. Against this argument, however, the following may occur to us: in the market for such a good as electricity there is at no time any stock. The *quantity existing* at any instant is zero. Yet there is a price, validly looked upon as depending on the confrontation of supply conditions and demand conditions. Evidently a price can be determined by the comparison of the potential sizes of two flows, each depending on this price, which must be such as to equalize them. Yet is it not true that the quantity supplied in any interval tends to zero with that interval, just as the growth of a stock in some time-interval becomes negligible if that interval is taken short enough? The answer plainly is that, when we are simply concerned with two flows, both the quantity supplied and the quantity demanded vanish to the same order, and thus, in a

* 'Sequence Analysis and the Theory of the Rate of Interest', *Economic Journal*, vol. LXVI (September 1956).

familiar way, we can think of the ratio of these two flows as remaining finite while we carry to the limit the shortening of the interval of measurement. In the measurement of a stock, of course, no time-interval is in any way relevant, and thus a flow which requires some finite lapse of time to be accumulated into some finite quantity cannot influence the size or price of a stock *at some instant*.

It is an argument of this sort which I take to underlie Mr R. W. Clower's* disposal of the problem:

> The aggregate quantities of various assets existing in an economy in any given period of time are inherited from the past. These quantities can be altered only gradually as a result of future economy decisions, so that if we consider appropriately short time periods, current additions to (or depletions of) aggregate asset stocks can be ignored.

Mr Clower's purpose is to show that productivity and thrift do play an essential role in the interest rate's historical course. By regarding the rate at any moment as depending purely on the stock situation at that moment, namely the size of the bond stock, the expectations of individuals about future bond prices, the current prices of other assets, Mr Clower can maintain that new issues of bonds, and retirements of existing bonds, occurring today, do not affect the rate today, unless they alter expectations. But when we look at two dates separated in time, the interest rate at the later date will be what it proves to be partly because of the change in size of the bond stock which new issues and retirements in the interval have brought about. The time rate at which such new issues and retirements will have taken place will be influenced by changes in productivity and thrift.

Changes in productivity may arise, as Mr Clower points out, from inventions or other sources, and thrift also is subject to many influences. Indeed, we may say that these are in a sense only names for certain superficial aspects of the whole complex course of economic history, and Mr Clower's aim is not, I think, to isolate productivity and thrift because they are more important than other strands in that skein, but because he wishes to get these recurrently self-assertive explanations of interest permanently filed away in the right box.

* 'Productivity, Thrift and the Rate of Interest', *Economic Journal*, vol. LXIV (March 1954).

Despite the solutions to which we may resort for a practical means of handling, in our theoretical discussions, the co-existence of a 'stock' mechanism and a 'flow' mechanism in the market where money and bonds are exchanged for each other, this co-existence remains the most serious theoretical problem concerning the interest rate. In his article 'The Equivalence of the Liquidity Preference and Loanable Funds Theories and the *New* [italics in original] Stock-flow Analysis',* Mr Cliff Lloyd concludes that it is at present unsolved. He presents the matter formally, in the frame of Professor Hicks's demonstration that the liquidity preference and loanable funds theories are equivalent:

> In a consistent $n$-good system, two of the goods being bonds and money, if any $n-1$ excess demand equations are satisfied, the $n$th must also be satisfied, thus the $n$th may be dropped.... The loanable funds theory drops the money equation, the liquidity preference theory drops the bond equation, but the two are equivalent.... This is quite a simple and clear-cut proof, provided that each of the goods in the system is represented by only one excess demand equation, but...in an explicit stock-flow theory any stock-flow good will be represented by two excess demand equations.†

A stock-flow good is one whose quantity, existing as a stock at each instant, can be different at different instants because a flow of the good is produced and another flow consumed, and because these flows, each measured as so and so many units per time-unit, can differ from each other. By equilibrium in respect of such a good, Mr Cliff Lloyd means constancy of the stock. However, a price for the good which makes equal the stock existing and the stock desired to be held is not necessarily the same as the price which makes equal the flow produced and the flow consumed. The difference between the desired and existing stocks, considered as a function of price, gives us an excess stock demand equation; the difference between desired consumption flow and flow of production forthcoming, considered as a function of price, gives us the excess flow demand equation. Unless the difference between production and consumption is zero, the stock will be changing; that is to say, the market for the good will not be in equilibrium. The converse, however, is not true.

* *Review of Economic Studies*, vol. XXVII (June 1960). † Op. cit.

Equality between the flows of production and consumption does not imply equality between the desired and the existing stocks. 'Thus according to the "new" stock-flow economics a stock-flow good, that is, one which is produced, consumed and held, must be represented in a general equilibrium system not with one but with two excess demand equations.'* Hence Mr Cliff Lloyd infers that, whether or not in fact the liquidity preference and loanable funds theories are one and the same, Professor Hicks's proof that they are so does not hold in regard to a good which is produced and consumed as well as being held in stock. He is careful *not* to infer that no proof can ever be found.

Mr Cliff Lloyd's argument calls for one or two comments. He does not appear to be justified in saying that Clower and Bushaw† were the first to study the equilibrium of a good which is produced and consumed as well as held in stock. Contrary to his assertion, Karl Brunner's article‡ referred to above deals with this case. Mr Cliff Lloyd's particular problem is the same as that posed by Mr Llewellyn Wright,§ but Mr Cliff Lloyd sees no *general* solution. He shows that special assumptions will give us a model where the two excess demand equations are in effect one and the same, so that Professor Hicks's proof would apply. His way of specifying the two excess demand equations of the general case appears to us to be open to criticism. In our paraphrase of his argument we have been speaking, first, of an excess flow demand equation (as he does), but, secondly, of an excess stock demand equation (as he does not). He prefers to add together the stock and flow demands and so define his second equation as 'the market excess demand equation which shows the total market demand, both stock and flow, for the good'. All the difficulties we have referred to in earlier pages, of justifying any particular choice of the length of the period of measurement of the flow, and, more fundamentally, the doubtful propriety of adding together two quantities of different dimension, a stock with no time-denominator and a flow which is necessarily expressed as so much per unit of time, are involved in

* Op. cit.

† R. W. Clower and D. W. Bushaw, 'Price Determination in a Stock-flow Economy', *Econometrica*, vol. XXII (July 1954).

‡ 'Stock and Flow Analysis: Discussion'.

§ 'Sequence Analysis and the Theory of the Rate of Interest'.

Mr Cliff Lloyd's method, which we have therefore chosen to re-express.

In an article* later than his book Professor Patinkin has argued as follows: Each individual has some stock of money 'now', and desires the prospect of having some particular stock at the 'next' date when the matter will arise, which date we may (by a usual convention) take to be the same for everyone. Thus each individual's attitude may be *alternatively* expressed, either as a desire for some future *stock* or as a desire for some particular *change*, between now and then, in his existing stock. Dividing this change by the number of time units in the interval, we have a flow. (Professor Patinkin in this particular article does not make explicit the need for this latter step.) Thus, says Professor Patinkin, stock analysis and flow analysis are alternative ways of looking at the matter, and we have not two equations, but one.

This argument seems to us fallacious. The size which a thing has at some instant and its speed of change at that instant are two distinct things, each separately subject to choice. If Professor Patinkin prefers to regard the individual as choosing the size that his money stock shall have at the 'next' date rather than 'now' he must allow him to choose *also* the speed at which that money stock shall be growing, or about to grow (or decline) at that next date. However, he writes:

> Before concluding this part of the paper, I should like to re-state its general argument in the following way: Stock analysis, as well as flow analysis, pre-supposes a period of time: namely the period between the moment *at* which the individual is making his plans, and the moment *for* which he is making them. Hence if the periods pre-supposed by the analysis are the same, the excess-demand function of stock analysis must be identical with that of flow analysis. This proposition holds also in the limiting case where the period is an instantaneous one.

Why does Professor Patinkin think that the individual, in making his plans *for* a particular moment, must only concern himself with the change which will then *have occurred* and not with the one which will then be about to occur? Why, in other words, should the individual concern himself only with *one* future

* Don Patinkin, 'Liquidity Preference and Loanable Funds: Stock and Flow Analysis', *Economica*, vol. xxv (November 1958).

moment? Is it because Professor Patinkin is in this passage concerned only with 'static equilibrium'? But in static equilibrium analysis do we speak of plans and distinguish the moment when they are made from the moment when they apply? The really essential point, however, is that stock equilibrium can be achieved *instantaneously* by *price changes*, e.g. of bonds, without the price which effects this equality between desired and *existing* stocks necessarily bringing about an equality between the stocks desired for the 'next' relevant date and the stocks which, comprising existing stock and impending 'production', will exist on that next date.

Patinkin's position of 1958* has been criticized by Mr Hugh Rose,† who refers in a short note published in 1959 to a 1957 article‡ of his own. In that earlier article Mr Rose interprets and contrasts the Keynesian and loanable funds theories of interest. Professor H. G. Johnson§ had suggested that the Keynesian theory is 'static', seeking only to explain the state of affairs in a short-period equilibrium and how changes in circumstances will alter the equilibrium values, while the loanable funds theory is dynamic and seeks to explain precisely how interest and income move from one equilibrium to another when circumstances have changed. In contrast with this position of Professor Johnson's, Mr Rose sees Keynes's theory also as dynamic.

In Mr Rose's general dynamic model (providing a formal frame within which both Keynesian and loanable funds theories can be dynamically interpreted) it is assumed that the expenditure plans of both households and business are always realized, any discrepancy between the total of these plans, on one hand, and current production, on the other, falling on the buffer stocks of finished goods held by producers. Such a discrepancy is the excess demand (positive or negative) for goods. The excess demand for money is the difference between the stock of money which the public desires to hold and the stock which exists. The loanable funds theory says that the interest rate will change if

* 'Liquidity Preference and Loanable Funds: Stock and Flow Analysis'.

† 'The Rate of Interest and Walras's Law', *Economica*, vol. XXVI (August 1959).

‡ Hugh Rose, 'Liquidity Preference and Loanable Funds', *Review of Economic Studies*, vol. XXIV (February 1957).

§ 'Some Cambridge Controversies in Monetary Theory', *Review of Economic Studies*, vol. XIX, no. 49 (1951–2).

the sum of the two excess demands is other than zero. The Keynesian theory (in Mr Rose's view) says that the interest rate will change if, and only if, the excess demand for money is other than zero. If, then, we believe that the excess demand for loans is the sum of the excess demands for goods and for money, Keynes appears to be maintaining that the interest rate can change even if the excess demand for loans (the excess supply of securities) is zero, and remain constant even when the excess demand for loans is not zero. Mr Rose's solution of this dilemma is twofold. First, he rejects 'Walras's Law' that the algebraic sum of the excess demands for goods, money and securities is zero. Secondly, he shows that in Keynes's construction the excess demand for loans is always equal to the excess demand for money.

This latter result arises in the simplest fashion. Producers finance the whole of their production (of consumption goods and investment goods taken together) by sales, made concurrently with the production itself, of consumers' goods and securities. If the total of consumers' goods and securities which income-receivers want to buy is smaller than the total that producers want to sell, the difference is plainly an excess demand for money, and this excess demand for money is exactly the excess of the securities offered by producers over the securities demanded by income-receivers: the excess demand for money and the

$$\begin{pmatrix}\text{excess supply of securities}\\ \text{excess demand for loans}\end{pmatrix}$$

are equal. An even simpler statement of the matter is as follows: In the Keynesian system the excess demand for goods *in any one period* is identically zero; for we are to conceive of decisions how much of this and that good to produce within, say, the coming month being taken at the beginning of that month and always adhered to. When goods have been produced someone has in a sense bought them, whether they wanted to or not; for someone has done the work and has a claim to the result. The lack of sufficient effective demand shows itself, in the minds of enterprisers, *before* they take their decisions as to how much to produce in the coming month; and naturally they are much influenced in their production decisions by reflecting on how much of last month's production has been left, contrary to their plans, on their own hands and been 'bought' by themselves.

There is no doubt in the present writer's mind that Keynes thought of the interest rate as adjusting itself to the nut-cracker squeeze of the quantity of money existing and the quantity desired, by changes in the price of fixed-interest securities, as these were offered or demanded by those who wished for extra money or had more money than they wanted. Liquidity preference can, of course, be influenced by very many circumstances and considerations, including the prices and price changes of consumers' goods or producers' goods; all markets are in some degree interdependent. But it is on the securities market that the interest rate actually *emerges* as, for example, the quotient of Consol coupon rate over Consol market price.

None the less, we must maintain that it is an essential part of Keynes's vision that the interest rate *can* change without any transactions in bonds at all, and without any emergence on the Stock Market of an excess demand or supply of bonds. If it happened that every holder of bonds or money said to himself at some moment: 'If the rate of interest were one point higher, my present holding would be just what I should choose to have', and if a testing of the market revealed this consensus of opinion, then the rate might be found to have moved up one point without any transactions. This is made virtually explicit in the *Treatise on Money*.

Professor H. G. Johnson's highly condensed and wide-ranging survey article on 'Some Cambridge Controversies in Monetary Theory' is remarkable for the contrast between the ease with which he is able, on Keynesian lines largely made explicit by Mrs Joan Robinson, to handle every kind of shift in the macro-economic situation and show what sequence of changes will be undergone by the interest rate, the net investment flow, income and the rest, when some autonomous psychological, technical or political transition disturbs an equilibrium, on one hand; and on the other, the awkward and artificial air of his account of them in terms of a Robertsonian dynamics. Professor Johnson says that 'the Keynesian theory...is a static theory; it is not concerned with the succession of changing [partial] equilibrium positions but only with the position which represents an equilibrium of all the forces at work'. This may be formally true; I am sure it does not represent the spirit or purpose of Keynes's thought. To be formally correct, Keynes ought, no doubt, to have carefully specified the precise character and mode of operation of the influence exerted by prosperous conditions on the inducement to invest, and to have pointed out in so many words that prosperous conditions arise when, for any reason, employment, output and income are increased; and so on. He did not do so. The accelerator, the 'investment coefficient' and all such are markedly absent from the *General Theory* (though not, in substance, from the *Treatise on Money*). In chapter 22 of the *General Theory*, however, Keynes indicates plainly his conception of the way in which wide shifts of the *schedule* or curve of the marginal efficiency of capital induce abrupt and great changes in investment and hence in all its dependent variables.

Is it then better to have highly special, arbitrary and clanking mechanical systems, in which our assumptions single out one or two variables, make expectations, confidence and the whole gossamer fabric of investment incentive to depend on these alone, and tell us precisely what effect a change in these variables will have on investment; or is it better to recognize that the inducement to invest is influenced by countless subtle aspects of the recent past and the 'news' (all taking colour and meaning, of course, from the historical background which has conditioned men's minds and bequeathed them their resources) and leave ourselves freedom to analyse these from case to case as best we may by *formally* treating (as Keynes did in effect) the inducement to invest as autonomous or exogenous? Again, when we try to understand the effects of changes in the quantity of money, is it better to chase packets of money in and out of the labyrinth of balances held or spent at different times for different kinds of purpose, at the greatest risk of muddling the identities of the various packets and the dates of the various transactions, or is it better to consider a *stock* of money, existing at a particular moment and matching or failing to match the stock desired at that moment; desired for a list of motives which we can make short or long at convenience: payments reserve, speculative asset, 'finance' marshalled for impending investment or what you will; and thus to show what market forces, at that same moment, will bear on the prices of bonds and thus push up or down the rate of interest? Keynes's critics have discussed whether his system is static or dynamic: they have not seen that it is *dramatic*, and that this quality arises from his method of cornering many problems and complications in one concept and dealing with them by a radical simplification. That this is the true Cambridge secret has been well understood by Mr Lawrence E. Fouraker.* Writing of Marshall and Keynes, he says:

Their intellects were too proud, resourceful and thorough to go on with the thesis without firmly establishing the connections. Having satisfied themselves, however, they employed a curious device when it came to recording the results of their pursuits. Instead of leading the reader through the intricate analytical processes that their own minds had recently traversed, they would provide a short cut, in the form of an assumption whose purpose was to eliminate consideration of the difficult problem they had faced and solved.

If all Keynes's critics had possessed Mr Fouraker's insight, what seas of ink could have been saved!

## 4. *The classical system: incomplete or over-determined?*

The question 'What determines the interest rate?' has been in post-war years one of a group of intimately linked problems which in the course of debate have seemed to swing round each other continually in a sort of whirlpool, now one, now another becoming central as article succeeds article from writers with different viewpoints. Among these problems is the question, discussed with brilliant clarity by Becker and Baumol,† whether, as Lange‡ and Patinkin§ have maintained, the Lausanne School and other neo-classicals so defined their systems that *either* these systems were incomplete through asserting the *identical* equality of total commodity demand and supply

* 'The Cambridge Didactic Style', *Journal of Political Economy*, vol. LXVI (February 1958).

† Gary S. Becker and William J. Baumol, 'The Classical Monetary Theory: the Outcome of the Discussion', *Economica*, vol. XIX (November 1952).

‡ Oscar Lange, 'Say's Law: a Restatement and a Criticism', in *Studies in Mathematical Economics and Econometrics*; in memory of Henry Schultz (O. Lange, F. McIntyre and T. O. Yntema, eds.) (Chicago University Press, 1942).

§ Don Patinkin, 'The Indeterminacy of Absolute Prices in Classical Economic Theory', *Econometrica*, vol. XVII (January 1949); 'The Invalidity of Classical Monetary Theory', *Econometrica*, vol. XIX (April 1951); 'A Reconsideration of the General Equilibrium Theory of Money', *Review of Economic Studies*, vol. XVIII (1949–50); 'Relative Prices, Say's Law and the Demand for Money', *Econometrica*, vol. XVI (April 1948).

(Say's *identity*) and thus being able to show only how inter-commodity exchange rates are determined and unable to show how absolute money prices are determined, or *else* that they were self-contradictory through assuming, in addition to Say's identity, that stocks of money are wanted for their own sake, so that the total stock of money can be other than just what, at given money prices of commodities, is desired, and can thus affect the demand for these commodities and make it other than equal to the supply. In brief, are the commodity market and the money market entirely separate from each other, so that the one determines in a wholly self-contained manner the *relative* prices of commodities and the other determines nothing because there is in it only one good, and this is always available (being not a real money but a mere *numéraire*) in just the quantity required, just as runs in cricket are available to the man in the scorer's box in just the quantity he requires for recording the events in the field of play? Or, on the contrary, are the markets connected so that when there is an excess supply of money there is *ipso facto* an equal excess demand for goods?

Becker and Baumol argue (with the support of much evidence by quotation) that what the classicals had in mind was not Say's identity but Say's *equality*. At first sight we might be inclined to think that Say's equality is a mere definitional truism to the effect that in equilibrium demand and supply are equal. But Becker and Baumol mean by it the assertion that if an equilibrium is disturbed, as by an arbitrary increase or reduction in the existing quantity of money, a new equilibrium will be found through such changes in the price level as will make the new quantity of money just sufficient. For if the desired and existing money stocks are unequal, people will offer a greater, or smaller, total money value of commodities than they demand, in order to acquire, or dispose of, stocks of money. When money prices of commodities have been given time to adjust themselves to this pressure the desired stock of money, which depends on the prices of commodities, will have adjusted itself to the quantity existing.

The question which here interpolates itself is this: if we add to the assumed system a bond market, will a change in the price of bonds, that is, a change of the interest rate, help to adjust the desired to the existing money stock? From Ricardo to Patinkin, some have said that the long-period *equilibrium* interest rate will be unaffected, and will therefore have no effect on the equilibrium of the rest of the system. Keynes, being uninterested in the long period (in which, by definition, all prices including those of productive factors are perfectly flexible), said nothing about long-period equilibrium, but said instead, like Ricardo, that in the short period the interest rate will be different and will affect other things.

Becker and Baumol do not themselves consider any role of an interest rate, but conclude that the neo-classicals did not treat the economic system as divided into two entirely separate enclaves, the non-monetary and the monetary, but instead believed, as Becker and Baumol express it, that 'money derives a "utility" from the goods it can buy, it is true, but because it can buy them at the moment the buyer considers convenient'.

From a conventionally simplified frame for the question whether or not an economic system, given time, will adjust itself to any change in the size of its money stock so as to reach a new equilibrium not differing in essentials from the old, the ripples have spread out towards answers based on more and more subtle and complex assumptions. Mr E. J. Mishan* distinguishes between a 'cash balance effect' and an 'asset-expenditure effect', and charges Patinkin with having treated them as one, at first under the name 'Pigou effect' and later as 'real balance effect'. When the price level falls, even a person who happens at that moment to have no cash balance may feel a desire or a freedom, because his assets are now worth more in terms of the kinds of goods he desires, to spend more per time-unit on such goods. If, however, his assets consist partly in cash, he will have an additional incentive to increase his expenditure per time-unit. For now he has in hand a larger stock of cash than is needed for convenience in bridging the time gap between receipts and outgoings of cash, and so it will be natural to get rid of some of the surplus cash. Once we introduce bonds and a bond market into our system, it is plain that surplus cash may be spent either on commodities (encouraging their output and raising their prices directly) or on bonds (lowering the interest rate and encouraging investment, and so other output, *indirectly*).

* 'A Fallacy in the Interpretation of the Cash Balance Effect', *Economica*, vol. xxv (May 1958).

Because of such considerations, it is exceedingly difficult to justify any particular line of separation between monetary theory and interest theory.

In the brilliant article of 1956 by S. C. Tsiang* we find carried a stage further the policy of generalizing the analysis so as to embrace the mutual influence of interest, employment, output, income and velocity of circulation. Mr Tsiang's first purpose is to show, in a manner quite different from that of Walras's Law, that the liquidity preference and loanable funds theories of the determination of interest are identical 'in the sense that the two sets of demand and supply functions, i.e. the demand for and the supply of loanable funds, and the demand for money to hold and the stock of money in existence, would determine the same rate of interest in all circumstances, if both sets of demand and supply functions are formulated correctly in the *ex ante* sense'.

Mr Tsiang rejects the approach via Walras's Law on the ground that it links interest no more intimately with money than with any of the other multifarious goods of the general equilibrium system. Walras's Law, which simply says that the demand for everything, including money, is necessarily identical with the supply of everything, including money, shows that in the general equilibrium system we have one redundant demand and supply equation which follows from all the rest, and that accordingly some one equation, *no matter which*, may be dropped. Such an argument leads to no more explicit theory of interest than the mere statement that interest is included in the general determinate equilibrium. To invoke the Law is, says Mr Tsiang, to use an *ex post* definition of the demand and supply of money.

Mr Tsiang's criticism of Fellner and Somers† concerns the very fundamental question of how to combine stock and flow demand in one analysis. Fellner and Somers, he says, define the total supply of money as total money expenditures on goods and services as well as on the purchases of 'claims' plus the amount of money held unspent.

This total of the so-called 'supply of money', the main components of which are flows over time, does not necessarily equal the total

* 'Liquidity Preference and Loanable Funds Theories, Multiplier and Velocity Analyses: a Synthesis', *American Economic Review*, vol. XLVI (September 1956).

† 'Note on "Stocks" and "Flows" in Monetary Interest Theory'.

stock of money in existence (which is the usual meaning of the supply of money in the liquidity preference theory) unless the period of time over which the flows of money expenditures are measured is so defined as to make them equal.

Mr Tsiang in his positive analysis does in fact define a 'period' with this special purpose in view. But his 'period' is in effect an instant, his payments are merely the allocation to various uses, by each holder of money, of all the money he possesses at that instant. In fact, Mr Tsiang is simply adopting that definition* of the total quantity of money in existence which says that it equals the total of all payments that can be made by all money-holders *simultaneously*. By compelling all the economic subjects in his system to make payments at such discrete instants, Mr Tsiang combines the notion of stock of money existing *at* an instant with flow of payments made during some time *interval*, viz. the interval separating two of his discrete instants. Thus he shows that when people want to hold money, *for whatever reason*, and there is in total only just so and so much money for them all to hold, something must adjust their desires to this circumstance. That something is the rate of interest, and it is a matter of indifference whether we call his system a liquidity preference or a loanable funds system.

We said, however, that Mr Tsiang's construction allows people to desire to hold money 'for any reason'. This, in his view, is the crux of the matter and the point on which he thinks liquidity preference theorists took a distorted view. Perhaps he is doing them an injustice. His starting-point (where surely everyone can agree) is that demand and supply schedules are *ex ante* concepts. It is indeed obvious that, since they express potential reactions, conditional decisions as to what will be done should this or that circumstance arise, they must refer to intended, future action; they are descriptions of people's forward-looking states of mind, even if we happen to be studying those states of mind from a viewpoint which places them in our past. Now Mr Tsiang fastens upon Keynes's admission, in his article† called 'Alternative Theories of the Rate of Interest', that intended acts of large-scale investment may provide a special motive for liquidity preference,

* John Maynard Keynes, 'Alternative Theories of the Rate of Interest', *Economic Journal*, vol. XLVII (June 1937).

† Op. cit.

that is, for desiring to accumulate or marshal large money balances ready for the execution of these investment schemes. Such mobilizing of money 'at the ready' for investment, Keynes called the motive of 'finance'. It was, in his view, just one more source of a desire to hold money rather than to be the possessor of someone else's I.O.U.s. Now Mr Tsiang says that this 'finance' motive is merely a part of the ordinary 'transactions demand' for money. We can wholeheartedly agree with him, and so would Keynes have done, and so does Professor Hicks in his famous 'Suggestion for Simplifying the Theory of Money'. Professor Hicks says, in effect, that when your desire for money arises from the transactions motive, it is a desire to have money *ready* to make payments, because the time which will elapse between your receipt of the money and the need to pay it out is, or may be, too short to make the lending of a small sum worth while. Of course, the transactions motive is an *ex ante* motive. Whoever said it was not? Only proponents of a mechanical quantity theory of money.

Mr Tsiang concludes his sections on interest with these words:

> All the disagreements between the loanable funds and liquidity preference theories on practical issues seem to arise from the failure on the part of liquidity preference theorists themselves to perceive the dependence of the aggregate liquidity preference (or demand for money) function upon the consumption and investment functions.

We feel bound to say that this statement betrays a misunderstanding of the *methodology* of the liquidity preference theory. That theory elects to concentrate on the question: Given the expectations, plans, uncertainties, hopes and fears, as well as the distribution of resources, which exist *at some moment*, where must the price of bonds stand to equilibrate the resulting market impulses? Those expectations and plans have been shaped by past history and by the most recent 'news', but they have been so shaped by an interplay so complex and subtle as to defy explicit analysis. We can, if we wish (and Mr Tsiang is one among many who have wished), make assumptions which will enable us to trace explicitly the emergence of today's market situation from yesterday's. Such a model will be a mind-clearing stereotype of certain aspects of how things happen in the economic world. But in what sense, or under what conditions, can they serve as predictive models?

Mrs Joan Robinson introduces her article on 'The Rate of Interest'* with a definition of 'a dynamic analysis' which will surely never be bettered. Its characteristic is, she says, 'that it cannot explain how an economy behaves, in given conditions, without reference to past history; while static analysis purports to describe a position of equilibrium which the system will reach no matter where it started from'. She further explains the paradox of Keynes's *General Theory*: 'Short-period analysis is concerned with the equilibrium of a system with a given stock of capital and with given expectations about the future. Past history is thus put into the initial conditions, so that the analysis is static in itself, and yet is part of a dynamic theory.' Thus we have, from Cambridge itself, a sanction and confirmation of Mr Fouraker's thesis.†

Disposing first of the role of productivity and thrift, Mrs Robinson shows that these govern the answer to the question 'What rate of interest will bring about full employment?' For a fall of the interest rate stimulates investment, and the degree to which investment needs stimulation, in order to make employment full, depends on the size of the saving gap to be filled, and this gap itself is, if anything, made smaller by a fall in the interest rate. If the market rate of interest ever stands below the full-employment rate there will be inflation which will drive the market rate up to equality with the full-employment rate. The latter thus provides a 'floor' for the market rate.

Turning to the short period, Mrs Robinson ascribes the relation between the income expected from each kind of asset, and the price of that kind, to the varying types and degrees of illiquidity which those kinds involve. These types of illiquidity she distinguishes as *inconvenience*, *capital uncertainty*, *lender's risk* and *income uncertainty*. Inconvenience is the lack of a perfect market, depriving the asset-holder of 'the power to realize its value in cash, whatever the value may be at the moment'. Here we have perhaps some ambiguity about the meaning of 'the' value. This sounds like 'market value'; but the market value *at any moment* is what can *immediately* be obtained, and if the market is limited

* In Joan Robinson, *The Rate of Interest and Other Essays* (London: Macmillan, 1952).

† 'The Cambridge Didactic Style'.

and imperfect this may be nothing. It might be better to define inconvenience as the asset-holder's lack of assurance that whatever (now unknown) value he shall attach to his asset at some future moment he will be able at that moment without delay or cost to sell it for that price. Uncertainty concerning future capital value can be otherwise expressed as uncertainty about what rate of interest will rule at future moments. Keynes, Mrs Robinson says, 'regards the rate of interest primarily as a premium against the possible loss of capital if an asset has to be realized before its redemption date'. Lender's risk is the fear of the borrower's default. Income uncertainty exists for the lender when he lends on short term and will have soon to re-lend at he knows not what rate of interest.

Different assets, Mrs Robinson says, are affected in different degrees by each of these qualities. Bills are very little, and bonds very much, subject to capital uncertainty, while the case is reversed for income uncertainty. Thus the relative prices and yields of bills and bonds will depend, given the supply of each, on the relative (weighted) number of 'widows and orphans' who desire certainty of *income* and financial institutions who set great store by their balance sheets and desire certainty of capital values. 'The general pattern of interest rates depends on the distribution of wealth between owners with different tastes, relatively to the supplies of the various kinds of assets.'

On this basis Mrs Robinson discusses the kinds of ripples or of permanent changes of level which will occur in the interest-rate pond when various disturbing events, such as changes in the quantity of money, in expectations, in thriftiness, in the size of the investment flow, and such as the adoption of a cheap-money policy, are thrown into it. Far the most intractable of these influences is expectations, and these she treats by a masterly and highly realistic *tour de force*, that of assuming that at all times, with greater or less conviction, people assume that interest rates will sooner or later return to some 'normal' level which more or less recent experience has established in their minds. This accepted 'norm' can itself be changed, and a cheap-money policy ill timed or too recklessly pursued, which has therefore to be abandoned, may strengthen the general belief in a norm which is higher than the one that might have been established by a more canny approach.

There was, until 1930 or thereabouts, a 'Cambridge' approach to monetary theory, in which the names of Marshall, Lavington, Robertson and Keynes suggested distinct but harmonious variants. In 1926, indeed, Sir Dennis Robertson's *Banking Policy and the Price Level* lit up the horizon of professional economics and heralded the great era of monetary theory that lasted until the War. The generous acknowledgement it made of suggestive discussions with Keynes promised a Cambridge school as closely knit as the Vienna or the Stockholm school. Unhappily the cave was not big enough to hold two giants. Sir Dennis's apparatus, with its refreshing terminology of 'splashing', 'lacking' and so forth, was aimed at a careful unravelling of the monetary skein. It has its lasting place in the history of thought, it typically illustrates its inventor's ingenious power to match the closest analysis with the freest fancy, and it explains the delight which his style has given to thousands of hearers and readers. Keynes's ultimate method, by contrast, was the sword of Alexander. He cut, not unravelled, the monetary tangle of ideas.

The Cambridge concert of ideas was split by the *General Theory*, and even Professor Hicks's powerful synthesizing habit of mind has been unable to close the gap. That gap, we are therefore entitled to assume, is unclosable. We cannot here avoid an expression of view. The Keynesian whale under Mrs Robinson's management can swallow with ease all fish which come to its jaws. To play them with Robertsonian hook and line, with no matter what ingenious shifts and stratagems, is much more laborious.

In his review* of Maurice Allais' *Economie et Intérêt*, Professor Kenneth Boulding has shown with what brevity and verve the heart of interest may be penetrated:

What is determined in the market [he writes] is not strictly the rate of interest but the price of certain 'property rights'...stocks, bonds or items of physical property. Each of these...represents to an individual an expected series of future values, which may be both positive and negative. If this expected series of values can be given some 'certainty equivalent'...then the market price of the property determines a rate of interest on the investment. This rate of interest,

* Kenneth E. Boulding, 'M. Allais's Theory of Interest', *Journal of Political Economy*, vol. LIX (February 1951).

however, is essentially subjective and depends on the expectations of the individual; the objective phenomenon is the present market price of the property.

As basic theory this, we think, is irreproachable. It is true too, as Boulding later hints, that nothing in life can in strictness be justifiably taken as certain: for what sort of guarantees does the human situation offer? None the less, we must qualify Boulding's position, for the practical necessities of life drive us to accept some things as unquestionable: sunrise and sunset, eventual personal dissolution and the payment of due interest by the British Government! The series of future payments to which a gilt-edged security gives the right is still, and with entire good sense, *treated in practice* as certain, even though the whole civilized fabric to which such arrangements belong is now destructible. Thus the yields of gilt-edged securities of various terms, short, medium or long, come very near to being 'objective' interest rates. Professor Boulding has, strangely, omitted to mention the basic uncertainty which afflicts even the holder of gilt-edged, and which ultimately explains the very need for positive interest, namely, the impossibility of knowing *when and at what price* he will be driven by circumstances to sell his security. His main contention surely is invincible: the search for a 'pure' interest rate in abstraction from 'risk, liquidity, convenience, etc.' is meaningless, 'a search [in a dark room] for a black cat that isn't there'.

In the foregoing we have tried to illustrate, by a commentary on selections from the post-1945 literature, those of the central problems in the determination of interest which have mainly engrossed attention since wartime preoccupations receded. In addition to this debate on fundamentals, there have been a number of more special contributions. Mr F. P. R. Brechling,* Dr Börje Kragh† and Mr Ralph Turvey,‡ to mention them in alphabetical order, have pointed out that 'the amount of money which people desire to hold as a store of wealth depends

* 'A Note on Bond Holding and the Liquidity Preference Theory of Interest', *Review of Economic Studies*, vol. XXIV (1956–57).

† 'Two Liquidity Functions and the Rate of Interest: a Simple Dynamic Model', *Review of Economic Studies*, vol. XVII (1949–50).

‡ 'Consistency and Consolidation in the Theory of Interest', *Economica*, vol. XXI (November 1954).

not only on the rate of interest but also on the *total* amount of wealth available'. Thus in order to describe the effect of an increase in the existing quantity of money, two kinds of 'reaction curves' are needed, one showing the reaction of the rate of interest to increases in the money stock effected by open-market operations which merely *exchange bonds for money* and leave the total stock of wealth unchanged, and the other showing the reaction of the rate of interest to *ceteris paribus* changes in the money stock. 'The two curves will co-incide if the marginal propensity to hold money is zero.'

Upon the results of his skilful empirical research into the finance of small businesses, Mr N. J. Cunningham* has built a theoretical analysis of great ingenuity. His first basic finding is that the opportunity cost to a firm of investing its own ploughed-back reserves in the purchase of equipment is, for a variety of reasons, less than the cost of borrowing funds for the purpose. The most important of these reasons is that, by borrowing, an entrepreneur endangers his firm in a manner, and to a degree, which does not arise when he lays out his own undistributed profits which have been held in the form of cash or easily marketable securities. It is impossible in a few lines to do justice to Mr Cunningham's subtle and thoroughgoing discussion, but he points mainly to the fact that, so far from being able to borrow unlimited funds at a constant market interest rate, the entrepreneur is acutely aware that the cost per unit of his borrowings will increase with the size of his total debt and that these borrowings will eventually reach an absolute limit, which will, moreover, become narrower at those very times of difficulty for the firm when borrowing may be most necessary to it. This power to borrow, Mr Cunningham urges, is looked upon by the business man, and should be treated by the economist, as a form of liquid reserve, a means of satisfying his precautionary and speculative motives for desiring liquidity. The 'subjective' cost to the entrepreneur of using borrowed funds for the purchase of durable equipment must therefore reflect a *double illiquidity*. It requires the lender to substitute an illiquid asset (viz. an I.O.U.) in his portfolio, for a liquid asset, viz. cash; and it deprives the borrower of one possible source of liquid funds which he could

* 'Business Investment and the Marginal Cost of Funds', *Metroeconomica*, vol. x (1958).

otherwise resort to in emergency or in face of an unforeseen profit opportunity. The consequence of this difference of implication between owned and borrowed funds is that the curve of *marginal cost of funds for investment* is likely to have a step or jump-discontinuity at the point where 'owned' funds are exhausted and resort must be had to borrowing. This vertical segment of the curve is the most striking of several features of the situation, all of which lead, in one set of circumstances or another, to the conclusion that changes of the market interest rate may quite visibly leave the firm's inducement to invest in equipment unaffected. These considerations are an important theoretical complement to the argument advanced in Part II of this article.

Mr George Clayton* has considered the very interesting problem of the *velocity of circulation of real balances*. When the velocity of circulation of money is slow, as in a business depression, can the banking system of its own power do anything to increase the frequency with which given quantities of *real purchasing power* change hands? His article points out how in some circumstances the public's desire for larger nominal balances regardless of the loss of income involved, with the resulting divorce of the long-term from the short-term interest rate, added to the insensitiveness of investment to any fall of the long-term rate which may be achieved, can frustrate the speeding up of the 'real' velocity of circulation even in a depression with heavy unemployment of resources. When there is full employment the banks' attempt to increase their outstanding loans merely results in higher prices. One way of expressing these well-recognized facts is to say that the banking system's power to increase the nation's nominal stock of money is by no means necessarily a power to increase the nation's money income, still less its real income. In introducing the notion of 'real velocity of circulation' Mr Clayton has, we think, greatly contributed to ease of discourse on these matters.

Mr J. K. Eastham, in a very valuable article,† has traced the fluctuating historic distinctions between the interest and the

* 'A Note on the Banking System's Power to Lend', *Metroeconomica*, vol. VII (1955).

† 'A Redefinition of the Boundary between Interest and Profit Theories', in *Dundee Economic Essays*, J. K. Eastham, ed. (Dundee, 1955).

profit components of the earnings of 'capital', and has shown the importance, for a theory of accumulation, of keeping interest among the obstacles and profit among the inducements to investment, that is, to the construction of specialized, concrete equipment.

From this survey of recent tendencies in the theory of how interest is determined, we turn now to consider the state of opinion, and to make some suggestions of our own, about the role of interest in the theory of the inducement to invest.

## PART II. THE ROLE OF INTEREST

### 5. *The investment horizon*

A change in an interest rate can, like a change in any other economic variable, transmit with more or less effect, and more or less delay, an impulse from one part of the economic system to another. Theory suggests that its more powerful effects are likely to be upon the demand for durable goods and upon the balance of payments. Demand for durable goods, whether by producers or householders, is investment, and the question whether interest-rate changes do or do not appreciably affect investment has been actively studied by observation, question and analysis from the 1938 attempt by the Oxford Economists' Research Group onwards.

A necessary tool for any such study is a clear conception of the *formal* role of the interest rate in the *formal* structure of a profitability calculation. Since money in hand can be lent at positive interest wherever an organized loan market exists, money in hand is equivalent on today's market to a larger sum of deferred money. Expected instalments of profit, or of services (such as enjoyment of a house) having a market value, are deferred money, and in order to find today's market worth of a series of such instalments, each must be adjusted for its deferment and, in some cases, also for its uncertainty. Any such instalment which is treated as free from uncertainty must accordingly be divided by: one plus the annual interest rate: and must be thus divided once for each year of deferment.

Since the interest rate thus occurs in the denominator of a fraction, this fraction, which is the 'present' or 'discounted' value of a deferred, but certain, unit instalment, will be smaller, the larger the interest rate. Thus today's demand price for any asset or object which is counted upon with certainty to yield specified deferred instalments will be lower, the higher the interest rate. If other relevant circumstances are unchanged, and if in particular the cost of production of such an asset is independent of the interest rate, fewer such assets will be demanded in each time-unit after than before a rise of the interest rate.

This scheme of analysis can be refined. We can suppose that the supply price of any type of equipment (any 'machines') rises as the number of units ordered per time-unit increases. We can suppose that the series of deferred instalments attributed to the asset is a different one in the minds of different individuals, each relying upon some information, and some interpretive background of experience, private to himself. Each will then have his own demand price and, we may suppose, his own convenient number of machines which he will order per time-unit provided the supply price is less than his demand price. When the number of machines being supplied per time-unit is such that the corresponding supply price is just low enough to evoke that number of orders per time-unit, we have an equilibrium.

But suppose that we wish to express such an equilibrium as consisting in the equality of a 'rate of return', on the one hand, and the loan interest rate, on the other? The appropriate formal algebraic equation looks exactly like the one by which, given the loan interest rate, we calculate the present value of a given series of annual deferred instalments. The meaning of the letters in this equation, however, is different. Instead of a present value or *demand price* we now have on the left-hand side a *supply price*, and instead of the loan interest rate prevailing in the market, we have on the right-hand side an *unknown* whose numerical value is to be determined by solving the equation. This unknown percentage, or, if we prefer, vulgar fraction or decimal fraction, is the marginal efficiency of capital. In equilibrium, the marginal (or 'lowest effective') demand price of each sort of machines, and their supply price, will have been driven to equality by the search for profit. In equilibrium, therefore, the marginal efficiency of capital will have been driven, by rising supply price, to equality with the interest rate on loans. This means that, in equilibrium, the personal demand price entertained by the least sanguine of those business men from whom an order for machines is actually elicited, will be equal to the supply price, and that therefore the percentage per annum at which this marginally sanguine placer of orders must discount his expected profits, to make their present value equal to the supply price of machines, is equal to the loan rate he must pay on money borrowed to buy these machines.

We need not, however, suppose that there are any intra-marginal investors. If we assume that the series of deferred instalments, which a machine is counted on, by the potential investor, to yield to him if he buys it, depends itself upon the number of machines ordered, and that each of these instalments is a decreasing function of that number, we can suppose *each* business man to carry the number of orders he gives per unit of time up to that level where his own ('personal') demand price for machines is no greater than their supply price. Thus a much more interesting sense is given to the word 'marginal' when we speak of the marginal efficiency of capital. If, in this case, we cease to assume implicitly that loans of no matter what term carry one and the same rate of interest, and suppose instead that each deferred instalment of profit or service is discounted at the particular rate appropriate to its own deferment, then we can accommodate in our scheme of thought the idea that some business men will value more highly than others the prospect of recovering relatively early the money they propose to invest in machines. Such men will direct their orders to machines of types which offer an *early* concentration of instalments, each large relatively to the total amount of the whole series of instalments promised by such a machine.

In all this there has been no mention of depreciation or amortization. Have those notions any relevance for investment decisions? Depreciation is loss of value or prospective earning power by a durable good. When a potential buyer of such a machine looks forward to a date at which some particular set or portion of the deferred instalments which it promises will have been obtained from it he will see it as destined to have, at that future date, a lesser value than it has now, and a value which he can reckon on the basis of the deferred instalments lying *beyond* that date and the interest rates which, by inference from the rates prevailing *now* for loans of various terms, he can reckon to prevail on that future date. This gradual ebb of value, as it occurs, will have to be somehow reflected in the book-keeping of his business and in the published condensations of those accounts, and for this purpose it may suit him to represent this decay by a conventional 'depreciation allowance' whose annual amount may be a constant or a term of a geometric series or what not. What has this convention of book-keeping to do with the basic profitability of the investment? Nothing.

It is a pity that a number of writers on the question whether the size of the investment flow is responsive to changes of interest rates, or not, still feel it necessary to encumber their analyses with irrelevant discussions of amortization. An interesting debate followed the publication of the evidence obtained on that question by Professors M. D. Brockie and A. L. Grey,* who had concluded therefrom that the interest-elasticity of firms' demand for equipment was low. Professor W. H. White† interpreted their figures differently, but failed to convince them, and the debate must be called inconclusive. It did, however, raise the exceedingly interesting question of the lengthening which Brockie and Grey‡ believe to have occurred in the 'pay-off period'. If the yearly profit which a proposed investment is counted upon to earn is taken as constant for all years there will be some number of years such that the total profits of those years equal the first cost (construction cost) of the investment. As a more refined definition, we may take the pay-off period to be that number of years whose total *discounted* profits equal the construction cost of the investment. In the Oxford Economists' 1938 study§ business men were often heard to say that they would not order equipment unless it promised to 'pay for itself in 3 (sometimes even 2) years'. Grey and Brockie‖ found that 85 per cent of their respondents used either the 'pay-out period' method or 'an alternative formulation amounting to virtually the same thing (the percentage of initial cost of the investment

* 'The Marginal Efficiency of Capital and Investment Programming', *Economic Journal*, vol. LXVI (December 1956).

† 'The Rate of Interest, the Marginal Efficiency of Capital and Investment Programming', *Economic Journal*, vol. LXVIII (March 1958).

‡ 'The Rate of Interest, the Marginal Efficiency of Capital and Investment Programming—A Rejoinder', *Economic Journal*, vol. LXIX (June 1959).

§ J. E. Meade and P. W. S. Andrews, 'Summary of Replies to Questions on Effects of Interest Rates', *Oxford Economic Papers*, No. 1 (October 1938).

‖ 'The Marginal Efficiency of Capital and Investment Programming'.

recovered out of earnings each year)...for evaluating prospective investments'. White* comments upon this:

Because the pay-out-period method requires that initial cost be recovered during a very small number of years, it connotes very short economic horizons, very high required rates of return and unscientific investment planning; consequently, the investment plans of 85 per cent of large firms may be assumed unaffected by the cost of capital.

Any economic theoretician will readily sympathize with Professor White's attitude. Nevertheless, we must beware here of letting pure theory kick aside too much of practical realism. Can it be truly called scientific to base profitability estimates on years too far ahead for knowledge about the observable *present* to throw any light upon their circumstances? Professor White is correct, as we showed many years ago,† in saying that interest-rate changes will be almost powerless to change the inducement to invest, when the planning horizon is only two or three years into the future. But this is not a reason for pretending that we can see beyond the horizon.

Why do‡ business men place their horizon at only two or three years ahead, and *ignore* deliberately the possibility that their proposed equipment may still, in the years beyond that horizon, prove capable of making goods which will sell for more than the running costs of the machines? It is because they cannot be *sure* that these profits will be earned, they cannot brush aside the threat that newer inventions will enable their rivals to undercut them or to oust their product with a better one. The present throws light on the immediate future, but that light dims rapidly as we peer farther ahead. The business men are not 'unscientific', they are cautious. Now plainly no equipment is worth buying if the money to be spent on it will not be recovered, let alone any return for 'enterprise', 'decision-making', 'risk-taking' or the general services of the enterpriser. If only three years' profit can be counted on, that profit must be at a

* 'The Rate of Interest, the Marginal Efficiency of Capital and Investment Programming'.

† G. L. S. Shackle, 'Interest-Rates and the Pace of Investment', *Economic Journal*, vol. LVI (March 1946).

‡ See ch. 15, 'Business and Uncertainty', p. 160, and Shackle, 'Interest-Rates and the Pace of Investment', *Bankers' Magazine*, vol. CLXXXIX (March 1960).

rate equal to one-third, at the very least, of the first cost of the machine. A minimum requirement of 34 per cent per annum may seem, at first glance, to be a deliberate rejection of countless profit opportunities which might yield, say, 20 or 15 per cent, still much in excess of the *loan interest rate.* In such an argument two wholly different ideas are being utterly confused. To spend £1 million and to get back £150,000 in each of three years, and then nothing, is not to make a profit.

The true relation between the crude annual profit, assumed to be the same from year to year and to be earned for just so and so many years and then to relapse to nothing, and treated as a proportion of the first cost of the equipment, on the one hand; and the rate of return which can be legitimately compared with the loan rate of interest, on the other; is simply the following. Each year's assumed profit is to be divided by : one plus an 'unknown' fraction : divided once for each year of deferment; the answers thus obtained are to be summed, and their sum is to be set equal to the machine's first cost. The resulting equation is then to be solved for the 'unknown' fraction, and the numerical value obtained is the 'marginal efficiency of capital' which can be compared *meaningfully* with the interest rate. There is still no mention of amortization. An example* will illustrate the matter. Let the first cost of a machine be 100, and the assumed earnings (excess of sale proceeds of product over *running* costs, no mention of amortization) in each of the next three years be 40, with nothing thereafter. Then the marginal efficiency of capital is 10 per cent per annum, and *it will not pay* to buy this machine with loaned money on which a rate of interest of more than 10 per cent per annum has to be paid, notwithstanding the appearance that the machine is going to earn '40 per cent per annum' of its first cost.

In any such calculation the air of precision and certainty are entirely bogus. We have deliberately spoken of 'assumed' profits. What is in question here is the need for some basis of argument, something to be set against the background of fact, news, experience and technical knowledge which the business man has at command. We have avoided speaking of expected profits, for the reason that 'expected' can cover everything from a feeling of conviction to the merest toying with a wild

* See Shackle 'Interest-Rates and the Pace of Investment'.

hope. The business man who resolves to count on nothing beyond three years ahead is well aware of the open door to good fortune which he will thus offer. If all goes well, the machine which has earned 40 per cent of its first cost in each of the first three years of its life may continue to do so, thus realizing a large overall gain.

By contrast with these uncertainties, the powerlessness* of interest rates, within the ordinary range of 2–8 per cent per annum, to influence the demand price of *near-horizon* equipment by undergoing any change of a size which may be supposed to occur within months, is a matter of plain arithmetic. It is plain for anyone to see what kind of difference is involved when we divide the supposed profit of three years hence by $(104/100)^3$ instead of by $(105/100)^3$, that is by 225/200 instead of by 232/200. This is the sort of difference made when the interest rate changes by a whole percentage point, from 5 to 4 per cent per annum.

The ineradicable uncertainty of enterprise, the nearness of the horizon thus imposed, the powerlessness of interest-rate changes, are all intimately bound together. Where this uncertainty is less (it is, of course, a subjective thing, a judgement or a state of mind, we are not called upon to justify a feeling that some forms of durable goods are more confidently counted on than others to yield profits in the distant future) the interest rate may have a powerful leverage. A house which is counted on to yield £100 per annum for eighty years has, at an interest rate of 4 per cent per annum, a present value of £2,400; at 2 per cent per annum it has a present value of £4,000. Upon which of the equal annual instalments, counted upon with certainty to be received from some durable good, does a small change of the interest rate used for discounting have the largest *absolute* effect in altering the present value of that instalment? The answer† may at first surprise a reader who has not come across it. The greatest absolute change in the present value of any one equal instalment affects that instalment whose deferment, in years, is equal to the reciprocal of the annual interest rate. Thus if that rate is 3 per cent per annum the largest gain in present value, due to a change to 2⅞ per cent per annum, will be achieved by the instalment due in thirty-three years' time. It would be for our children or our children's children to say whether or not we

* Op. cit. † Op. cit.

should allow a change in the yield of Consols to tempt us to build houses for them, could we but consult their future knowledge now!

## 6. *Harrodian dynamics*

We turn to a broader canvas. Sir Roy Harrod's *Towards a Dynamic Economics** reverts in its broad style and spirit to the classic models, where the whole darkling plain of human affairs was in view, but its economic features were emphasized by the lamps of settlement. A different metaphor suggests its character in detail.

Rivers, tides and ocean currents irresistibly present themselves as an image and analogy of the economic process. There are the short-period waves and the idiosyncratic storms, there are tides and more constant, one-way currents acting slowly over great stretches of time. This picture is brought to mind by the view of interest which underlies Sir Roy's economics of long-period growth or decline. No one better understands Keynes's short-period pre-occupations or his view of interest as the hourly and momently fluctuating equilibrator of Bull and Bear expectations. Yet in his *Towards a Dynamic Economics*, written immediately after the War, Harrod is concerned with the slowest, most deep-seated and steady forces which bear upon, and are transmitted by, the rate of interest. The view that liquidity preference and expectations (the speculative motive), however important and spectacular their effects, are waves on the surface of a deep tide representing the 'real' forces of thrift and productivity, is one shared in some degree by writers as widely separated as Sir Dennis Robertson and Mrs Joan Robinson. Like Mrs Robinson, Harrod, in discussing the long-term forces, reverts in effect to the older usage whereby 'interest' covered any gain due to the possession of a stock of wealth, other than the market appreciation of the assets themselves. Saving is the continual or repetitive act by which wealth is permitted to accumulate. What considerations in the income-receiver's mind must be overcome by a positive interest rate, in this older sense, if he is ever to save?

There are two quite distinct reasons for spending now rather than waiting for a larger sum later. One is that the larger sum may veri-

* London: Macmillan, 1948.

tably have less utility than the smaller sum now, the other the lack of telescopic faculty whereby we fail to estimate justly the utility that the larger sum will have.

In the secure and virtually tax-less Victorian world the well-to-do no doubt looked upon 'the family' and its 'fortune' as everlasting, only provided each successive generation took seriously its duty of maintenance and improvement. But can we, even so, argue as though life were a space within which there is free movement for the human individual; as though he were provided with some sort of fix-point and a mental theodolite, by which he can survey the country of life and make some objective comparison of the utility a given expenditure would give him at different parts of that life?

A man may choose to sacrifice 2 units of utility—of utility not money—in 20 years from now for the sake of 1 unit now; but in 20 years' time he will presumably regret having done so.

At the later date, we might by this reasoning equally well argue, he will regret not having lived for twenty years at subsistence level in order at last to be rich. In so far as *any* current consumption impoverishes my later years, I ought to live in a garret in order to be buried in a Pharaoh's tomb. But in what sense can the actual, experienced and not merely imagined utility of one moment be compared with that of a different moment? What common ground, what fix-point is there, in the time not of the sophisticated outsider but of the living individual in his moment-to-moment experience? Every comparison of *my own* utility (not that of the 'economic subject' under my microscope) which I can *in fact* make is inevitably made at some one moment. Who has the right to tell me that this comparison is ill judged? What sense will it make, in forty years' time, if my then self says, 'That young man ought to have saved for my old age instead of spending to enjoy his youth?'

These are intensely difficult matters and we may perhaps be forgiven for taking an unusual view of them. In doubting the meaningfulness of that sort of intertemporal comparisons which underlie Böhm-Bawerk's 'first ground' for the existence of interest we are saying only that a man cannot stand outside of time and of his own immediate present, and weigh the relative expediency, by some objective, impersonal, omnitemporal standard, of this act or that. Comparisons of 'then' and 'now' are made *now*. There is no 'third point' in time, no neutral, a-temporal common ground, from which the comparison can be made so as to leave the individual still free to act 'now' in whatever way that comparison suggests.

The central and continuous theme of *Towards a Dynamic Economics* is the search for those various sets of circumstances, any one set among which, once attained, would carry the economy on a path of steady enrichment of each and all of its subjects; and if such circumstances seem too precarious or elusive, then a search for the policy and means by which the economy can be consciously held to such a path. Sir Roy looks upon a steady, slow secular fall of the interest rate as able, to some extent, to take the place of the accelerator in providing an inducement to invest strong enough to keep the economy at full employment along a rising ceiling of output. The accelerator, if relied upon alone to maintain full employment, might require a pace of growth of output *greater* than the upward slope of the ceiling; a pace of growth, that is to say, which it would be impossible to maintain. Therefore the rate of interest must be pushed ever downward in order that a steady *deepening* of the structure of capital equipment may reinforce the *widening* induced by the growth of output. Besides the problem of a chronic tendency to under-employment equilibrium there is, however, a second problem, that of the business cycle, and here Sir Roy regards the interest rate as wholly ineffective. He compares as follows the two problems:

While the fall in the long-term rate may not produce any strong immediate effect by making entrepreneurs reconsider their productive methods or by making durable goods more attractive to the consumer, it is not inconsistent with this to hold that in due time, that is after there has been time for the lower rate to sink in and become part of the furniture of the mind of entrepreneurs and others, the various adjustments consequent upon it may add up to a sizeable amount.

But

This does not help us with our trade cycle problem. What we there want is responsiveness preferably within a few months, but, at the very worst, within a year or two... I am inclined to attach great weight to the views of those who urge us not to expect a very great increase of capital outlay in the period immediately following a change in the long-term rate of interest.

Interest is the most paradoxical of all economic quantities. At first sight it seems to present us with the opportunity of doing calculations, and of obtaining in this way results which are at once quantitatively exact, logically inescapable and theoretically interesting. It is one of the main pillars of the claim of economics to be Queen of the Social Sciences, the only one of those sciences reducible to mathematical statement and analysis. It runs in an unbroken thread through the whole theory of accumulation of wealth, both on the saving and on the investment side, and thus seems to reign over the theories of employment, of money, of growth, of the general price level and of the balance of payments. It can appear, from this viewpoint of pure theory, as the pivot of the entire system, the sun in the midst of its planets. Yet when examined closely, these claims dissolve. It has been admitted from Marshall's time at least that the influence of the interest rate on saving is doubtful even as to its algebraic sign. More recently its influence on investment has been denied on the basis of business men's own testimony. Bank rate is still nominally the Bank of England's leading-rein for the commercial banking system, but it has had to be reinforced by 'directives', special deposits, hire-purchase regulations and what not. It seems likely that the interest rate, or the system of rates, will continue to receive from theoreticians the homage due to a ceremonial monarch, without in fact counting for more than such a monarch in the real affairs of Western nations.

weight to the views of those who urge us not to expect a very great response of capital outlay in the period immediately following a change in the long-term rate of interest.

Facts and figures must play a part in all economic enquiries. At first sight it seems to present us with the opportunity of doing calculations and of obtaining in this way results which are at once quantitatively exact, logically inescapable and theoretically interesting. These are the main pillars of the claim of economics to be the queen of the Social Sciences, the only one of these sciences which seems wholly suited to measurement and analysis. Yet in this fundamental area, through the whole theory of accumulation of wealth, both on the saving and on the investment side, and thus seems to interlock the theories of employment, of money, of growth, of the general price level and of the balance of payments, it can appear, from this sort of pure theory, as the pivot of the entire system. Yet, in the midst of an elementary world, a continued scrutiny these claims dissolve. It has been admitted for a long time at least that the influence of the interest rate on saving is doubtful even as to its sign. And, what is more, its influence on investment has been doubted on the basis of business men's own testimony. Bank rate is still officially the Bank of England's chief weapon for the commercial banking system, but it has had to be augmented by directives, special deposits, hire-purchase regulations and what not. It seems likely that the interest rate, or the system of rates, will continue to receive from theoreticians the homage due to a fundamental mechanism, without its fact counting for more than such a movement in the real affairs of Western nations.

# VI

# CRITICAL REFLECTIONS

# 20

# BATTLES LONG AGO*

## A REVIEW ARTICLE

Controversies in economic theory have a life-cycle somewhat resembling that of household equipment. When first invented they are eagerly explained and counter-explained by the more ardent spirits and nervously heard about by the more conservative ones. After a decade or so they are completely relegated to limbo, and argument turns to different problems or adopts a different apparatus of thought. But when fifty years have gone by, these old disputes are rescued from obscurity by a new generation, to whom their quaint antique convolutions seem delightful and nostalgic, and who can see in them, perhaps, something far closer to their own current practical perplexities than the 'detours' which economic theory has taken in the meantime. To be fascinated with past disputes, we must not be too close to them in time, for then we shall simply look on them as a tiresome groping after truths that seem to us simple and straightforward, and if we are compelled to read about them, we shall feel ourselves, as Keynes put it in another context, to be 'chewing over a lot of cold mutton'.

If the danger of giving rise to such feelings does, in fact, confront those who contemplate gathering a thirty-year span of their own articles between hard covers, they should not allow it to deter them, especially if they were themselves in the forefront of the battle and were amongst the inventors of some of the ideas and theories which were under dispute. For these books of gathered articles are not for one generation only. Those who come after us will turn eagerly to them, grateful for these 'symposia' at which a man sits round a table with his earlier selves and drinks to his own past. When a writer has been as incandescent, as protean and as enormously fruitful as Mr Kaldor,

* Nicholas Kaldor, *Essays on Value and Distribution* (London, 1960: Gerald Duckworth and Co.).

Idem. *Essays on Economic Stability and Growth* (London, 1960: Gerald Duckworth and Co.).

he is under an obligation to make of his long thoughts a continuous, evolving drama in one book.

The present reviewer, engaged elsewhere in an effort to unravel the threads of those very debates of the last thirty-five years, in some of which Mr Kaldor took so intimate a part, is doubly grateful for these two volumes in which we find conveniently not only what Mr Kaldor said but an indication of what he would now repeat or repudiate. He no longer believes that a useful economics can be built on 'a few self-evident postulates alone' but thinks that it 'can only be reached as a result of empirical hypotheses'.* This is, of course, the road along which economics has been marching ever faster since the war brought its great hunger for statistics and the electronic computer its giant power to process them. Yet how does one tell whether a hypothesis is 'empirical' or merely 'self-evident'? Are there hypotheses which are self-evidently empirical? There can be more than one view, too, about the nature and proper use of economic theory. It is nowadays expected to be a more intelligible edition of the Sibylline books, telling us the future if only, unlike Tarquin, we are ready to buy it. But is this really what it can do? The econometricians, priests of this particular oracle, talk about 'incomplete information'. But they never tell us how they would know that their information was complete, if it ever was. Theory can serve a quite different purpose, that of organizing thought about the nature and *possibilities* inherent in the economic world, so that the student feels that at least he has a method of attack on any problem. Used in this way, theory is not predictive but descriptive, and it needs no elusive distinction between 'empirical' and 'self-evident' postulates.

The great efflorescence of theory in the 1930's included, amongst at least three new branches which the tree of economics then put out, the enormously fertile subject of Imperfect Competition. Mr Sraffa, Sir Roy Harrod and Mrs Joan Robinson amongst the economists of England were the chief gardeners in this case, but Mr Kaldor was there with four mainly critical papers which he now reprints. It must be confessed that criticism reads with less ease and perspicuousness at a distance in time from the debate. One is no longer constantly handling and discussing the ideas in such a way that a question can be taken

* *Value and Distribution*, p. 3.

up at any moment without preparation or definition. The host of subquestions and byways of thought that were open to the minds of the original protagonists are now lost, and implicit references to them are obscure and frustrating. The task of reconstructing such a debate in one's own mind, from written sources and the memories of others, is all but impossible, and the present writer, engaged at that time on one of the other branches, was an observer and not a participant. I doubt whether today's student will be able to follow all those paths along which Mr Kaldor with such assurance picks his way, but the reader will find some intriguing judgements: 'We see therefore that the mathematical economists in taking perfect competition as their starting point, weren't such fools after all.'* 'This is a question of business psychology rather than economics.'† (What, dare one ask, is economics about if it is not about business psychology?)

It was in another great debate that Mr Kaldor played the central or initiating role, that of the New Welfare Economics. (Where are the snows of yesteryear?) The subject which, in Professor Pigou's day, was a burning and emotional issue of practical political economy, has in recent years been utterly made over. It is now an abstract and elegant but useless application of symbolic logic, telling us that if everybody's welfare can be simultaneously increased, everybody will be better off. If (and I pray that this may be the case) your happiness makes me happy, then the welfare of the world (*my* world) can be increased by improving your happiness, and the welfare of the world (*your* world) can similarly, perhaps, be increased by improving my happiness. But where, in all this, does interpersonal comparison and *addition* come in? Mr Kaldor and the mighty band who followed his path-breaking track cleared an immense amount of undergrowth, but they did not quite come full-circle to re-instate Pigou on a more secure and less question-begging foundation. Welfare is a value judgement made for himself by each individual, and not necessarily made *selfishly*, but, on the contrary, sometimes with a perfect altruism, but made by each man for himself, *unaddably*.

It is said that there are certain places in the sea, such as the central Baltic, where in certain states of the wind tremendous

* Ibid., p. 71. † Ibid., p. 75.

waves and currents drive together from all directions and clash with a fearful yet fascinating violence. In the intellectual world certain institutions at certain historical junctures, through their topographical location and high prestige, seem likewise to be the natural scene of great clashes of thought, so that for a time they enjoy a super-normal activity and seething intensity of life. Such a place was the London School of Economics in the middle 1930's. Driven by adversity or oppression or visiting more normally, brilliant men in a great stream poured into it from all directions, bringing an immense diversity of ideas to be traded and cried up against each other like the wares of merchants at a medieval fair. Amongst these collisions of thought, one of the most enigmatic is described by Mr Kaldor in one of his 'Value' essays and two of his 'Growth' essays. The present reviewer as a research student had as his supervisor, ever thought of in gratitude for his imaginative fostering of work belonging to 'the other camp', the protagonist of this strange passage of intellectual history. Mr Kaldor (in 1942) wrote:

> The term 'fascination', though perhaps slightly unacademic, aptly describes the effect of the *first impact* of Professor Hayek's ideas on economists trained in the Anglo-Saxon tradition (and [Mr Kaldor] has no wish to conceal that he was among the fascinees) to whom it suggested aspects of the nature of capitalistic production they were never taught to think of. In comparison with Professor Hayek's 'triangles', 'distorted price margins', and unduly-elongated production periods, the [then] prevailing concern with price-levels, and with banks doing this or that, must have appeared facile and superficial.*

How did this 'first impact', to which the present reviewer was strongly subject, come to be repudiated by Professor Hayek's colleagues, his students and, in a different way, himself? There is in the Austrian theory of capital a paradox and a mystery which still intrigues economists. At first sight, the basis of this theory is an inspired simplification which seems to dissolve a crippling theoretical difficulty. This difficulty is, how can we measure the 'quantity of capital', when capital by its nature consists of a countless diversity of incommensurable objects? Böhm-Bawerk's idea, and Jevons's in some degree, was that all this collection of utterly various tools, machines, buildings and

* *Stability and Growth*, p. 148.

stockpiles is the concrete manifestation of the part played in production by the *lapse of time*. The greater the total role of time in making some given stream of output, the larger the quantity of capital (equipment) engaged in the making of that output. The longer the 'average period of production', the weighted average lapse of time between doing work and getting the fruits of that work, the greater at any moment must evidently be the number of objects, each requiring given hours of labour to make it, which have been made in the past but not yet destroyed in an act of consumption, and so the average period of production measures the quantity of capital. It is tragic that an idea of such arresting beauty and simplicity should fail to work, yet that has been the experience of many of those who sought to work out its detailed application; not least, I think, of Professor Hayek himself, whose fame derives nowadays from his work in other directions. Mr Hugh Gaitskell is among those who have concluded that the average period of production is not a serviceable tool of analysis. The moral of a sad tale is that in economics one can set too great a store by detailed precision. Economics is not a precise subject, either in its definitions or its measurements, and we get on better if we recognize this fact. The Austrians were too profound in elaborating their theory, the English too fastidious in criticizing it. That 'capital is time' is *still* a good idea, used as a general illuminator, not as a piece of mathematical logic.

Keynes's tremendous impact on economic theory is well measured by the number of first-rate minds who have been content, or by the very success of his ideas have been compelled, to take his work as the basis of their own constructions. Had there been no Keynes, economic theory might still have attained much of its present power. Streams of thought from several directions were converging to carve out a new river-bed for economics; Myrdal and Lindahl with their Wicksellian inspiration had an impulse of immense importance to contribute; Frisch had provided an oscillation model which only waited for the multiplier concept; Kalecki alone, but for the barriers of language and situation, might have propagated a quasi-Keynesian system of his own. Harrod, Hicks and Kaldor (not to speak of Professor Kahn and Mrs Robinson, who actually bore up the prophet's arms) were ready to dash off at full speed with the Olympic torch, once it had been lighted; and Mr Kaldor has carried it as fast and as far as any, still proclaiming (and not all Keynes's followers have been so scrupulous) by whom the flame was lit. Keynes drew all these lines of force together as by a giant magnet; needles which would have taken much time to settle down were all drawn quickly to point in the same direction and give the same guidance; Keynes contributed not only his ideas but an ascendant charisma which marshalled and accelerated the forces of change.

Any notable work will attract a host of refiners and expositors with little of their own to contribute; what is unique in Keynes's case is the calibre of his supporters, men who would in any case have greatly advanced their subject. Mr Kaldor's 'Growth' essays include many illustrations of a brilliant virtuosity, and perhaps most strikingly of all, his own trade-cycle model and his superb comparison of the Marxian and the Keynesian systems, the latter essay designed for and delivered to an audience in Peking, upon whom surely the impress must have been profound even if, inevitably, they could not fully fathom the incomparable blend of tact and temerity with which the message was conveyed.

What a proud record of achievement and what a reflection of a unique personality is gathered between the covers of these two volumes; and what an item for inclusion in that list of 'books I would take to a desert island'!

# 21

# THE STAGES OF ECONOMIC GROWTH*

## A REVIEW ARTICLE

'This book presents an economic historian's way of generalizing the sweep of modern history. The form of this generalization is a set of stages of growth.'

Thus, in his opening sentence, Professor Rostow states by implication a whole philosophy of history. When we wish to study the nature, origins, motives, and consequences of human action, we have to study history, for history is what men have done, and there is no other genuine raw material. Broadly, in writing history, two rival methods, based on two mutually antagonistic presuppositions, are possible. The historian can describe, in such detail as the scale of his work allows, what seems to him to have happened, and leave his readers to interpret and explain the story for themselves on any principles they like. Or he can try to supply such principles. He can try to say what history means, to find in the factual record a structure, a recurring pattern, a mechanism. To do this is to treat human affairs as a part of nature, capable, therefore, of being studied by the methods of the natural scientist. But the natural scientist's declared aim is to fashion a predictive tool. Is the historian, then, to become a prophet? How is he to explain, according to some formal scheme, what did happen, and still escape the argument that, since in his view things were bound to happen in the way they did, he must logically be able to tell us what is bound to happen next? Professor Rostow refers to Marx, the most famous of those who have accepted this challenge as a matter of course and, in explaining past history, have exposed themselves with eager, dedicated certainty to the verdict of future history. He might perhaps have mentioned also Professor Toynbee who has, however, been cautious to the point of inconsistency in drawing inferences from his own approach. Professor Rostow calls his book 'A Non-Communist Manifesto', and he

* W. W. Rostow, *The Stages of Economic Growth* (Cambridge University Press 1960).

has the courage of his method in drawing conclusions about the future from his formalization of the past.

Mankind evolved, we are told by the paleontologists, from ancestors who rested, like other animals, upon their hands as well as their feet. The decisive change when it occurred took, geologically speaking, the mere twinkling of an eye, perhaps some fifty thousand years, and men suddenly began to stand erect, so that, having their hands free, they could hold things, bring them close to their eyes for interested inspection, and wield them as weapons, and then as tools. Since then they have seldom looked back, and never for long. For perhaps a million or perhaps ten million years men have been moving from the oldest Old Stone Age to the nuclear age. Has this progress been smooth or jerky? Have there been, in various societies, periods of stagnation, separated from each other by spurts of sudden virtuosity, enterprise, ambition, and glimpsing of far horizons? Has one such spurt been spreading over the world from an epicentre in Britain, during the last two centuries? What has been the mechanism of this propagation, and, above all, why and how did the earthquake start in Britain? Professor Rostow does not spend much time on the question *whether* since 1760 there has been a spreading industrial revolution, but is concerned only with the *how* of the one which, so obviously, has taken place.

But perhaps a longer perspective would have been in order here. Fire and the cutting edge, animal husbandry, agriculture, the wheel, the sail, the alphabet, positional notation in arithmetic; all these inventions or discoveries were as great and revolutionary as any that have been made in the last two centuries, and our list has omitted printing, the greatest liberator and social solvent, the indispensable foundation of modern technological mass-competence. Did these inventions give rise to a 'take-off into self-sustained growth' (or continuing change)? If not, why not? If Newton succeeded in giving science its necessary mathematical take-off, why did Archimedes, so near him in spirit and power, not succeed? Professor Rostow does not look into the dark backward and abysm of time. Yet the modern take-off needs to be put into a deep and general vista of human history and prehistory, if we are not to get exaggerated notions of our superiority.

Professor Rostow's famous article, 'The take-off into self-sustained growth', published in the *Economic Journal* of March 1956, will remain a landmark in economics. A book of the present length might well have been devoted to giving a series of close-ups of historical instances ofthe take-off and of particular aspects and details of it, to studying the mechanism at short range, to constructing a theory in the more stringent meaning oı the word, to filling in a flesh-and-blood picture, to amassing statistical evidence. It is the *agencement*, the fitting-together-so-that-it-works, of his central idea that seems, to a theoretician, to ask for more precise treatment. Truth, indeed, is not always vouchsafed to the man who gets closest to the trees rather than surveys the wood. Need we fear that the snowy peaks on Professor Rostow's skyline will turn out to be but clouds? I do not for a moment think it. But some relevant thoughts are worth a glance. Professor Rostow refers constantly to 'the powerful arithmetic of compound interest'. A compound-interest curve is one whose gradient is everywhere proportional to its ordinate. Thus if I have only £10 in the savings bank I shall still be a poor man after ten years, even if I am getting 8 per cent per annum on my money, for I shall have only gained another £10. But during a second 10 years I shall have gained another £20, my third ten years will bring me in £40, my fourth £80 and my fifth £160. Were I a Methuselah, having started eighty years ago with 10 *pence*, the process of accumulating £10 in eighty years might not have impressed me on the neighbours as a budding Rockefeller. Yet if I can last another century and two-thirds I shall be a millionaire in pounds sterling. Do I happen, then, just at this particular moment, to be at my 'take-off', the critical moment between £10 in eighty years and a million pounds in only twice as long again? The exponential curve has its psychological and subjective aspects, it appears, for all this happens at a constant 8 per cent per annum. Even a rocket to the moon starts slowly off its pad.

By all odds, however, it is humanly unlikely that progress would be steady and smooth. A new tool or technique, once it has been clearly demonstrated, is likely to spread rapidly through an economy. Sometimes a series of such innovations, with the accompanying bursts of necessary investment, will be closely echelonned and give the overall effect of a general revolution. Professor Rostow's great achievement and lasting glory lie in his having dramatized, to use his own word, the need to study how this sort of thing happens, so that we can manipulate it in favour of those 'uncommitted' nations which we are so eager to align with the West. Acknowledging this, even a reviewer who is no historian may be permitted to regret that Professor Rostow did not risk boring his Cambridge audience with a patient unravelling of the skein, instead of rather conversationally sketching his 'five stages of economic growth'.

Professor Rostow's discussion contains one strange lacuna. If your working population is ten men, just able by devoting themselves wholly to farming to keep themselves and their dependants alive, and if you then wish to transfer two of them to making machines, the eight who remain as farmers will have somehow to increase their output per head by a quarter. This is the simple reason why a subsistence-farming economy, unless it can get large gifts of imported food, can only establish industries on condition of an increase in its farming productivity. It is most unlikely to be able to do this without help from outside, in the form of gifts or very long-term loans, as well as technical advice. Professor Rostow devotes most of pages 22 to 24 to a vague and roundabout discourse on farming's role in the take-off, without ever plainly putting down this primal, basic piece of arithmetic. The plain logic of the matter is incisively discussed in Professor B. S. Keirstead's *Capital, Interest and Profits*, where the example of Newfoundland's fisherfolk economy is described in moving terms from first-hand knowledge.

When new ideas, new ambitions and new technical knowledge reach a conservative economy from other countries, income and influence may have to be redistributed, by taxation, inflation or revolution, before the economy can begin to industrialize itself. Professor Rostow sketches convincingly enough, and perhaps a little repetitively, the sort of difficulties and resistance that have to be overcome in order that the tide of industrial revolution may sweep in. But this is not the nub of the matter. From the viewpoint of the theory of history, the great question is: How did the *first* industrial revolution begin, the British one? and here he has nothing to say. Brilliant insights and intuitions have made Professor Rostow justly famous. But now there is heavy spadework to be done.

# 22

# VALUES AND INTENTIONS

## A REVIEW ARTICLE

A book* which so abounds as this one does in grace and wit, in telling and vivid illustration, in seductive charm of manner and in that charismatic power which comes from originality of thought drilled and marshalled by long meditation for maximum tactical effect, is a most dangerous one for any but the hardened sceptical expert to read. I am no such expert but only an economist powerfully driven by the exigencies of his own subject's dilemmas to seek a deeper insight into human nature and 'the human condition'. It is, I believe, no accident that such a one should find in the earlier part of this book a discussion with which he can feel an instinctive sympathy, a discussion which he can follow and largely accept because it states, in a very unfamiliar but recognizable way, some aspects of some of the difficulties he had discovered for himself.

I shall not pretend that I have been everywhere convinced. The author's grip upon his reader's mind varies in its strength, and I am sure that this variation reflects the degree of the author's own conviction and reposeful satisfaction with what he is saying. In some passages he uses much italic, a practice which can be variously interpreted. Most often in this book it is plainly the desire to punch home a meaning or a logical inference which in speaking would be conveyed by tone of voice: a perfectly legitimate, indeed a necessary resource. For Professor Findlay's style is that of a writer who writes by ear and not merely by mechanical selection of words and constructions; the cadence, the almost choreographic pattern of his long sentences, guides the reader in understanding them. Indeed, it is astounding to find how swiftly one is borne along on this deep current of subtle thought.

For those who can accept them, Professor Findlay's outlook and method provide a great liberation of thought. He would

* J. N. Findlay, *Values and Intentions* (London, 1961: George Allen and Unwin Ltd.).

have us free ourselves from sole acceptance of the strict and, as he convincingly says, static and immobile logic of entailment and of mathematics, vital as is their role of expanding, revealing and restating the import of propositions, and would have us recognize the legitimacy, and the prevalence in the actual working of our minds, of a looser logic of analogy, of consonance and the mutual sympathy of ideas, by which we may advance from one complex of ideas to another:

A logically necessary thought-development is, by its nature, a thought-development which hovers round one spot, [and] which may illuminate it from a variety of angles, but which does not, in an important sense, move on to other points by transitions whose illumination and informative worth depends on the fact that they are *not* strictly necessary. Though few genuine thought-transitions, even the most obvious in their necessity, quite deserve the dispraise conveyed by the Wittgensteinian term 'tautological', yet there are some thought-transitions which, in an important sense, and by a vast expenditure of energy, contrive not to advance but to remain stationary, while others are, in a related sense, ampliative, engaged in covering new territory. It is a strange fact that the energy of philosophers has to a large extent been directed to the absurd project of trying to turn thought-changes which involve this kind of advance into those which are elaborately stationary, or to regarding the former as a *faute de mieux* for, or an approximation to, the latter, not the latter as a queer limiting case of the former. Even those who, like Hegel and the British idealists, have most stressed the systematic coherence involved in genuine thought-progressions and the deliberate stationariness of logistical and mathematical thinking, have still sought to give the former the ineluctable character proper to the latter, failing to see that genuine movement generally involves a choice among a variety of directions [p. 106].

May it not be that in its *explorations* the mind is almost bound, because of the measureless and unplumbed complexity of the cosmos it is trying to understand, and indeed by the very nature of exploration, its character of unguided groping, to make non-logical transitions; but that *after* some stage of these explorations it is legitimate and obligatory to try to 'tidy up', to make the scheme of thought which has been evolved, as the upshot of the almost random groping procedure, reflect the *assumed* all-embracing systematic *unity* and coherence of the underlying reality? Surely this is the object, for example, of the mathematical physicists' search for a unified field theory, a simultaneous explanation of gravity and of electrical phenomena. It is what a colleague in my own subject, Professor Kenneth Boulding, was seeking to do for the whole human or even the whole biological and social aspect of things, in his book *The Image*; it is the natural and necessary outcome of a belief that the cosmos, animate and inanimate, is ultimately *orderly* and *explicable*. For if so, there surely must be the ultimate possibility of representing this cosmos by an *axiom system* (one of many or perhaps of infinitely many which would serve equally well), and so of being in fact able to explain all phenomena by a logical appeal to a few basic postulates. I am reminded of the brilliant saying which Sir Isaiah Berlin has preserved for us: 'The fox knows many things, but the hedgehog knows one big thing.' Professor Findlay's philosopher, stepping *across* the tracks of entailment or of mathematical calculus instead of proceeding along them, is like the fox with his varied armoury of schemes; but he may still wish to become like the hedgehog with his one all-conquering idea.

After his basic survey of the nature of consciousness and of the means of insight into it, Professor Findlay turns to study the nature of belief, and offers a perspective of great splendour which, despite its unqualified scope, I found to shed only a tantalizingly partial light on those problems on which I should most like to consult him. Yet he starts direct towards what is for me the central focus. Many writers have spoken of 'degrees of belief', and for the economist, or at any rate for myself, some notion under this heading has long seemed indispensable. Yet Professor Findlay has many cautions to offer, and shows us pitfalls and an important distinction:

And it is furthest at variance with the fact that we do not at all characterize beliefs, as we do colours, in terms of quality or intensity: of quality they exhibit no significant variations, and of the 'more or less' they in one dimension exhibit only a 'completeness' or 'fullness' and a companion 'partiality' or 'approach to completeness', which can only by a complete misunderstanding be regarded as a case of psychic intensity, and in another dimension only a variation in 'fixity' and 'firmness' which both obviously have a reference to the *other* beliefs in which a given belief is rooted, or to the other belief-tendencies that compete with it, and have some power to drive it from the field. The 'degrees of belief' are on the one hand degrees of approximation to a perfect type, and on the other degrees of ability to withstand attrition or destruction: they are in no sense proper cases of intensity.

I had myself long since come to the idea that we cannot *directly* measure degrees of belief as degrees of feeling: but can we not *map* degrees of belief upon some suitable, intimately linked feeling or response? I have tried elsewhere to express this idea as follows:

A degree of belief is not in itself a sensation or an emotion; but a high degree of belief is a condition of our being able to feel a high degree of surprise. The concrete mental experience which corresponds to any given degree of belief in some particular hypothesis is, I think, the degree of surprise to which this belief exposes us (supposing it to remain unchanged until the truth will be known) and will subject us in case the hypothesis proves false.*

I hope Professor Findlay and the reader of these lines will forgive this interpolation; I wish merely to explain the gratification that his own assertion gives me, showing that at least my doubts were well founded whether or not my solution is accepted. This is not the place to enlarge on the details of that solution, but it is proper to admit that, so far as I can judge, Professor Findlay is not himself likely to approve of them. His problem and mine are, in fact, distinct. He is concerned with the search, which surely every man pursues throughout his life, for some glimpse of the meaning and essential conditions of that life and of the nature of the reality which resides somewhere in the presentations of sense and thought. My concern was with the pragmatic assumptions of one deciding upon action, the degree to which he takes this or that hypothesis about the outcome of each rival available act to be nearer or further from 'certainly right' or 'certainly wrong'. The insight which the philosopher in every one of us strives for is something which, inevitably, is meditated and modified endlessly so long as life lasts; for this task there is 'world enough, and time', there is no hurry. But decision is for now, for if I do not now decide what to do in the imminently approaching moments or hours they will decide it for themselves. This distinction is not merely one of degree,

* *Expectation in Economics* (Cambridge University Press, 1949), p. 11.

for it means that any claim I might wish to make, to have considered a complete ring of all possibilities, is even more grotesquely absurd in the case of pressing decision than in that of the search for scientific explanation. The splendid conception of Charles Peirce which Professor Findlay praises (p. 118) looks down an altogether different vista of human concerns than that of the choice of action. One is the sage's tranquil choice of world theory, the other the soldier's choice of action in the heat of battle.

Professor Findlay distinguishes the 'more' and 'less' of belief into two kinds or dimensions. I am not sure that I have fully understood him in this:

> Partial belief has one sort of magnitude, essentially relative and fractional, representing the extent to which it *is* partial, the degree to which it is near to or far from ousting competing claims from the field. To the partial believer this shows in the degree to which an alternative 'looms large' on the horizon of the possible, like the moon on the physical horizon, the extent to which it appears to co-incide with a wider spread of difference among distinct alternatives, and so in a sense to come on him from more directions than alternative possibilities.—It is impossible to express this sort of magnitude of belief in any wholly non-metaphorical manner: the image of a *Spielraum* or space of possibilities seems as indispensable to the full development of partial belief as does the image of a spatialized past and future to the fully developed consciousness of time.—Partial belief will also have a second sort of magnitude, generally covered by such terms as 'strength', 'firmness' or 'fixity', which depend on the general power of a partial belief to resist reduction or modification by other partial beliefs.—It will be a magnitude distinct from the first, for what we believe *more* we need not believe very firmly, as is shown by the rapid yielding to novel alternatives or considerations, whereas a belief inconsiderable in its spread may also be stable and firm.

I quote this passage for the sake also, however, of its reference to 'the image of a spatialized past and future'. Here also I recognize the impact, on another man's thought, of a matter which has greatly exercised my own.

The reader of such a book as this, which everywhere manifests its author's serene humanity of outlook, is bound to look eagerly forward to those passages which will treat of the idea of *freedom*. How will a writer upon moral values, upon modes of human action, upon responsibility and duty, resolve the basic dilemma of *cause* or *choice*? It is best to begin by letting our author speak for himself:

The notion of causation is simply the notion of the *growing* of later stages of things *out* of earlier ones, a notion senseless if not involving recognizable continuance of pattern. It is, further, a notion so central to the interweaving of things in a common world, without which nothing could be conceived believingly, that all our beliefs suggest or imply it. There is something monstrous, *a priori* unlikely, in the thought of anything *not* born out of proper antecedents in regular fashion, a monstrousness which leads us to look for such antecedents even when no trace of them is apparent, and to accept only with the last reluctance anything that would block or end this search. This notion of causal determination requires, in its first rough form, only that whole phases should grow out of whole phases, not that every distinct feature of them, every distinct light in which they may be regarded, should have its own individual aetiology. But as the movement towards abstraction turns the aspects of things into things of a sort, the monstrousness of seeing something grow out of nothing becomes transferred to each abstract aspect, so that we become deeply reluctant to think of the least feature of things without a complete causal permit of entry.—This reluctance then comes into a frontal clash with our pointed notion of freedom: we begin to feel that, if an A emerges out of the mere capacity for being an A or B, it in a sense arises out of nothing. And with this feeling goes a threat to our whole cognitive security, the emergence of something which, if once admitted, may make it impossible to believe or affirm anything whatsoever. And this threat must be exorcised, either by modifying our original ideal of freedom so as to accord with our notion of exhaustive causal explanation, or by modifying our notion of causal explanation so as to accord with our notion of freedom [pp. 198, 199].

To say that all things are caused, that every event, every transition from one state of affairs to another, can be accounted for in its every aspect and detail by reference to circumstances accompanying it or preceding it, is to say that a man's sense of playing an *independent* part in even the obscure and humble details of total history is an illusion. By this embracing universal and complete causation we bring ourselves face to face with complete determinism: there is no choice which is really choice, no spontaneity, no claiming credit or accepting responsibility, there is no *decision*. To decide is to create, in some measure. Yet in this double dilemma and central mystery of the human condition we cannot simply opt for a non-causal world. For a world without regularities of sequence, without 'laws of nature', without natural order, would be a world without possible knowledge of the effects of given actions. It would be a world where choosing of this action rather than that would be purposeless and pointless, since its consequence could not be even guessed at. It would be a world where we could take decisions, but they would be *powerless*.

I have not found in Professor Findlay's book a clear confrontation of this 'dilemma behind a dilemma'. He shows us with admirable candour the clash between cause and freedom, but behind this clash there is a curtain which he does not draw aside, a curtain which hides from us, in our everyday speech and thought, the problem of how we can each of us be, as we suppose, in the strictest sense an *ultimate source* of some part of the shape of history.

No review can do justice to the warm and rich humanity, the fine distillation of thought from a long and intense cultivation of the deepest problems that face the philosopher, and the limpid, flowing style which fill Professor Findlay's pages.

# INDEX